Psychology and Gender Dysphoria

Psychiatry and psychology have a long and highly debated history in relation to gender. In particular, they have attracted criticism for policing the boundaries of 'normal' gender expression through gender identity diagnoses, such as transvestism, transsexualism, gender identity disorder and gender dysphoria.

Drawing on discursive psychology, this book traces the historical development of psychiatric constructions of 'normal' and 'abnormal' gender expression. It contextualizes the recent reconstruction of gender in the 5th edition of the *Diagnostic and Statistical Manual of Mental Disorders* (DSM-5) and its criteria for gender dysphoria. This latest diagnosis illustrates the continued disagreement and debate within the profession surrounding gender identity as 'disordered'. It also provides an opportunity to reflect on the conflicted history between feminist and transgender communities in the changing context of a more trans-positive feminism, and the implications of these diagnoses for these distinct but linked communities.

Psychology and Gender Dysphoria examines debates and controversies surrounding psychiatric diagnoses and theories related to gender and gender nonconformity by exploring recent research, examples of collaborative perspectives, and existing feminist and trans texts. As such, the book is relevant for postgraduate and postdoctoral researchers of gender, feminism and critical psychology as well as historical issues within psychiatry.

Jemma Tosh is a Research Manager at the Faculty of Health Sciences at Simon Fraser University and a Postdoctoral Research Fellow at the Institute for Gender, Race, Sexuality and Social Justice at the University of British Columbia. She is the author of *Perverse Psychology: The Pathologization of Sexual Violence and Transgenderism* (Routledge, 2015).

Psychology and Gender Dysphoria

Feminist and transgender perspectives

Jemma Tosh

Routledge
Taylor & Francis Group
LONDON AND NEW YORK

First published 2016 by Routledge

2 Park Square, Milton Park, Abingdon, Oxfordshire OX14 4RN
711 Third Avenue, New York, NY 10017

Routledge is an imprint of the Taylor & Francis Group, an informa business

First issued in paperback 2017

British Library Cataloguing in Publication Data
A catalogue record for this book is available from the British Library

Library of Congress Cataloging in Publication Data
Names: Tosh, Jemma, author/
Title: Psychology and gender dysphoria: feminist and transgender perspectives/Jemma Tosh.
Description: New York: Routledge, 2016. | Includes index.
Identifiers: LCCN 2015036725 | ISBN 9781138013926 | ISBN 9781315794938 (ebk)
Subjects: LCSH: Sex differences (Psychology) | Femininity. | Transgender people – Identity. | Gender identity disorders. | Sex change.
Classification: LCC BF692.2 .T67 2016 | DDC 155.3/3 – dc23
LC record available at http://lccn.loc.gov/2015036725

ISBN: 978-1-138-01392-6 (hbk)
ISBN: 978-0-8153-5996-8 (pbk)

Typeset in Bembo
by Swales & Willis Ltd, Exeter, Devon, UK

For my parents

To define is to limit . . . How shallow were the arbitrary definitions of ordinary psychologists!

(Oscar Wilde, 1891)

Contents

Acknowledgements

I would like to thank Mary Bryson for supporting my work through the Institute for Gender, Race, Sexuality and Social Justice at the University of British Columbia. I would also like to thank Jamie Veale for welcoming me to Vancouver and introducing me to the Institute. I am very grateful for the immense support and critical insights from Ian Parker and Erica Burman, and everyone at the Manchester Discourse Unit. I would also like to thank Geoff Bunn and Asiya Siddiquee for their guidance during my PhD studies, where this project began. Many thanks to China Mills for being wonderfully supportive and for providing helpful feedback on an earlier version of this text. I am also grateful to Maya Gislason, for supporting my work so wholeheartedly and for the many interesting conversations we have had on the creative blending of topics and disciplines regarding gender and social justice.

Thank you to others who have inspired my research and continue to do so with their challenges to the pathologization of gender diversity, Jake Pyne, Natacha Kennedy, Ann Travers, Anne Pullen Sansfaçon, Meg John Barker, Brenda LeFrançois, Gavi Ansara, Karl Bryant, Peter Hegarty, and many more. I am also grateful to Lauren Wroe, who helped me to combine my academic work and activist campaigns, and I would like to thank members of the Psychology of Women Section of the British Psychological Society for their ongoing support and commitment to an anti-oppressive and inclusive feminism.

I would like to thank my family and friends for understanding my commitment both to writing and to campaigning for gender and sexual minority groups. Even when you don't know what I'm writing about, you know that it is important to me and that's enough. You forgive my absence when I am hidden away in a room writing for hours, days, weeks, and months, and you celebrate with me when it's done. Thank you to my Mum, Dad, and my partner James. Don't worry, I won't make you read this one either. Thanks to my sister Nikki and her children Jared and Madison, for reminding me that I'm not a 'proper' (i.e. medical) doctor - it's actually more of a compliment than you think it is! Thank you to my friends Kelly, Fionnuala and Krista, for our long and amusing discussions about feminism, sexism, and life in general. Thank you to my grandmother Mary, here's another one to show your friends.

Jem

Chapter 1

Introduction

> Gender Dysphoria . . . a marked incongruence between one's experienced/ expressed gender and assigned gender.
>
> (American Psychiatric Association [APA], 2013, p. 452)

The definition of gender dysphoria provided by the American Psychiatric Association is from the latest edition of the *Diagnostic and Statistical Manual of Mental Disorders* (DSM). It is a diagnosis that can be applied to those who do not conform to Western gender 'norms' (see Chapter 3). Currently in its fifth edition, the DSM is meant to represent a consensus of diagnostic terms and criteria for psychology and psychiatry to use for clinical and research purposes. It provides a universal language for those working in therapeutic contexts to describe and diagnose people experiencing emotional distress. To ascertain what kind of distress, professionals need only consult this comprehensive 'Bible' of psychiatry (Kutchins & Kirk, 2003), to see which term best describes the presenting 'symptoms'. However, the DSM has also represented an intersection of competing perspectives, being the target of much criticism since its inception in 1952 (Boyle, 2007; Caplan, 1996; Cooper, 2004; Crowe, 2000; Frances, 2013; Gornall, 2013; Kutchins & Kirk, 2003; Wakefield, 1997; Zur & Nordmarken, 2008). This has been in relation to its conceptualization of homosexuality, bisexuality, asexuality, gender identity, femininity, hearing voices and 'race' (Barker, 2007; Conrad & Angell, 2004; Kim, 2014; Phoenix, 1994; Sedgwick, 1991; Ussher, 2011; Winters, 2009; Wise, 2004), to name a few examples.

Psychiatry and psychology, then, are highly contested areas. They define 'normality' and label all that fall outside of this narrowly assigned category as 'mentally ill'. The diagnosis of gender dysphoria is no exception. It is a contentious concept as those who try to define and diagnose come up against counter-narratives and concepts based on lived experience, activism and research focused on social justice (Ansara & Hegarty, 2012; Hill, 2012; Meyer & Sansfacon, 2014; Tosh, 2011c; Winters, 2009). Debates regarding gender have an equally conflicted history within feminist and transgender studies (see Chapters 4 and 5) that often run parallel to psychological and psychiatric perspectives. Consequently, the diagnosis of gender dysphoria is at a cataclysm of numerous debates and disagreements – it is at the epicentre of long-standing arguments originating from many different directions. The purpose of this book is to navigate this complex terrain, to examine the tensions between and within these discourses, and consider how these relate to lived experiences of an embodied gender-related distress.

The tendency to focus on abstract concepts means that the very people being talked about can be left behind in these debates (Hill, 2012; Namaste, 2000). Often considered an opportunity to develop gender theory, or a new population for study, the high rates of suicide attempts, hate crime, murder and rape of gender nonconforming people (Clements-Nolle, Marx, & Katz, 2006; Goldblum et al., 2012; Grant et al., 2010; Jauk, 2013; Lee & Kwan, 2014; Stotzer, 2008; Turner, Whittle, & Combs, 2009) fall to the side while psychiatrists debate which treatment is best for 'the prevention of transsexualism' (Zucker et al., 2012) and some feminists argue whether it is safe to use public toilets (e.g. Jeffreys, 2014). More time is spent talking about gender nonconformists as being a threat, than talking about the threats they face from a society that positions conformity as the 'norm'. Responses to the perceived threat of gender nonconformity have included online and offline harassment, the deliberate 'outing' of trans people, which puts them at risk of violence, discrimination and suicide (Molloy, 2014; Moore, 2014), and the promotion of legislation that stops access to medical and social services (Stryker, 2009). Moreover, this sole focus on the pathologization and victimization of trans people can overlook their celebration, success and happiness. From protests and petitions, to threats of violence, the debates regarding gender dysphoria have well surpassed academic discussion (Tosh, 2011a, 2011c; Woolbert, 2014).

With this volatile context in mind, I will describe the role psychology and psychiatry have played in defining gender 'normality' and 'abnormality', as well as the responses and challenges posed by those more likely to be positioned in the latter category: women (cisgender and transgender) and those with gender identities and bodies that exist outside of the binaries of man/woman, male/female. I do this with an appreciation of the historical and changing contexts in which these perspectives occurred. I echo the aim of many who have positioned the *'psy' disciplines* as the subject of study and analysis (Foucault, 1975; Rose, 1979). I provide a genealogical tracing as well as a critical questioning of present assumptions and misconceptions (Pilgrim, 1990). I show how long-standing problems within the psy professions impact on present discourses and experiences.

This can be a challenging endeavour, particularly if histories contradict current understandings of psychology and gender:

> Revelations about Jung's 'collaboration' with the Nazis (Masson, 1993) or Burt's invented data, or the psychologist Cattell's frank espousal of eugenic

> beliefs can be profoundly unsettling to psychotherapists and psychologists who have based their own careers, in good faith, on the work of these early pioneers.
>
> (Newnes, 1999, p. 21)

The same can be said for feminism, where individuals join a movement with ambitions of contributing to social change, challenging oppression, helping women and ending sexism. It can be difficult to acknowledge the limitations of previous work that has had such positive implications for feminism in some areas, or of oppression perpetuated by some feminists, especially if one has been complicit in such actions on the assumption that it was for 'the right reasons'.

Therefore, rather than outline a 'traditional' history that conveys psychology and psychiatry as progressing through its development of 'science' to its modern place of 'expertise', I provide a brief overview of how psychology and psychiatry have constructed, categorized and medicalized human experience and simultaneously positioned that knowledge as authoritative and 'truth' (Foucault, 1975; Scull, 1982; Shorter, 1998). I also highlight the role of violence, oppression and coercion in 'treatment' approaches, as this element is often lacking in historical accounts that convey psychology and psychiatry as 'science' (Szasz, 2007), and is key when looking at how different forms of oppression intersect.

Psychiatric classification

When someone experiences emotional distress, they may come into contact with a wide range of professionals, including psychologists, psychiatrists, psychoanalysts, psychotherapists and so on. There are many sub-disciplines within psychology and psychiatry, each emphasizing a different perspective on 'mental illness'; from neuropsychology (the study of brain and behaviour) to parapsychology (the study of human experience and the paranormal), the possibilities for the study of human experience are vast. Psychology draws on sociology, philosophy, queer theory, business, history, education, feminism, animal behaviour, medicine and many more (Ayers & Visser, 2010; Brown & Stenner, 2009; Burman, 1997a; Clarke & Peel, 2007; Dickins & Donovan, 2012; Goto & Martin, 2009; Kaila, 2006; Kaluger, 1969; McInerney, 2013; Rogelberg, 2009; Suls, Davidson, & Kaplan, 2010). Despite this eclectic maze of (inter/dis)connected disciplines, medical and biological approaches to human experience and distress predominate. A wealth of criticism targeting the medical model of 'mental illness' and 'mental health' (Bentall, 2009; Boyle, 2007; Burstow, LeFrançois, & Diamond, 2014; Conrad, 1992; LeFrançois, Menzies, & Reaume, 2013; Mills, 2014; Newnes, Holmes, & Dunn, 1999; Rose, 2009; Szasz, 1960) has failed to bring an end to the dominance of medical diagnosis (Pilgrim, 2007).

Medical categorizations of human behaviour may seem necessary and enduring, but they are only one way that we have framed human diversity. Madness has been linked to the physical body since the classical period of ancient Greece (500–336 BC, Blundell, 1995) (Bentall, 2009), such as hysteria's initial conceptualization as a 'wandering womb' (Wetzel, 1991). However, in the global North, the care of those considered 'mad' was within the realm of the layperson prior to the introduction of medical asylums (Boyle, 1990), the Church when people were thought to be possessed by a demon (Szasz, 2007), and law enforcement if their behaviour was framed as illegal (particularly in the case of criminalized sexualities, such as homosexuality) (Bullough, 1982; Robb, 2003). By the end of the seventeenth century, 'trade in lunacy' was 'a flourishing new industry' (Szasz, 2007) and a symptom-based classification system of madness was later introduced in the 18th century following similar moves in botany. François Boissier de Sauvages's (1732, 1763) *Nouvelles Classes de Maladies de Maladies dans un Ordre Semblable a Celui des Botanistes* and *Nosologie Méthodique* listed 'mental illnesses' as 'folies', and was credited by William Cullen (1785) as the first successful attempt at the systematic classification of disease.[1] Vogel (1764) added to this with the publication of *Definitiones Generum Morborum* and Cullen (1784, 1785) produced a category of 'neuroses' that included 'mania' and 'melancholia' (Bynum, 1981). The last of these 18th-century 'landmark works' (Munsche & Whitaker, 2012) was Philippe Pinel's *Memoir of Madness* published in 1794, outlining an argument for the need for humane treatment and asylums (Weiner, 1992).

However, it was not until the mid-19th century that psychiatry developed as a medical specialism (Bentall, 2009), due to the influence of Kraepelin's (1883) empiricist approach to classification that continues to define the profession today (Pilgrim, 2007). Kraepelin (1883) produced *Compendium der Psychiatrie*, credited as including the first conceptualization of 'dementia praecox', meaning 'senility of the young' (Bentall, 2009) and later renamed 'schizophrenia' by Bleuler (1911).[2] Kraepelin's influence was greater than the introduction of a new psychiatric category; he also promoted the theory that all mental 'illnesses' were a result of degeneracy – a biological inheritance of 'abnormality'.

While research continues to look for evidence of the connection between genetics and 'mental illness' (Andreassen, Thompson & Dale, 2014; Flint & Kendler, 2014), the profession has admitted it has been unable to identify biologically based indicators related to the development of emotional distress, or 'mental illness' (Kupfer, 2013). Even so, the underlying medical naturalism of the approach remains influential. It assumes 'that current medical terminology describing mental abnormality is valid and has global and trans-historical applicability' (Pilgrim, 2007, p. 359). This is instead of the many different ways that unusual experiences, hearing voices and emotional distress can be understood from diverse perspectives from within and outside of psychology, and as a result, the very different possibilities for alleviating distress (Cromby, Harper & Reavey, 2007; Scott, 1997). An unfortunate consequence of the predominance of biomedical models of emotional distress is that it can often be assumed that for someone's suffering to be considered 'real', it needs to have a biological basis. Those who research violence and abuse know this to be untrue.

During the early 20th century, organizations began collecting and analysing statistical data regarding the categories that had been produced earlier. The first edition of the *International List of Causes of Death* was initially published by the International Statistical Institute (1900), and was based on the work of a committee led by Jacques Bertillon and the earlier *Bertillon Classifications of Causes of Death* (American Public Health Association, 1899). Both included 'insanity' as a cause of death, with the latter listing a range of conditions under 'mental alienation' from the very familiar (e.g. 'homesickness' and 'nostalgia'), to the long-standing and well-known (e.g. 'melancholia', 'nymphomania', 'megalomania' and 'dementia'), to the less well-known (e.g. 'lycantrophy' – transformation into a werewolf, or a 'madness' where one believes themselves to be a werewolf, depending on the context and time period when the term is used, and 'andromania' – women's obsession with men) (p. 22). Each edition expanded the list of 'mental illnesses', including its current edition: the *International Classification of Diseases 10* (ICD-10) produced by the World Health Organization (2010). The American Medico-Psychological Association (1918) produced the *Statistical Manual for the Use of Institutions for the Insane* in 1918, which included 'a system of uniform statistics in institutions for mental diseases' with an aim to 'promote the introduction of the system throughout the country' (p. 3). The American Medico-Psychological Association became the American Psychiatric Association (APA) in 1921, but didn't publish the first *Diagnostic and Statistical Manual of Mental Disorders* (DSM) until 1952. Prior to this, the influence of the World Wars had led to a reconceptualization of mental 'illness' as a response to returning soldiers who were experiencing emotional distress. Consequently, the *DSM-I* (APA, 1952) more closely reflected the military's Medical 203 (War Department, 1946). Rather than frame 'madness' as biologically inherited, it emphasized mental health problems as 'reactions to extraordinary circumstances' (Houts, 2000, p. 941), which coincided with the rising popularity of psychoanalysis in the US (Houts, 2000). Therefore, by the time the first DSM was published, human behaviour had been categorized within the context of medicine for centuries with a recent reconceptualization based on the experiences of soldiers.

Bentall (2009) noted that prior to Kraepelin's work, there were almost as many ways of describing 'mental illness' as there were psychiatrists, each with their own diagnostic system. This made for difficult comparisons of case studies, theories, or therapeutic interventions. For example, 'How was a psychiatrist working in, say, Edinburgh, to know that he was studying the same kind of patients as his rival in Boston?' (Bentall, 2009, p. 31). This process of collecting statistical data for the production of a universal text provided another move, then, from theories proposed by multiple authors, to a single authoritative text that described and defined 'norms' of behaviour promoted for use by everyone – a single and uniform language to describe and define human diversity. Consequently, it suppressed pluralism in the discussion and development of multiple understandings of emotional distress and human experience; the profession of psychiatry sought to bring order to madness. It also redefined human experience and diversity within medical terms – a 'medicalization of madness' (Szasz, 2007, p. 57) that became an authoritative discourse and an accepted 'truth'. Or as Boyle describes it:

> . . . it was not that psychiatry developed more humane ways of dealing with the 'mentally ill' or more scientific ways of understanding 'mental illness' but that medical dominance over deviant behaviour contributed to the later widespread adoption of the idea that it should be viewed as illness.
>
> (Boyle, 1990, p. 4)

At present, the DSM is one of the most influential psychiatric texts, as it contains the most comprehensive account of diagnostic categories used by the profession,[3] which is further legitimized by the influence of the pharmaceutical industry in promoting the diagnostic model and biomedical treatments of emotional distress (Healy, 2012; Moncrieff, 2008). Nevertheless, the DSM is highly controversial and its contents have been heavily debated for decades (Caplan, 1996; Cermele, Daniels & Anderson, 2001; Cooper, 2004; Cotten & Ridings, 2011; Frances, 2013; Johnson, 1998; Kutchins & Kirk, 2003; Malhi et al., 2014; Stoppard, 1991; Zur & Nordmarken, 2008).

Numerous controversial diagnoses demonstrate not only the widespread disagreement regarding the definition of 'mental illness', but also the politics involved in categorizing human experience and behaviour as 'normal' or 'abnormal'. Noteworthy diagnoses include 'homosexuality' and 'paraphilic coercive disorder'. Homosexuality was initially positioned by psychiatry as a 'perversion' or form of 'sexual deviance', and featured in the first two editions of the DSM. During revisions for the third edition, however, protests from both inside and outside the profession and years of challenges to psychiatry's conceptualization of sexuality resulted in its removal from the DSM in 1973 (APA, 1973). 'Paraphilic coercive disorder' is a diagnosis that the profession has tried to include in the DSM since the 1980s, without success. It refers to individuals who rape as a preferred form of sexual activity. Protests and challenges from feminists and forensic psychiatrists and psychologists showed the level of concern and disagreement regarding this problematic concept also (Tosh, 2011c, 2014; Zander, 2008). Historically, we can see how behaviours become classified as 'mental illness' and declassified at different times, depending on the social context (rather than research into biological causes of 'madness'), such as the 'masturbation panic' of the 19th century, where 'onanism' was considered a cause of insanity and to be avoided at all costs (Hunt, 1998). Another example is the diagnosis of 'drapetomania', which was applied to black individuals who tried to escape from slavery before the North American civil war, but lost favour with the profession when slavery was abolished (Hoberman, 2012; Myers, 2014). Therefore, as Pilgrim (2007) notes, 'the DSM can be read as a revisable political manifesto for the psychiatric profession, as well as a scientific document' (p. 638). In its fifth edition, it has been on the receiving end of protests, petitions, open letters dropping the publication from a variety of professions and more (DCP Position Statement, 2013; *DSM-5* Response, n.d.; Insel, 2013; Speak Out Against Psychiatry, 2013; Tosh, 2011c).

Psychological measurement

While psychiatry emerged as a sub-discipline of medicine, psychology separated from philosophy in the late nineteenth century (Cheshire & Pilgrim, 2004; Rose, 1979). Psychology had a different focus than psychiatry; as Burt (1927) noted, rather than categorize instances of apparent 'abnormality', psychology moved from considering 'man-in-general' within philosophy to the psychological study of individual differences, and it pursued this line of enquiry via the means of measurement (Rose, 1979), influenced by German models of experimental analysis (Cheshire & Pilgrim, 2004). Whether assessing cranial bumps in phrenology, or intelligence testing in schools and asylums, psychology has a long history of aspiring to quantify human abilities (Gould, 2006). For pioneers like Binet, co-author of 'La psychologie individuelle'/'the aim of individual psychology' (Binet & Henri, 1895), the purpose of such measurement was primarily for comparison, that is, to differentiate between humans in terms of measurable and observable behaviour. This was something that Galton wanted compared to an 'ideal' based on a 'mobile, eager, energetic, [and] well-shaped' man (Galton, 1890, pp. 320–81), which highlighted the sexist and ableist perspective that positioned able-bodied men as the ideal standard for all humans (Gould, 2006).

Research in this area centred around the concept of 'intelligence' as defined and produced by psychology during the early 20th century by well-known pioneers of the profession including the already mentioned Alfred Binet, Cyril Burt and Francis Galton, as well as Charles Spearman and Karl Pearson. However, it also developed out of long-standing concerns regarding degeneracy (Rose, 1979). Thus, the endeavour to measure human ability had long been tied to biology and heredity through theories of degeneracy in psychiatric discourse. Research and theories on intelligence testing were then used to explicitly make the connections between 'intelligence', biology and 'race' and were promoted by psychologists connected to the US and UK eugenics movements (Kamin, 1974; Rose, 1979).[4] Francis Galton, a British evolutionary theorist and cousin of Darwin, introduced the term 'eugenics' (an approach aimed at 'improving' the human race through selective breeding) in 1883 in *Inquiries into Human Faculty and Development* (Cheshire & Pilgrim, 2004; Rose, 1979). In this publication, Galton highlighted the relationship between (random) individual differences and (systematic/predictable) variations within and across populations. The result was the 'ogive', or 'bell curve', where human abilities were placed on a graph based on their distance from a statistical 'norm', and as a consequence, chance became consolidated as 'scientific law' (Rose, 1979, p. 18).

The translation of 'degeneracy' from an ethical/moral issue to a medical/scientific problem opened up the possibility (and justification) for measures of population control, such as compulsory sterilization, limits on immigration, increased regulation, and at its extreme, termination of those considered 'feebleminded' (e.g. those who scored low on intelligence tests). As Rose (1979) explained, 'feeblemindedness' was thought to be a 'social danger' that was passed on via reproduction. Therefore, measures to control reproduction were introduced to reduce the perceived 'danger' to society.

The 'norm' was central to 'Galtonian discourse' (Rose, 1979, p. 17), and to statistical approaches within psychology from this point onwards. Thus, the underlying foundation that paved the way for the eugenics movement was the quantifying of human behaviour and experience in terms of degrees of 'normality'/'abnormality', which became a fundamental concept in psychology. This was in addition to the adoption of medical naturalism and evolutionary theory (Cheshire & Pilgrim, 2004). Training in the discipline retains this keen focus on the statistical analysis of human variation and the assumption that human experience falls within a 'normal' distribution with 'deviations' the focus of study and 'treatment', as well as biological determinants of behaviour. Psychology promotes an ideal and statistical 'norm' that does not accurately represent the diversity evident within a vast range of human cultures (Rogers & Pilgrim, 2014). I remember being told explicitly during my own training in psychology that 'we learn about normal development to make it easier to spot the abnormalities.' This is despite numerous calls for a diversification of research methods to be taught to students in order to move away from the rigidity and dangerous myth of 'objectivity' that masks underlying values (Hager, 1982; Harding, 1986) that can result in scientific racism, sexism and ableism (Bibeau & Pedersen, 2002; Campbell, 2009; Jordan-Young, 2011).

Removing the need to reflect on the impact of research or treatments on society (i.e. framing research as apolitical or objective) can place researchers at the risk of causing further harm. Thus campaigns against pathologization are closely tied to movements towards the diversification of research methods within psychology, as statistical concepts are the very basis from which students learn to reduce human complexity to quantifiable data for the purposes of comparison to a constructed 'norm', with 'deviations' positioned as Other/'abnormal' from the outset. The hostility and difficulties documented from those engaging in active challenges to the predominance of quantitative methods and theory within psychology (Burman, 1997b; Luttrell, 2005; Povee & Roberts, 2014) illustrate the importance still held for these problematic concepts within the discipline, as well as the resistance to acknowledging psychology's role in the perpetuation of human suffering.

Therefore, while psychiatry was committed to categorizing human experience, psychology was set on measuring it. Psychiatry developed 'norms' through the process of creating categories of 'abnormality', and producing a 'normal'/'abnormal' dichotomy. Psychology, on the other hand, produced a similar concept based on statistical analyses, with extremes (too much of something or too little) being framed as 'unusual', 'atypical', or 'abnormal'. Both disciplines promoted a concept of 'normality' that reflected the experience of white, middle/upper class, able-bodied, gender-conforming men (Ali, 2004; Caplan & Cosgrove, 2004; Cermele et al., 2001; Metcalfe & Caplan, 2004; Tosh, 2013; Ussher, 1992). This is where the professions of psychology and psychiatry began, and while there has been much change and development since, they still promote this narrow view of 'normality' and attract much criticism in relation to their representation and treatment of women, gender nonconforming people, sexual diversities, race, dis/ability, and people from working-class or long-term unemployed groups (Barker, 2007; Goodley, 2014; Lott & Bullock, 2006; Richards, 2003; Tiefer, 2009, 2006; Ussher, 1992, 2011; Winters, 2009). Unfortunately, due to the definition of 'abnormality' centring heavily on these groups, they are more likely to be the focus of psychological and psychiatric theories, research and treatment. This is why it is important to talk about power, privilege and oppression in relation to psychology.

Psychiatric violence

Rose (1979, 1985) describes a 'psychological complex', a matrix of agents, discourses and practices that is not a result of 'objective' 'science', but deeply embedded in power relations. It has the potential to operate both negatively (i.e. by excluding and restricting) and positively (i.e. by producing discursive objects and subjects). Therefore power can be conceptualized as a dominant force acting upon others (such as restricting freedoms), as well as in the form of the production of knowledges and 'truths' (Foucault, 1975). Within psychology and psychiatry, mental health professionals have the ability to impact on the physical freedoms of an individual through civil commitment, as well as forced medication and intervention that remove an individual's bodily autonomy and their right to consent to treatment (Breggin, 1993; Pescoslido et al., 1999). Additionally, the production and authentication of dominant 'norms' (as 'truth') feeds into a culture where nonconformity is punished through ridicule, harassment, exclusion and violence (Feder, 1997).

There are countless examples of psychiatric intervention that invite us to question the role of coercion and abuse in therapy, as well as illustrate how once framed in authoritative discourse by medicine and law, violence can continue unquestioned in the guise of 'treatment'. As Bentall (2009) describes, a medical director of the New Jersey state hospital in 1907 believed that because infection was the cause of disease, the same could be true for madness. Through a range of surgeries (such as the removal of teeth, tonsils, testicles, ovaries, gall bladder and colon), this doctor attempted to rid individuals of infection; however, up to 45 per cent of those treated in this way died as a result of the surgery.

Lobotomies were also common: originally developed in 1930s Italy, they involved drilling holes in a patient's skull, inserting a blade, and severing nerve fibres connected to the frontal lobe of the brain. Other methods included 'transorbital lobotomy' introduced by Freeman in 1946, where 'he used a mallet to pound an ice pick through the patient's eye socket into the brain then moved the pick around blindly to sever the nerve fibers' (Lerner, 2005, p. 119). These surgeries were completed on 'unwilling patients' under restraint. Rather than reflect an unusual practice, this was 'business as usual' for psychiatry (Lerner, 2005). During the 1960s and 1970s, brain surgery (or 'psychosurgery') was used in attempts to reduce violent behaviour, but masked the political uses of the method on those involved in 1960s protests (Breggin, 1975). Also developed in the 1930s was electro-convulsive therapy (ECT):

> ECT is a procedure that consists of passing sufficient electricity through the head (100–190 volts) to produce a grand mal seizure. In unilateral or modified shock, both electrodes are placed on one side of the head; in bilateral or unmodified shock, one electrode is placed on each side.
>
> (Burstow, 2006b)

A method more frequently used on women, with well-documented consequences such as memory loss and permanent brain damage (Breggin, 2007), ECT has been described by patients as 'torture', 'punishment' and 'traumatizing' (Burstow, 2006a, 2006b). It can also be routinely used without anaesthetic, for example in the global South (Chanpattana et al., 2005). It is highly contested by professionals and survivors alike (Breggin, 1979). However, it is important not to relegate such practices to history, as increasing interest in the treatment of depression and other mental 'illness' with 'psychosurgery' and ECT never went away. It received renewed interest in the 1970s during the remedicalization of psychiatry (Breggin, 1992), and as a result, invasive and controversial practices are still psychiatry's 'business' (Lerner, 2005). Assumed to be a necessary cruelty in the elimination of madness, they also illustrate that madness is viewed as a fate worse than death, as risks of physical pain, permanent injury and loss of life have all been considered at one time or another acceptable in the 'treatment' of mental 'illness'.

Similarly, from the 1950s to the 1970s, psychologists and psychiatrists drew on a range of theories in the development of 'treatments' that aimed to 'cure' homosexuality (and transvestism, e.g. Lambley, 1974; Marks & Gelder, 1967; Marks, Gelder & Bancroft, 1970; Marquis, 1977; Rosen & Kopel, 1977; Serber, 1977). Behavioural therapies attempted to associate attraction to men's bodies[5] with pain, distress, or discomfort. This was done through a variety of strategies, including electric shock treatments and being given pharmaceutical drugs to induce vomiting (Feldman & MacCulloch, 2013; Freund, 1960): such interventions were openly acknowledged by the profession as ineffective in converting homosexual individuals to heterosexuality (Bancroft, 1974; Davison, 1976). Psychoanalytic approaches were also used at this time, based on the assumption that homosexuality developed during childhood and thus could be changed (Beiber et al., 1962). The professions of psychology and psychiatry have since condemned such reparative therapies (e.g. APA, 1973), but some continue to practice within religious contexts (e.g. Nicolosi, 2009) and recent research in the UK found that 17 per cent of therapists had tried to change a client's sexual orientation (Bartlett, Smith & King, 2009).

Women's sexuality has been another area where abuses (or 'psychiatric violence' – LeFrancois, 2012) have been documented in treatments that aimed to increase or decrease sexual desire. Historically, clitoridectomies (the surgical removal or reduction of the clitoris) were recommended for a wide range of 'conditions' applied to women, including hysteria (see Chapter 2) and nymphomania (Groneman, 1994; Studd & Schwenkhagen, 2009). Sexual intercourse was recommended for those deemed 'frigid' (Potts, 2002). This is not just historic abuse, as surgeries continue to be recommended for 'female sexual dysfunction' or 'female arousal disorder', despite such diagnoses being highly contested, and in some cases, openly admitted as a creation of the pharmaceutical industry for profit (Moynihan & Mintzes, 2010). Canner's (2008) illuminating documentary showed unsuccessful invasive treatments in medical attempts to ensure women orgasmed during penetrative intercourse, such as experimental spinal surgery. This is despite the long-standing acknowledgement that most women do not orgasm during heterosexual penetration (Hite, 2004). Similarly, the newly named 'penetrative disorder' that pathologizes fear and pain during penetrative intercourse[6] can incur medical treatments such as surgery, botox injections, and the regular insertion of dilators – all based on the problematic and heterosexist assumption that penile penetration is the 'norm', 'healthy', and the predominant aim of sexual activity (Tosh & Carson, in press). Therefore, sometimes, the 'helping professions' can be anything but helpful (Tosh & Golightley, under review).

Sanism

In addition to restricting personal freedoms, the production of a narrow concept of 'normality' positions all that do not fit this definition as 'abnormal' and Other, and as a result, the labels psychology and psychiatry produce take from that individual the ability to have control over their life and body. Their voice is no longer believed; whether it is the voicing of sexual abuse reframed as a 'delusion' or a 'lie' as part of their diagnosis (e.g. 'schizophrenia' or 'borderline personality disorder'), or the declaration of gender identity reframed as criteria for 'gender dysphoria', the stance is that 'doctor knows best' (Emke, 1992). Szasz (2007) refers to this as the 'infantilization of the insane', where adults with diagnoses of 'mental illness' are treated like children, their rights taken away, and psychiatrists given the role of decision maker and guardian.

Psychiatry was initially viewed as a sympathetic and non-judgmental approach compared to prior discourses that positioned such people as 'evil' or 'monstrous' (Oosterhuis, 2000), but the consequences of framing certain groups of people as 'pathological' has since been well documented in terms of discrimination and stigma, where those with a diagnosis of 'mental illness' can be at high risk of violence and victimization. However, others describe this issue in terms of oppression, a systematic victimization of a social group, rather than focusing on individual experiences (Poole et al., 2012).

Psychology and psychiatry's oppression of individuals has been conceptualized as 'sanism' (Birnbaum, 1960; Perlin, 2002, 2006), or sometimes 'mentalism' (Chamberlin, 2005). It comprises of systemic and individual discrimination, prejudice, fear and hatred:

> Sanism impacts negatively on their entire world – socially, politically, economically, physically, personally, intellectually and emotionally. Generally, the impact of sanism is far-reaching and devastating, more devastating than the experiences that bring us into contact with psychiatry in the first place.
> (LeFrancois, 2012, p. 7)

Sanism can also result in microaggressions, such as assuming that those with a diagnosis are incompetent, irrational and aggressive, and requiring supervision and assistance at all times (Poole et al. 2012). The concept was first described by Birnbaum (1960) in his work as a legal representative for Edward Stephens and Kenneth Donaldson. He stated that understanding sanism was better from the standpoint of those diagnosed as 'mentally ill', 'from the viewpoint of the oppressed' rather than from the oppressors (Birnbaum, [1974], cited in Ingram, 2011, para. 11).

Like other 'isms', sanism is interconnected with other forms of oppression (Ingram, 2011). For instance, despite the removal of homosexuality as a 'mental illness' from the DSM, heterosexuality is still positioned as the 'norm' within psychology, psychiatry and sexology (Tiefer, 2009). Therefore homophobia and heterosexism are still entangled with sanism (LeFrancois & Diamond, 2014; Sedgwick, 1991). Diagnoses position gender minorities and gender-diverse individuals in the oppressive confines of sexism, cisgenderism, heterosexism and sanism – furthering their experiences of inequality through its removal of their voice and bodily autonomy. As Fabris (2011) states, 'the "mad" can't speak for themselves is the standard rebuttal' (p. 27).

The problems with psychology and psychiatry can be masked by medical discourse and a perception that the very altruistic purpose of these professions is to help. Instead, some use the term 'psychiatrized' to describe the effects of diagnosis, as something that is done *to* someone. They reject the labels of 'mental illness' and 'mental health' which are considered 'a sloppy attempt to hide the oppressive nature of psychiatry, to make it seem more palatable, even to make it seem friendly' (LeFrancois, 2012, p. 7). Similarly, for Perlin, sanism is of more concern as a form of oppression because it is:

> . . . (a) largely invisible (b) largely socially acceptable; and (c) frequently practiced (consciously or unconsciously) by individuals who regularly take

> 'liberal' or 'progressive' positions decrying similar biases and prejudices that involve sex, race, ethnicity, or sexual orientation. It is a form of bigotry that 'respectable' people can express in public.
>
> (Perlin, 2002, p.22)

For example, popular phrases such as 'that's crazy' or 'that's so insane' are often used by those critical of other forms of derogatory language, but who fail to interrogate the sanist connotations of these terms (Ingram, 2011). For those less familiar with psychology, this brief overview provides information to consider regarding the role of psychology and psychiatry in the oppression of others – as we can all too easily look to other disciplines for solutions.

The limits of theory

> Every solution to a human problem generates a new set of problems.
>
> (Szasz, 2007, p. 66)

There are many problems with psychology and psychiatry, as well as abuses and questionable treatments that have attracted condemnation over many decades. Nevertheless, a sudden retraction of support, or the assumption that the professions never help can result in the promotion of a 'one size fits all' ethos that can be just as problematic. It can also assume an 'us' and 'them' stance that overlooks the existence of those who identify as both 'mad' (or other pathologized positions) *and* clinician (Richards et al., 2014). Just as forcing people to undergo unwanted and non-consensual treatments is harmful (Szasz, 2007), so too is the forced removal of support, or the insistence that those who choose to seek such therapies should stop. For example, Claridge describes an account of an anti-psychiatrist letting down someone who came to them for help:

> Anna, the tragic story of an individual schizophrenic who was persuaded by a Laingian doctor to face up to her madness without drugs and whose slow, painful death from self-inflicted burns symbolizes in the most awful way the end of an era in psychiatry.
>
> (Claridge, 1990, p. 157)

While the casualties of psychiatry are high in number (Breggin, 2006; Gotzsche, 2013; Joukamaa et al., 2006), stories like this highlight the importance of careful challenges to such an influential system in the wake of prevalent emotional distress. There are also many groups and individuals who value and embrace the diagnostic system (Pilgrim, 2007), for many reasons, including its relationship to the access of services and financial support. Such is the case for the diagnoses of gender dysphoria for trans individuals (Lev, 2006) and post-traumatic stress disorder for feminists campaigning for support for rape victims (Wasco, 2003). Simply removing a source of support or intervention can have drastic consequences. While one form of intervention may be highlighted as harmful, we must be careful with recommendations and conclusions not to inadvertently introduce something just as harmful in a new guise. Thus, the relationship between abstract theorizing about madness and gender and the lived realities of those experiencing distress and gendered oppression must be reciprocal.

Language and discourse

Writing about a topic that has conflict and disagreement as its foundation is a difficult task to undertake. The language is contradictory, hostile, pathologizing and ever-changing. It requires an appreciation that there are multiple perspectives occupying the same space simultaneously and an engagement with their diversity. It also illustrates the importance of language – its power, abuse and impact on the lives of many people. This area of research is one where the changeability of terms is a notable constant. Within psychiatry, there are diagnoses from 'metamorphis sexualis paranoica' to 'transvestic fetishim' and 'gender dysphoria', all applied to people who do not conform to 'norms' of gender. Within transgender activist spaces, and people's descriptions of their own identity, there are just as many terms – such as 'transexual', 'transgender' and 'genderqueer'. Therefore, one thing is certain: that the terms used in this book will change over time and they will mean different things to different people, in different contexts. It is a wonderful example of social constructionism in action, but it can feel uncertain for those who find comfort in clear conclusions and precise answers. For this reason, I provide definitions of terms I use as I go through the book. These are not given as 'the' ultimate meaning of the word, but are simply provided to show how I am using the term. These words and labels may change in the future as they are taken up and appropriated for different purposes. What is important is that we change our ways of speaking and writing within the changing context of transgender and feminist campaigns for social justice. Consequently, my words represent a particular perspective, at a particular time.

It is also important to differentiate between 'gender dysphoria', the problematic psychiatric concept produced and constructed through texts like the DSM, and gender dysphoria, the embodied experience of gender distress experienced by people whose gender identity does not conform to Western expectations of gender 'norms' or is incongruent with their physical body. I critique, trace and challenge the former, a label that positions gender diversity as mental 'illness' and results in transgender and non-binary identities being labelled as 'mad', 'sick' and 'perverse' – a concept that undermines the decisions and choices of individuals due to questions of 'mental capacity' or are explained away as part of a 'sickness'. This does not mean that the distress is not 'real'; it means that I question the need to frame such distress as a biological abnormality for it to be seen as valid. Like Hacking (1999) argues, analysing a social construction does not mean that the phenomenon is 'not real'. There is the construction of transgender people by multiple viewpoints (e.g. psychiatry, feminism and transgender perspectives), and then the lived reality and existence of trans people and trans identities. I do not conflate the two. I do not question, critique, or challenge the existence of gender distress, as there is much evidence for its existence, prevalence and intensity (Bochenek & Brown, 2001; Clements-Nolle et al., 2006; Lee & Kwan, 2014; Maguen & Shipherd, 2010; Rymer & Cartei, 2015; Stotzer, 2009; Wyss, 2004). Instead, I analyse how it is framed and explained in psychological, feminist and transgender texts.

In this book, I will be drawing on a wide range of theory and research, predominantly focusing on feminism and transgender scholarship and activism, as well as critical psychology and discursive approaches. Critical psychology (Parker, 2007; Parker & Burman, 2008) draws on philosophy, sociology and feminism in its analysis of psychology, power and oppression. It developed from, and includes, psychiatric survivor (Burstow, 2004; Chamberlin, 1994; Cresswell & Spandler, 2013) and anti psychiatry perspectives (Cox & Kelly, 2002), as well as qualitative methodologies such as discourse analysis (Burman & Parker, 1993; Burman, 2004; Parker, 2013). The method applied in this book includes (but is not limited to) a 'free association' of selected texts. Identification of objects and subjects that are constructed and naturalized[7] within the text is done in conjunction with an examination of how these particular constructions disadvantage/oppress certain groups, promote others and support particular institutions. This subsequently invites an analysis of power and its social, cultural and political contexts (Burman, 2004), as well as the role of institutions and ideology (Parker, 1998). Examining contradictions and contestations is an important part of the analysis. As Burman states:

> Rather than formulating a monovocal account, good discursive analyses acknowledge the multiple and contested character of the interplay of discourses by showing how different discursive representations are built to interact with and ward off others.
>
> (Burman, 2004, para. 16)

Drawing on qualitative methodologies is not only important for the reasons outlined in this introduction, such as the problems of quantifying human behaviour and experience, but also due to the particular relevance of language in this topic area. This is in addition to its suitability for the study and understanding of lived experiences and subjectivity – often lacking in pathologizing approaches (i.e. those that frame diversity or nonconformity as mental 'illness').

Book outline

This book examines the debates and controversies surrounding psychiatric diagnoses and theories related to gender and gender nonconformity. It does this through an examination of competing feminist and trans texts, as well as examples of collaborative perspectives. Drawing on discursive psychology, it traces the historical development of psychiatric constructions of 'normal' and 'abnormal' gender expression and contextualizes the recent reconstruction of gender through the *DSM-5* criteria for gender dysphoria (Chapters 2 and 3). Following this examination of psychiatric constructions, Chapters 4 and 5 turn to feminist and trans texts to examine how these frame gender dysphoria and their responses to psychiatric discourse. Chapters 4 and 5 also address the complex relationship between feminist and trans perspectives, reflecting on their long history of hostility, as well as areas of mutual overlap and alliance. A book describing these interconnected and complex issues is difficult to structure, as the connections and relationships between different perspectives and issues are dense and volatile. Therefore, addressing issues regarding feminism does not imply that trans people are not a part of that discourse, movement, or category. Similarly, discussing trans issues does not exclude feminism or feminist perspectives. Ultimately, the following chapters represent complexity, interconnectedness and a rejection of binary thinking.

Notes

1 Although the classification of the medical causes of death began a century earlier (World Health Organization, 2010).
2 Boyle (1990) opposes the view that Kraepelin observed a pattern of behaviours or 'symptoms' justifying the theory of dementia praecox (p. 9). She describes evidence that the concept of schizophrenia defined in the 19th century actually described a different group of people than it does today; perhaps those experiencing the effects of the infectious disease encephalitis lethargia, due to the similarity in symptoms.
3 The WHO's ICD is also used and over time has aimed to be more consistent with the DSM's terms and structure, although its next edition is likely to move away from the DSM's diagnosis of 'gender dysphoria' (see Chapter 3).
4 At the same time, some first-wave feminist arguments echoed this narrative of the need to take control over the production of the 'race' in social purity movements, within the context of campaigning for reproductive rights for women (Klausen & Bashford, 2010). However, this was a complex relationship between feminism and eugenics (Devereux, 2006), where taking a 'maternal' role as 'guardians of the race' included misunderstanding and fear regarding 'madness' and 'feeblemindedness' (Moss, Stam & Kattevilder, 2013).
5 As the focus was primarily with homosexual men.
6 Which can include those who have experienced sexual violence.
7 Parker (1998) defines 'naturalization' as constructing objects or subjects in a way that makes challenging their existence appear 'nonsensical' (p. 103).

References

Ali, A. (2004). The intersection of racism and sexism in psychiatric diagnosis. In P. Caplan & L. Cosgrove (Eds), *Bias in psychiatric diagnosis* (pp. 71–6). Oxford: Rowman & Littlefield.
American Medico-Psychological Association (1918). *Statistical manual for the use of institutions for the insane.* New York: Author.

APA (American Psychiatric Association) (1952). *Diagnostic and statistical manual of mental disorders first edition (DSM-I)*. Washington, DC: Author.
APA (American Psychiatric Association) (1973). Position statement on homosexuality and sexual orientation disturbance: Proposed change in *DSM-II*. Washington, DC: Author: http://www.torahdec.org/downloads/dsm-ii_homosexuality_revision.pdf (accessed 3 December 2015).
APA (American Psychiatric Association) (2013). *Diagnostic and statistical manual of mental disorders fifth edition (DSM-5)*. Washington, DC: Author.
American Public Health Association (1899). *Bertillon classification of causes of death*. Lansing, MI: Robert Smith Printing.
Andreassen, O. A., Thompson, W. K., & Dale, A. M. (2014). Boosting the power of schizophrenia genetics by leveraging new statistical tools. *Schizophrenia Bulletin*, *40*(1), 13–17.
Ansara, G., & Hegarty, P. (2012). Cisgenderism in psychology: Pathologising and misgendering children from 1999 to 2008. *Psychology & Sexuality*, *3*(2), 137–60.
Ayers, S., & Visser, R. (2010). *Psychology for medicine*. London: SAGE Publications.
Bancroft, J. (1974). *Deviant sexual behaviour: Modification and assessment*. Oxford: Oxford University Press.
Barker, M. (2007). Heteronormativity and the exclusion of bisexuality in psychology. In V. Clarke & E. Peel (Eds), *Out in psychology: Lesbian, gay, bisexual, trans and queer perspectives*. pp. 86–118. Chichester: John Wiley & Sons.
Bartlett, A., Smith, G., & King, M. (2009). The response of mental health professionals to clients seeking help to change or redirect same-sex sexual orientation. *BMC Psychiatry*, *9*, 11.
Beiber, I., Dain, P., Dince, P., Drellich, M., Grand, H., Gundlach, R., & Bieber, T. (1962). *Homosexuality: A psychoanalytic study of male homosexuals*. New York: Basic Books.
Bentall, R. (2009). *Doctoring the mind: Why psychiatric treatments fail*. London: Penguin UK.
Bibeau, G., & Pedersen, D. (2002). A return to scientific racism in medical social sciences: The case of sexuality and the AIDS epidemic in Africa. In M. Nichter & M. Lock (Eds), *New horizons in medical anthropology: Essays in honour of Charles Leslie*. (pp. 141–71). London: Routledge.
Binet, A., & Henri, V. (1895). La psychologie individuelle. *L'Année Psychologie*, *2*, 411–65.
Birnbaum, M. (1960). The right to treatment. *American Bar Association Journal*, *46*(5), 499–505.
Bleuler, E. (1911). *Dementia praecox oder gruppe der schizophrenien*. Leipzig: Deuticke.
Blundell, S. (1995). *Women in ancient Greece*. Cambridge, MA: Harvard University Press.
Bochenek, M., & Brown, A. W. (2001). *Hatred in the hallways: Violence and discrimination against lesbian, gay, bisexual, and transgender students in U.S. schools*. New York: Human Rights Watch.
Boissier de Sauvages, F. (1732). *Nouvelles classes de maladies de maladies dans un ordre semblable a celui des botanistes*. Avignon: D'Avanville.
Boissier de Sauvages, F. (1763). *Nosologie méthodique*. Lyon: Jean-Marie Bruyset.
Boyle, M. (1990). The non-discovery of schizophrenia? Kraepelin and Bleuler reconsidered. In R. Bentall (Ed.), *Reconstructing schizophrenia*. (pp. 3–22). London: Routledge.
Boyle, M. (2007). The problem with diagnosis. *The Psychologist*, *20*(5), 290.
Breggin, P. (1975). Psychosurgery for political purposes. *Duquesne Law Review*, *13*, 841–62.
Breggin, P. (1979). *Electroshock: It's brain-disabling effects*. New York: Springer Publishing Company Inc.
Breggin, P. (1992). The return of ECT. *Readings: A Journal of Reviews and Commentary in Mental Health*, 12–17.

Breggin, P. (1993). *Toxic psychiatry: Drugs and electroconvulsive therapy, the truth and better alternatives.* London: Harper Collins.

Breggin, P. (2006). How GlaxoSmithKline suppressed data on Paxil-induced akathisia: Implications for suicidality and violence. *Ethical Human Psychology and Psychiatry, 8*(2), 91–100.

Breggin, P. (2007). ECT Damages the brain: Disturbing news for patients and shock doctors alike. *Ethical Human Psychology and Psychiatry, 9*(2), 83.

Brown, S., & Stenner, P. (2009). *Psychology without foundations: History, philosophy and psychosocial theory.* London: SAGE Publications.

Bullough, V. (1982). The sin against nature and homosexuality. In V. Bullough & J. Brundage (Eds), *Sexual practices and the medieval Church.* (pp. 55–71). Buffalo, NY: Prometheus Books.

Burman, E. (1997a). *Deconstructing feminist psychology.* London: SAGE Publications.

Burman, E. (1997b). Minding the gap: Positivism, psychology, and the politics of qualitative methods. *Journal of Social Issues, 53*(4), 785–801.

Burman, E. (2004). Discourse analysis means analysing discourse: Some comments on Antaki, Billig, Edwards and Potter 'Discourse analysis means doing analysis: A critique of six analytic shortcomings'. *Discourse Analysis Online, 1*(2): http://extra.shu.ac.uk/daol/articles/open/2003/003/burman2003003-paper.html (accessed 20 November 2015).

Burman, E., & Parker, I. (1993). Introduction – discourse analysis: the turn to the text. In E. Burman & I. Parker (Eds.), *Discourse analytic research: Repertoires and readings of text in action.* (pp. 1–13). London: Routledge.

Burstow, B. (2004). Progressive psychotherapists and the psychiatric survivor movement. *Journal of Humanistic Psychology, 44*(2), 141–54.

Burstow, B. (2006a). Electroshock as a form of violence against women. *Violence Against Women, 12*(4), 372–92.

Burstow, B. (2006b). Understanding and ending ECT: A feminist imperative. *Canadian Woman Studies, 25*(1), 115–22.

Burstow, B., LeFrançois, B., & Diamond, S. (2014). *Psychiatry disrupted: Theorizing resistance and crafting the (r)evolution.* Montreal: McGill-Queen's Press.

Burt, C. (1927). *The measurement of mental capacities: The Henderson Trust Lecture No. VII.* Edinburgh: Oliver & Boyd.

Bynum, W. F. (1981). Cullen and the study of fevers in Britain, 1760–1820. *Medical History. Supplement,* 1, 135–47.

Campbell, F. K. (2009). *Contours of ableism: The production of disability and abledness.* Basingstoke: Palgrave Macmillan.

Canner, E. (2008). Sex, lies and pharmaceuticals: The making of an investigative documentary about 'female sexual dysfunction'. *Feminism & Psychology, 18*(4), 488–94.

Caplan, P. (1996). *They say you're crazy: How the world's most powerful psychiatrists decide who's normal.* Reading, MA: DaCapo Press.

Caplan, P., & Cosgrove, L. (2004). *Bias in psychiatric diagnosis.* Oxford: Rowman & Littlefield.

Cermele, J. A., Daniels, S., & Anderson, K. L. (2001). Defining normal: Constructions of race and gender in the *DSM-IV* Casebook. *Feminism & Psychology, 11*(2), 229–47.

Chamberlin, J. (1994). A psychiatric survivor speaks out. *Feminism & Psychology, 4*(2), 284–7.

Chamberlin, J. (2005). User/consumer involvement in mental health service delivery. *Epidemiologia E Psichiatria Sociale, 14*(1), 10–14.

Chanpattana, W., Kunigiri, G., Kramer, B. & Gangadhar, B. (2005). Survey of the practice of electroconvulsive therapy in teaching hospitals in India. *Journal of ECT, 21,* 100–104.

Cheshire, K., & Pilgrim, D. (2004). *A short introduction to clinical psychology*. London: SAGE Publications.

Claridge, G. (1990). Can a disease model of schizophrenia survive? In R. Bentall (Ed.), *Reconstructing schizophrenia*. (pp. 157–83). London: Routledge.

Clarke, V., & Peel, E. (2007). *Out in psychology: Lesbian, gay, bisexual, trans and queer perspectives*. Chichester: John Wiley & Sons.

Clements-Nolle, K., Marx, R., & Katz, M. (2006). Attempted suicide among transgender persons. *Journal of Homosexuality, 51*(3), 53–69.

Conrad, P. (1992). Medicalization and social control. *Annual Review of Sociology, 18*, 209–32.

Conrad, P., & Angell, A. (2004). Homosexuality and remedicalization. *Society, 41*(5), 32–39.

Cooper, R. (2004). What is wrong with the DSM? *History of Psychiatry, 15*(1), 5–25.

Cotten, C., & Ridings, J. (2011). Getting out/getting in: The DSM, political activism, and the social construction of mental disorders. *Social Work in Mental Health, 9*(3), 181–205.

Cox, R., & Kelly, P. (2002). From anti-psychiatry to critical psychology. *The Journal of Critical Psychology, Counselling and Psychotherapy, 2*(3), 148–52.

Cresswell, M., & Spandler, H. (2013). The engaged academic: Academic intellectuals and the psychiatric survivor movement. *Social Movement Studies, 12*(2), 138–54.

Cromby, J., Harper, D., & Reavey, P. (2007). Moving beyond diagnosis: Practising what we preach. *The Psychologist, 20*, 289.

Crowe, M. (2000). Constructing normality: A discourse analysis of the DSM-IV. *Journal of Psychiatric and Mental Health Nursing*, 7(1), 69–77.

Cullen, W. (1784). *First lines in the practice of physic, vol. III* (4th edition). Edinburgh: C. Elliot & T. Cadell.

Cullen, W. (1785). *A synopsis of methodical nosology in which the genera of disorders are particularly defined, and the species added with the synonimous of those from Sauvages*. Philadelphia, PA: Parry Hall.

Davison, G. (1976). Homosexuality: The ethical challenge. *Journal of Consulting and Clinical Psychology, 44*, 157–62.

DCP Position Statement. (2013). *Classification of behaviour and experience in relation to functional psychiatric diagnoses: Time for a paradigm shift*. Leicester: Division of Clinical Psychology.

Devereux, C. (2006). *Growing a race: Nellie L. McClung and the fiction of eugenic feminism*. Montreal: McGill-Queen's Press – MQUP.

Dickins, T., & Donovan, P. (2012). Animal behaviour fieldwork: Introducing psychology students to the process of science. In *Proceedings of the HEA STEM Learning and Teaching Conference*. The Higher Education Academy: files.eric.ed.gov/fulltext/EJ991403.pdf (accessed 15 November 2015).

DSM-5 Response. (n.d.). Statement of concern: from http://dsm5response.com/statement-of-concern/ (accessed 6 November 2013, no longer available).

Emke, I. (1992). Medical authority and Its discontents: A case of organized non-compliance. *Critical Sociology, 19*(3), 57–80.

Fabris, E. (2011). *Tranquil prisons: Chemical incarceration under community treatment orders*. Toronto: University of Toronto Press.

Feder, E. K. (1997). Disciplining the family: The case of gender identity disorder. *Philosophical Studies, 85*(2-3), 195–211.

Feldman, M. P., & MacCulloch, M. J. (2013). *Homosexual behaviour: Therapy and assessment*. New York: Elsevier.

Flint, J., & Kendler, K. S. (2014). The genetics of major depression. *Neuron, 81*(3), 484–503.

Foucault, M. (1975). *Madness and civilization: A history of insanity in the age of reason.* New York: Vintage Books.

Frances, A. (2013). *Saving normal: An insider's revolt against out-of-control psychiatric diagnosis, DSM-5, big pharma, and the medicalization of ordinary life.* New York: Harper Collins.

Freund, K. (1960). Some problems in the treatment of homosexuality. In H. J. Eysenck (Ed.), *Behaviour Therapy and the Neuroses,* (pp. 312–14). London: Pergamon Press.

Galton, F. (1890). Some remarks on Cattell's 'Mental tests and measurements'. *Mind, 15,* 380–81.

Goldblum, P., Testa, R. J., Pflum, S., Hendricks, M. L., Bradford, J., & Bongar, B. (2012). The relationship between gender-based victimization and suicide attempts in transgender people. *Professional Psychology: Research and Practice, 43*(5), 468–75.

Goodley, D. (2014). *Dis/ability studies: Theorising disablism and ableism.* London: Routledge.

Gornall, J. (2013). *DSM-5*: A fatal diagnosis? *BMJ, 346,* f3256.

Goto, S., & Martin, C. (2009). Psychology of success: Overcoming barriers to pursuing further education. *Journal of Continuing Higher Education, 57*(1), 10–21.

Gotzsche, P. C. (2013). *Deadly medicines and organised crime: How Big Pharma has corrupted healthcare.* London: Radcliffe Medical Press.

Gould, S. (2006). *The mismeasure of man.* New York: W. W. Norton & Company.

Grant, J., Mottet, L., Tanis, J., Herman, J., Harrison, J., & Keisling, M. (2010). *National transgender discrimination survey report on health and health care.* National Center for Transgender Equality; National Gay and Lesbian Task Force: http://www.thetaskforce.org/static_html/downloads/resources_and_tools/ntds_report_on_health.pdf (accessed 20 November 2015).

Groneman, C. (1994). Nymphomania: the historical construction of female sexuality. *Signs,* 19, 337–67.

Hacking, I. (1999). *The social construction of what?* London: Harvard University Press.

Hager, M. G. (1982). The myth of objectivity. *American Psychologist, 37*(5), 576–9.

Harding, S. G. (1986). *The science question in feminism.* Ithaca, NY: Cornell University Press.

Healy, D. (2012). *Pharmageddon.* Los Angeles: University of California Press.

Hill, D. B. (2012). *Trans Toronto: An oral history.* New York: William Rodney Press.

Hite, S. (2004). *The Hite report: A nationwide study of female sexuality.* New York: Seven Stories Press.

Hoberman, J. (2012). *Black and blue: The origins and consequences of medical racism.* Los Angeles: University of California Press.

Houts, A. (2000). Fifty years of psychiatric nomenclature: Reflections on the 1943 War Department Technical Bulletin, Medical 203. *Journal of Clinical Psychology, 57*(6), 935–67.

Hunt, A. (1998). The great masturbation panic and the discourses of moral regulation in nineteenth and early twentieth century Britain. *Journal of the History of Sexuality, 8*(4), 575–615.

Ingram, R. (2011). Sanism in theory and practice. Presented at the *2nd Annual Critical Inquiries Workshop,* Vancouver.

Insel, T. (2013). Director's blog: Transforming diagnosis: http://www.nimh.nih.gov/about/director/2013/transforming-diagnosis.shtml (accessed 20 November 2015).

International Statistical Institute. (1900). International list of causes of death. *Bulletin of the Institute of International Statistics, 12,* 280.

Jauk, D. (2013). Gender violence revisited: Lessons from violent victimization of transgender identified individuals. *Sexualities, 16*(7), 807–25.

Jeffreys, S. (2014). The politics of the toilet: A feminist response to the campaign to 'degender' a women's space. *Women's Studies International Forum, 45*, 42–51.

Johnson, M. (1998). Psychological differential diagnosis: Alternatives to the DSM system. *Journal of Contemporary Psychotherapy, 28*(1), 91–5.

Jordan-Young, R. M. (2011). *Brain storm*. Boston, MA: Harvard University Press.

Joukamaa, M., Markku, H., Knekt, P., Aromaa, A., Raitasalo, R., & Lehtinen, V. (2006). Schizophrenia, neuroleptic medication and mortality. *British Journal of Psychiatry, 188*, 122–7.

Kaila, H. L. (2006). *Industrial And organisational psychology*. Delhi: Gyan Publishing House.

Kaluger, G. (1969). *Psychology and sociology: An integrated approach to understanding human behavior*. St. Louis, MO: C. V. Mosby Co.

Kamin, L. J. (1974). *The science and politics of I.Q.* Potomac, MD: Routledge.

Kim, E. (2014). Asexualities and disabilities in constructing sexual normalcy. In K. Cerankowski & M. Milks (Eds), *Asexualities: Feminist and queer perspectives*. (pp. 249–82). London: Routledge.

Klausen, S., & Bashford, A. (2010). Fertility control: Eugenics, neo-malthusiasnism, and feminism. In A. Bashford & P. Levine (Eds), *The Oxford handbook of eugenics* (pp. 98–115). Oxford: Oxford University Press.

Kraepelin, E. (1883). *Compendium der psychiatrie*. Leipzig.

Kupfer, D. (2013). Statement by David Kupfer, MD: Chair of *DSM-5* Taskforce discusses future of mental health research. Washington, DC: American Psychiatric Association.

Kutchins, H., & Kirk, S. (2003). *Making us crazy. DSM: The psychiatric Bible and the creation of mental disorders*. New York: Simon and Schuster.

Lambley, P. (1974). Treatment of transvestism and subsequent coital problems. *Journal of Behavior Therapy and Experimental Psychiatry, 5*(1), 101–2.

Lee, C., & Kwan, P. K. Y. (2014). *The trans panic defense: Heteronormativity, and the murder of transgender women* (SSRN Scholarly Paper No. ID 2430390). Rochester, NY: Social Science Research Network.

LeFrançois, B. (2012). And we are still being psychiatrised. *Asylum, 19*(1), 7–8.

LeFrançois, B., & Diamond, S. (2014). Queering the sociology of diagnosis: Children and the constituting of 'mentally ill' subjects. *Journal of Critical Anti-Oppressive Social Inquiry, 1*(1), 39–61.

LeFrançois, B., Menzies, R., & Reaume, G. (2013). *Mad matters: A critical reader in Canadian mad studies*. Toronto: Canadian Scholars' Press.

Lerner, B. (2005). Last-ditch medical therapy: Revisiting lobotomy. *New England Journal of Medicine, 353*(2), 119–21.

Lev, A. I. (2006). Disordering gender identity: Gender identity disorder in the *DSM-IV-TR*. *Journal of Psychology & Human Sexuality, 17*(3-4), 35–69.

Lott, B. E., & Bullock, H. E. (2006). *Psychology and economic injustice: Personal, professional, and political intersections*. Washington, DC: American Psychological Association.

Luttrell, W. (2005). Crossing anxious borders: Teaching across the quantitative-qualitative 'divide'. *International Journal of Research & Method in Education, 28*(2), 183–95.

Maguen, S., & Shipherd, J. C. (2010). Suicide risk among transgender individuals. *Psychology & Sexuality, 1*(1), 34–43.

Malhi, G. S., Lampe, L., Coulston, C. M., Tanious, M., Bargh, D. M., Curran, G., . . . Fritz, K. (2014). Mixed state discrimination: A DSM problem that won't go away? *Journal of Affective Disorders, 158*, 8–10.

Marks, I., & Gelder, M. (1967). Transvestism and fetishism: Clinical and psychological changes during faradic aversion. *The British Journal of Psychiatry, 113*(500), 711–29.

Marks, I., Gelder, M., & Bancroft, J. (1970). Sexual deviants two years after electric aversion. *British Journal of Psychiatry*, *117*(537), 173–85.

Marquis, J. (1977). Orgasmic reconditioning: Changing sexual object choice through controlling masturbation fantasies. In J. Fisher & H. Gochros (Eds.), *Handbook of behaviour therapy with sexual problems*. (pp. 120–30). Oxford: Pergamon.

Masson, J. M. (1993). *Against therapy: Emotional tyranny and the myth of psychological healing*. New York: Athenaeum.

McInerney, D. (2013). *Educational psychology: Constructing learning*. Frenchs Forest, New South Wales: Pearson Higher Education AU.

Metcalfe, W., & Caplan, P. (2004). Seeking 'normal' sexuality on a complex matrix. In P. Caplan & L. Cosgrove (Eds), *Bias in psychiatric diagnosis* (pp. 121–6). Oxford: Rowman & Littlefield.

Meyer, E., & Sansfacon, A. (2014). *Supporting transgender and gender creative youth: Schools, families, and communities in action*. New York: Peter Lang Pub. Incorporated.

Mills, C. (2014). *Decolonizing global mental health: The psychiatrization of the majority world*. London: Routledge.

Molloy, P. (2014). Op-ed: The deadly effects of outing: http://www.advocate.com/commentary/2014/01/24/op-ed-deadly-effects-outing (accessed 20 November 2015).

Moncrieff, J. (2008). The creation of the concept of an antidepressant: An historical analysis. *Social Science & Medicine*, *66*, 2346–55.

Moore, T. (2014). Trans woman commits suicide amid fear of outing by sports blog: http://jezebel.com/trans-woman-commits-suicide-amid-fear-of-outing-by-spor-1503902916 (accessed 20 November 2015).

Moss, E., Stam, H., & Kattevilder, D. (2013). From suffrage to sterilization: Eugenics and the women's movement in 20th century Alberta. *Canadian Psychology/Psychologie Canadienne*, *54*(2), 105–14.

Moynihan, R., & Mintzes, B. (2010). *Sex, lies, and pharmaceuticals: How drug companies plan to profit from female sexual dysfunction*. Sydney: Greystone Books.

Munsche, H., & Whitaker, H. (2012). Eighteenth century classification of mental illness: Linnaeus, de Sauvages, Vogel, and Cullen. *Cognitive & Behavioral Neurology*, *25*(4), 224–39.

Myers, D. B. (2014). 'Drapetomania': Rebellion, defiance and free black insanity in the antebellum United States. *eScholarship*: http://escholarship.org/uc/item/9dc055h5 (accessed 20 November 2015).

Namaste, V. (2000). *Invisible lives: The erasure of transsexual and transgendered people*. Chicago, IL: University of Chicago Press.

Newnes, C. (1999). Histories of psychiatry. In C. Newnes, G. Holmes, & C. Dunn (Eds), *This is madness: A critical look at psychiatry and the future of mental health services*. (pp. 7–28). Ross-on-Wye: PCCS Books.

Newnes, C., Holmes, G., & Dunn, C. (1999). *This is madness: A critical look at psychiatry and the future of mental health services*. Ross-on-Wye: PCCS Books.

Nicolosi, J. J. (2009). *Shame and attachment loss: The practical work of reparative therapy*. Downers Grove, IL: IVP Academic.

Oosterhuis, H. (2000). *Stepchildren of nature: Krafft-Ebing, psychiatry, and the making of sexual identity*. Chicago, IL: University of Chicago Press.

Parker, I. (1998). Realism, relativism and critique in psychology. In I. Parker (Ed.), *Social constructionism, discourse and realism*. (pp. 1–10). London: SAGE Publications.

Parker, I. (2007). Critical psychology: What it is and what it is not. *Social and Personality Psychology Compass*, *1*(1), 1–15.

Parker, I. (2013). Discourse analysis: Dimensions of critique in psychology. *Qualitative Research in Psychology, 10*(3), 223–39.

Parker, I., & Burman, E. (2008). Critical psychology: Four theses and seven misconceptions. *Hellenic Journal of Psychology, 5*, 99–115.

Perlin, M. L. (2002). You have discussed lepers and crooks: Sanism in clinical teaching. *Clinical Law Review, 9*, 683.

Perlin, M. L. (2006). International human rights law and comparative mental disability law: The universal factors. *Syracuse Journal of International Law and Commerce, 34*, 333.

Pescoslido, B., Monahan, J., Link, B., Stueve, A., & Kikuzawa, S. (1999). The public's view of the competence, dangerousness, and need for legal coercion of person with mental health problems. *American Journal of Public Health, 89*(8), 1339–45.

Phoenix, A. (1994). Practicing feminist research: The intersection of gender and 'race' in the research process. In M. Maynard & J. Purvis (Eds), *Researching women's lives from a feminist perspective.* (pp. 49–71). London: Taylor & Francis.

Pilgrim, D. (1990). Competing histories of madness: Some implications for modern psychiatry. In R. Bentall (Ed.), *Reconstructing schizophrenia.* (pp. 211–33). London: Routledge.

Pilgrim, D. (2007). The survival of psychiatric diagnosis. *Social Science & Medicine, 65*(3), 536–47.

Poole, J., Jivraj, T., Arslanian, A., Bellows, K., Chiasson, S., Hakimy, H. . . . Reid, J. (2012). Sanism, mental health, and social work/education: A review and call to action. *Intersectionalities: A Global Journal of Social Work Analysis, Research, Polity, and Practice, 1*(0), 20–36.

Potts, A. (2002). *The science/fiction of sex: Feminist deconstruction and the vocabularies of heterosex.* London: Psychology Press.

Povee, K., & Roberts, L. D. (2014). Qualitative research in psychology: Attitudes of psychology students and academic staff. *Australian Journal of Psychology, 66*(1), 28–37.

Richards, C., Barker, M., Lenihan, P., & Iantaffi, A. (2014). Who watches the watchmen? A critical perspective on the theorization of trans people and clinicians. *Feminism & Psychology, 24(2)*, 248-258.

Richards, G. (2003). *Race, racism and psychology: Towards a reflexive history.* London: Routledge.

Robb, G. (2003). *Strangers: Homosexual love in the nineteenth century.* London: Picador.

Rogelberg, S. (2009). Journal of Business and Psychology: A new direction. *Journal of Business and Psychology, 24*, 1–3.

Rogers, A., & Pilgrim, D. (2014). *A sociology of mental health and illness.* Maidenhead: McGraw-Hill Education.

Rose, N. (1979). The psychological complex: Mental measurement and social administration. *Ideology & Consciousness, 5*, 5–68.

Rose, N. (1985). *The psychological complex: psychology, politics and society in England, 1869-1939.* London: Routledge & Kegan Paul.

Rose, N. (2009). Normality and pathology in a biomedical age. *The Sociological Review, 57*(2), 66–83.

Rosen, R. C., & Kopel, S. A. (1977). Penile plethysmography and biofeedback in the treatment of a transvestite-exhibitionist. *Journal of Consulting and Clinical Psychology, 45*(5), 908–16.

Rymer, S., & Cartei, V. (2015). Supporting transgender survivors of sexual violence: Learning from users' experiences. *Critical and Radical Social Work, 3*(1), 155–64.

Scott, B. J. (1997). Inner spiritual voices or auditory hallucinations? *Journal of Religion and Health, 36*(1), 53–64.

Scull, A. (1982). *Museums of madness.* Harmondsworth: Penguin UK.

Sedgwick, E. (1991). How to bring your kids up gay. *Social Text, 29*, 18–27.

Serber, M. (1977). Shame aversion therapy. In J. Fischer & H. Gochros (Eds), *Handbook of behaviour therapy with sexual problems.* (pp. 152–64). Oxford: Pergamon.

Shorter, E. (1998). *A history of psychiatry: From the era of the asylum to the age of Prozac* (1st edition). New York: Wiley.

Speak Out Against Psychiatry. (2013). *DSM-5* protest Tuesday 4th June 4.30pm onwards at the Institute of Psychiatry: http://speakoutagainstpsychiatry.org/dsm-5-protest-4th-tuesday-june-4-30pm-onwards-at-the-institute-of-psychiatry/ (accessed 20 November 2015).

Stoppard, J. M. (1991). Sexism and the *DSM-III-R. Canadian Psychology/Psychologie Canadienne, 32*(2), 148–50.

Stotzer, R. L. (2008). Gender identity and hate crimes: Violence against transgender people in Los Angeles County. *Sexuality Research & Social Policy, 5*(1), 43–52.

Stotzer, R. L. (2009). Violence against transgender people: A review of United States data. *Aggression and Violent Behavior, 14*(3), 170–79.

Stryker, S. (2009). *Transgender history.* Berkeley, CA: Seal Press.

Studd, J., & Schwenkhagen, A. (2009). The historical response to female sexuality. *Maturitas, 63*(2), 107–11.

Suls, J., Davidson, K., & Kaplan, R. (2010). *Handbook of health psychology and behavioral medicine.* New York: Guilford Press.

Szasz, T. (1960). The myth of mental illness. *American Psychologist, 15*(2), 113.

Szasz, T. (2007). *The medicalization of everyday life.* Syracuse, NY: Syracuse University Press.

Tiefer, L. (2009). *Sex is not a natural act and other essays.* Boulder, CO: Westview Press.

Tiefer, L. (2006). Female sexual dysfunction: A case study of disease mongering and activist resistance. *PLoS Med, 3*(4), e178.

Tosh, J. (2011a). Academic debate or transphobic hate? A response to 'Zuckergate'. *Clinical Psychology Forum, 221*, 51–4.

Tosh, J. (2011b). The medicalization of rape: A discursive analysis of 'paraphilic coercive disorder' and the psychiatrization of sexuality. *Psychology of Women Section Review, 13*(2), 2–12.

Tosh, J. (2011c). 'Zuck off!' A commentary on the protest against Ken Zucker and his 'treatment' of childhood gender identity disorder. *Psychology of Women Section Review, 13*(1), 10–16.

Tosh, J. (2013). The (in)visibility of childhood sexual abuse: Psychiatric theorizing of transgenderism and intersexuality. *Intersectionalities: A Global Journal of Social Work Analysis, Research, Polity, and Practice, 2*(1), 71–87.

Tosh, J. (2015). *Perverse psychology: The pathologization of sexual violence and transgenderism.* London: Routledge.

Tosh, J., & Carson, K. (in press). The desire to be normal? A discursive and intersectional analysis of 'penetration disorder'. *Intersectionalities: A Global Journal of Social Work Analysis, Research, Polity, and Practice.*

Tosh, J., & Golightley, S. (under review). The caring professions, not so caring? Bullying and emotional distress in the academy.

Turner, L., Whittle, S., & Combs, R. (2009). *Transphobic hate crime in the European Union.* Press for Change: http://www.ucu.org.uk/media/pdf/r/6/transphobic_hate_crime_in_eu.pdf (accessed 20 November 2015).

Ussher, J. (1992). *Women's madness: Misogyny or mental illness?* Amherst: University of Massachusetts Press.

Ussher, J. (2011). *The madness of women: Myth and experience.* London: Routledge.

Vogel, R. A. (1764). *Definitiones generum morborum.* Gottingae: Litteris Ioannis Henrici Schvlzii.

Wakefield, J. (1997). Diagnosing *DSM-IV* Part I: *DSM-IV* and the concept of disorder. *Behaviour Research and Therapy, 35*(7), 633–49.

War Department (1946). Nomenclature of psychiatric disorders and reactions: War Department Technical Bulletin, Medical 203. *Journal of Clinical Psychology, 2*, 289–96.

Wasco, S. (2003). Conceptualizing the harm done by rape: Applications of trauma theory to experiences of sexual assault. *Trauma, Violence & Abuse, 4*, 309–22.

Weiner, D. (1992). Philippe Pinel's 'Memoir on Madness' of December 11, 1794: A fundamental text of modern psychiatry. *American Journal of Psychiatry, 149*(6), 725–32.

Wetzel, J. (1991). Universal mental health classification systems: Reclaiming women's experience. *Affilia, 6*, 8–31.

Winters, K. (2009). *Gender madness in American psychiatry: Essays from the struggle for dignity.* Dillon, CO: BookSurge Publishing.

Wise, M. (2004). *Mad science: Discourses of 'schizophrenia' and 'therapy' for hearing voices* (PhD thesis). Murdoch University; http://researchrepository.murdoch.edu.au/411/ (accessed 17 November 2015).

Woolbert, A. (2014, June 18). TVTP declares Gender Identity Watch as hate group. From http://www.transviolencetracker.org/index.php/press-releases/99-gender-identity-hate-group (accessed 7 November 2014, no longer available).

World Health Organization. (2010). *International statistical classification of diseases and related health problems*, 10th revision. Washington, DC: Author.

Wyss, S. (2004). 'This was my hell': The violence experienced by gender non-conforming youth in US high schools. *International Journal of Qualitative Studies in Education, 17*(5), 709–30.

Zander, T. (2008). Commentary: Inventing diagnosis for civil commitment of rapists. *Journal of the American Academy of Psychiatry and the Law Online, 36*(4), 459–69.

Zucker, K., Wood, H., Singh, D., & Bradley, S. (2012). A developmental, biopsychosocial model for the treatment of children with gender identity disorder. *Journal of Homosexuality, 59*(3), 369–97.

Zur, O., & Nordmarken, N. (2008). DSM: Diagnosing for status and money. *The National Psychologist*, 15.

Chapter 2

Psychiatric constructions of women and femininity

Following the introduction and growth of psychiatry and psychology described in Chapter 1, I will now outline how women[1] have been framed as 'abnormal' in numerous ways. The pathologization of women has expanded with each edition of the DSM, and consequently there are many diagnoses and theories related to aspects of women and femininity. From the overly emotional to the overly aggressive, women have been the focus of much psychiatric and psychological theorizing with aims of 'correcting' those who veered too far from their ascribed gender role as well as those who conformed all too well. In addition to constructing women as 'abnormal', psychiatry and psychology have a long history of pathologizing women who have been victims of violence. Psychiatric discourse, then, functions to detract focus from the social causes of violence and abuse, and also produces several narratives that negate its impact, such as arguing that women derive pleasure from their victimization. As a result, psychiatric diagnoses have been highly criticized for their pathologization of women who conform to social and cultural expectations of femininity (e.g. Caplan, McCurdy-Myers & Gans, 1992; Cermele, Daniels & Anderson, 2001; Chesler, 1997; Jimenez, 1997; Metzl, 2003; Ritchie, 1989; Tiefer, 2009; Ussher, 2011), this is despite the reported negative impact that stereotypical gender roles (when restrictive and compulsory) can have on women's well-being (Friedan, 2010; Ussher, 2010). To examine this intersection of sexism and sanism, in this chapter I outline psychiatric constructions of gender-conforming women and femininity through a range of long-standing and influential diagnoses, as well as feminist critiques of them. I focus on 'hysteria', 'borderline personality disorder' and 'masochism', with reflection on some other ways that these professions frame women and their distress as pathological. I begin with a consideration of how similar concepts have been positioned historically to illustrate both the transient existence of psychological and psychiatric discourses, as well as how long-standing these negative portrayals of women are.

Witchcraft

> The modern psychiatric view of the witch as a mentally ill person is not merely a false interpretation of the historical record; it is a perverse denial of the true role of the witch as benefactor or therapist as well as malefactor or troublemaker.
>
> (Szasz, 1997, p. 82)

Prior to psychiatric conceptualizations of women, religious discourse was predominant in describing and intervening in occurrences of 'deviance'. Like psychology and psychiatry, religious discourse both delineated 'appropriate' gendered behaviour, as well as interventions designed to 'normalize' those who did not conform. During the Middle Ages (5th–15th centuries) in Europe and North America, those who experienced emotional distress or challenged societal 'norms' were labelled as sinners and witches, whose actions were thought to be due to possession by a demon or devil (Wetzel, 1991). Attempts to cast out such 'evil' included exorcism and magical rituals (Ussher, 1992). For women, a label of 'sinner' or 'witch' could be applied for a wide range of behaviours and activities deemed inappropriate and sinful, including homosexuality, being sexually active (or being perceived to be 'promiscuous'), living independently of a man, or not being married (e.g. the 'hag') (Ussher, 1992). Many of those labelled as such were women who were in positions of religious authority, something that was considered heretical and used as further evidence of their inherent 'wickedness' (Wetzel, 1991). It also included women healers, such as midwives, who were seen as a threat to male physicians (Becker, 2009) and the Christian Church, due to their perceived denunciation of God's authority in sickness and healing (Szasz, 1997), and as a scapegoat for the ills of society that could not be explained (Ussher, 1992). The woman healer, or witch, was a healer of those who experienced suffering and disease. People sought out their help voluntarily and reimbursed them for their services (Szasz, 1997).

Witchcraft, and the healing therapies that drew on women's long history as healers and midwives, were made illegal in the English Witchcraft Act in 1542. The punishment of death was cemented with further laws, such as the Scottish Witchcraft Act of 1563 (Szasz, 1997). This was in addition to texts that described in detail the 'wickedness' of women and witches that began a century earlier, such as Sprenger and Kraemer's (1496) influential *Malleus Maleficarum* ('Witch Hammer'). This culminated in the widespread mass murder of women during witch-hunts that began during the 14th century: 'The trials have been seen as the embodiment of a hatred of women, organized and ritualized through patriarchal dictate, resulting in the torture and death of millions of women under the catch-all term 'witch': the ultimate in misogynistic annihilation' (Ussher, 1992, p. 43).

While men were also punished for witchcraft, women were the more frequent victims, being labelled as 'witch', and subjected to abuse and murdered. Ussher (1992) describes how during the trials women were frequently stripped in public (allegedly for men to look for marks of the devil) and raped, prior to being drowned. These women were thought to be capable of killing with a single look, destroy crops and livestock, and control the minds of men (Ussher, 1992).

These well-documented constructions of 'sinful' and 'wicked' women apply to predominantly Christian perspectives within a context of colonization. Colonial discourse repositioned native or indigenous religions as feminized, barbaric (Carroll, 1990), backward and evil (McVeigh & Rolston, 2009). As Strmiska (2003) describes, 'Christianity did not simply "rise" – it conquered. Nor did Paganism merely "fall" – it was crushed' (p. 60). The Christian Church forced the version of

European witchcraft as being allied with the devil during the Middle Ages (Szasz, 1997), by transforming Pagan deities (such as the horned god) into the concept of Satan (Strmiska, 2003). Subsequently, Pagan understandings of gender and sexuality were prohibited. For instance, in Celtic Pagan Ireland, women were 'not simply other but often otherworldly' (Bitel, 1998, p. 19). Women and femininity were highly regarded in numerous myths and accounts of fae and goddesses, such as Brigit,[2] daughter of the Túatha Dé Danann god, Dagda (Cusack, 2007) and Cailleach Bhéarra the Celtic 'hag' (Crualaoich, 1995; Fhloinn, 2005). Moreover, while Aboriginal cultures are varied and diverse, they often shared a respect for women who were framed as the foundation of their communities, such as the Ojibwe. Women were central to the 'circle of life' and 'medicine wheel' (Stark, 2013). This was in addition to Warrior Women, such as those of the Blackfoot Ninawaki Society (Stevenson, 1989). Moreover, Caffrey (2000) describes how the culture of the Lenni Lanape was notably gendered, with specific customs for dress and work, but that women were highly valued and the power between men and women was 'complementary' (p. 44).

British colonization impacted on these prior conceptualizations, in Ireland through prohibitory laws and violence which aimed to eradicate Irish people and culture (McVeigh & Rolston, 2009; Sharkey, 1994; Ó Siochrú, 2008), while in North America, Aboriginal children were required to attend residential/boarding schools where violence and abuse were widespread, to disconnect them from their cultural heritage (Fast & Collin-Vezina, 2010; Smith, Varcoe & Edwards, 2005). Despite the difference between Aboriginal communities, and the contrast to European paganism, they too were labelled as 'witches' by colonizers (Dickason & McNab, 2008). Similarly, black women were targeted during the witch trails, with the infamous Salem witch trials beginning with the conviction of Tituba,[3] where such violence was tied to slavery and discourses of black communities as 'evil' users of voodoo and folk medicines (McMillan, 1994; Moss, 1999):

> The presupposition that Europeans brought from the Old World concerning the nature of African people and the colour black, combined with the novel situations to which the Europeans adapted in the New World, caused them to cast enslaved and free Blacks within the realm of the satanic.
> (McMillan, 1994, p. 100)

This was part of a broader colonial rhetoric at this time, that drew on discourses of 'wilderness, Indians and Africans' that tied Aboriginal spirituality with 'demon-possession' and black communities during slavery with 'demons' (Howard, 2011, para. 1), inciting fear and used as justifications for violence. Therefore, when women were targeted and murdered for witchcraft, this is one example of women being harmed not solely for their gender, sexuality, or their perceived 'deviance', but also due to the colonial eradication of older religions, practices, and cultural symbols.

However, it is also important not to view these older religions as exclusively historical or as no longer relevant. Framing alternative approaches to mental well-being as inferior to psychiatry and medicine invalidates and undermines a wide range of cultures and communities that are Othered by 'white' Western perspectives. We can critique and challenge oppression and violence that utilizes religious discourse to justify and excuse harmful actions, such as the murder of women during the witch trials (Ussher, 1992), the controlling of young women's sexuality in 'purity' balls (Valenti, 2009), or the harmful conversion therapies applied to homosexual individuals (Robinson & Spivey, 2007). However, our critiques and condemnations should not further oppress others who have coercively and/or violently had their religious practice condemned and restricted. For example, Aboriginal individuals have been institutionalized for their religious practices, labelled as 'mentally ill' and forcibly sterilized (Kanani, 2011). Black men in the UK and the US are disproportionately diagnosed with schizophrenia (Metzl, 2011; Ndegwa & Olajide, 2003; Whaley, 2004), and mental health professionals tend to interpret symbols and practices from numerous religions originating from African countries as 'symptoms' of psychopathology (Loewenthal & Cinnirella, 2003). Also, the expansion and influence of the psychopharmaceutical industry can subjugate local knowledge and indigenous interventions (Mills, 2014). These current ways of relating to emotional distress and unusual experiences show that while it can appear a linear trajectory from religious authority to psychiatry, this oversimplifies the changes that occurred as well as framing religious and spiritual approaches to emotional well-being as outdated and inferior.

Therefore, psychiatry did not replace such ways of viewing and responding to these experiences, but repositioned them as less valid and less authoritative, as part of a process of modernization that embraced rationality and science, and moved away from subjectivity and spirituality. This was in addition to a parallel move towards 'white' Western civility within professions dominated and defined by men, and away from local, native perspectives where women held key positions in the creation and dissemination of knowledge (Becker, 2009; Ehrenreich & English, 1973, 2013; Siddiqui, Lacroix & Dhar, 2014; Ussher, 1992).

Hysteria

> . . . control of women though allegations of witchcraft came gradually to be replaced by another potent means of social control – psychiatric diagnosis.
>
> (Becker, 2009, p. 4)

In the 19th century, there was a shift in the predominant way of describing women and 'deviance', from the religious authority of 'witchcraft' to the medical and psychiatric context of 'mental illness'. Where women were once labelled 'witch', they then became labelled 'hysterics' (Shaw & Proctor, 2005; Ussher, 1992). However, the concept of hysteria had a much longer history.

The term 'hysteria' was derived from 'hysteron', a Greek word meaning 'womb' (Szasz, 2007). This was due to early theories in ancient Greece that the 'disorder' was caused by a 'wandering womb', thought to be a consequence of not bearing children (Wetzel, 1991), or later, in the Middle Ages, due to 'excessive' sexuality (Becker, 2009). Treatments included surgery performed on the ovaries and uterus (Wetzel, 1991). Due to assumptions about gender and sexed bodies,[4] the proposed relationship between the womb and 'hysteria' embedded the cause of the 'disorder' in the body of women.

From the 16th century onwards, theories began to move away from the 'wandering womb' perspective, looking instead to the nervous system or mind for an explanation (Becker, 2009; Ussher, 2013). Briquet's (1859) *Traite de l'Hysterie* (Treatise on Hysteria) was based on the study of 430 individuals, and highlighted sexual 'excessiveness' and low social class as causal factors for 'hysteria' (also known as 'Briquet's syndrome'), in addition to youth and being a woman. Consequently, he recommended changes in social conditions for treatment (Mai & Merskey, 1980, p. 1401). This was in stark contrast to Weir Mitchell's (Mitchell, 1875, 1904, 1908) influential bed-rest cure, which included seclusion, no activities, a loss of autonomy over basic tasks such as eating, and has since been compared to solitary confinement (Ussher, 1992). Mitchell described his treatment of 'hysteria' as follows: 'She was put to bed, and left it for no purpose. At first she was fed and washed by others, and forbidden to read or use her hands, and even to talk' (Mitchell, 1875, p. 95).

In the 19th century, Charcot (1887) studied 'hysteria' through its physical and visual presentations, prioritizing the role of photography in documenting and analysing the behaviour of women who had been diagnosed and institutionalized. Such individuals were described as having trances, convulsions, rage, problems with speech, and sudden changes in mood (Becker, 2009; Showalter, 1987; Ussher, 2013). This included Blanche Wittman, who became known as 'Queen of the Hysterics' (Showalter, 1987). Charcot's work further removed constructions of 'hysteria' as directly tied to women's bodies (or to the womb) by also diagnosing men who had experienced railway accidents. Nevertheless, the diagnosis was still most often applied to women (Arnold, 2008; Ussher, 1992), and considered a 'female'/'feminine' disease (Showalter, 1987; Ussher, 2013), with the study of institutionalized women further assisting in this construction of 'hysteria' as a 'disorder' of women (Didi-Huberman, 2004). Although, women who defied strict gender roles were also diagnosed as 'difficult' (Wetzel, 1991) and those with 'uncontrolled' anger (or 'temper tantrums') came under the gaze of psychiatry as well (e.g. APA, 1980, 1994). It was also noted that the diagnosis of 'hysteria' was often applied to those who were active in the feminist movement (Showalter, 1987),

Freud revered Charcot for developing the concept of 'hysteria' and legitimizing it within the profession (Showalter, 1987); he even translated Charcot's work into German (e.g. Charcot & Freud, 1886). In *Studies in Hysteria*, Breuer and Freud (1955 [1895]) described case studies using psychoanalysis. Breuer's work with Bertha Pappenheim, known as the Anna O. case, led to his theory that 'hysteria' was due to an excess of emotion or excitement, as the result of an active mind living in a passive and monotonous role:

> *Studies in Hysteria* thus seemed to lay the groundwork for a culturally aware therapy that took women's words and women's lives seriously, that respected the aspirations of New Women, and that allowed women a say in the management of hysterical symptoms.
>
> (Showalter, 1987, p. 158)

This produced a more sympathetic account of 'hysteria' than the aggressive women described in Charcot's work (Showalter, 1987). Breuer and Freud's psychoanalytic perspective promoted the tracing of repressed memories (the perceived cause of the behaviour) and then converting the overexcitement through cathartic listening (or the 'talking cure') (Breuer & Freud, 1895). However, Freud's case study with Dora was different: rather than listening to the woman's thoughts and experiences, Freud interpreted them based on his theories of sexuality. This included the choice to frame disclosures of childhood sexual abuse as fantasy, and therefore the denial of widespread violence against women and girls (Masson, 2012; Shaw & Proctor, 2005).[5] Consequently, rather than viewing the cause of the behaviour as an interaction between an active mind with an unfulfilling (or abusive) environment, Freud viewed the cause as a result of internal desires and fantasies of incest and homosexuality, and removed the behaviour from its context, leaving women in their abusive situations (Showalter, 1987).

Despite the influence of psychoanalysis, its reconceptualization of hysteria was initially met with hostility and derision due to the promotion of a method that emphasized listening to women, rather than social confinement through bed-rest. Later, Freud's work was also criticized by feminists, for its phallocentric understandings of women's sexuality and distress, as well as the psychologizing of social and political issues such as abuse (Bernheimer & Kahane, 1990; Brennan, 2002; Buhle & Buhle, 2009; Chodorow, 1989; Hunter, 1983; Mitchell, 1974). However, Billig (1999) notes that viewing Freud as solely in a position of authority and privilege overlooks his position as a Jewish man in a society where anti-Semitism was increasing prior to the onset of Nazism:

> The description 'educated, bourgeois male' neglects a category which was central to Freud's political and social position. He was a member of a much discriminated minority; and so was Dora. Ultimately both Freud and Dora were to be driven from their society in fear of their lives.
>
> (Billig, 1999, p. 221)

While prominent psychiatrists in Europe dismissed Freud's work (Oosterhuis, 2012), psychoanalysis was influential in the US and in the development of the first edition of the *Diagnostic and Statistical Manual of Mental Disorders* (APA, 1952).[6] Excessive emotion was included in the 'personality disorders' section of the *DSM-I* (APA, 1952), as a category entitled 'emotionally unstable personality'. 'Hysteria' was included in the *DSM-II* (APA, 1968) as 'hysterical personality (histrionic personality disorder)'; however, from the *DSM-III* (APA, 1980, 1987) onwards, only the latter term was used, and this remains so in the latest *DSM-5* (APA, 2013).

Despite the change in name, 'hysteria' was consistently portrayed as 'exaggerated' or 'excessive' emotion that was unstable or poorly controlled. For example, the *DSM-II* (APA, 1968) described the 'disorder' as 'characterized by excitability, emotional instability, over-reactivity, and self-dramatization' (p. 43), whereas the *DSM-III-R* (APA, 1987) stated, 'The essential feature of this disorder is a pervasive pattern of excessive emotionality' (p. 348). It was also tied to seductiveness, vanity, immaturity, 'temper tantrums' and being too dependent on others (APA, 1968, 2013). The current criteria include: 'excessive emotionality', 'attention seeking', 'inappropriate sexually seductive' behaviour, a prioritizing of appearance that is used to get attention, and a view that "relationships [are] more intimate than they actually are" (APA, 2013, p. 667). Described as being charming, flirtatious, enthusiastic, and 'the life of the party' (p. 667), those who are diagnosed are pathologized for spending too much 'time, energy and money' on their clothing and personal appearance, being overly concerned with the opinions of others and distressed by 'unflattering' photographs (p. 667).

These criteria seem like an inevitability for women living in Western culture, where pressures to look 'good' and 'attractive' are immense (Gill, 2003, 2008). That these behaviours are associated with femininity has been noted by feminists such as Ussher, who asks, 'Isn't this how we are taught to "do girl" through teenage magazines, romantic fiction, and "chick flicks"?' (Ussher, 2013, p. 65). Reeds-Gibson (2004) argued that magazines aimed at women seemed like instruction manuals for 'hysteria', such as 'how to get him to notice you, how to dress for summer [and] whether or not you should sleep with your boss' (p. 205), which have been pathlogized as 'attention-seeking', 'overly concerned with physical attractiveness' and 'seductive' (APA, 1987, p. 348; APA, 2000, p. 711). The DSM recognized this relationship by describing 'histrionic personality disorder' as 'a caricature of femininity' (APA, 1980, p. 314). Consequently, it is almost unavoidable for women to be diagnosed with this label, with there being so many parallels between the psychiatric criteria and predominant constructions of normative or idealized femininity.

However, the social context is stripped from a diagnosis that frames the cause of such behaviours as an 'abnormal' personality. Feminist work has argued against the individualizing and pathologizing accounts of women subsumed under the label of 'hysteria', instead emphasizing the social context of gender inequality, as well as the unreasonable and contradictory expectations of femininity that are placed upon women in Western society (Shaw & Proctor, 2005;

Showalter, 1987). As a result, Gould (2011) states that 'histrionic personality disorder' is not a mental illness, but a 'cultural disorder', 'a result of attitudes toward traditionally feminine styles of interaction' (p. 26), and concludes that the diagnosis should be removed from the DSM. She states that women are responding to a 'disordered culture' (p. 37), one that is hierarchized in such a way as to position women as inferior and alienated, and therefore treatment should not be to change the woman, but to change the culture.

Borderline personality disorder

> The borderline is a site of contention, controversy, and struggle over boundaries, not only between the categories of disorder, but of the boundaries of madness itself, and the limits of psychiatry.
>
> (Wirth-Cauchon, 2001, p. 3)

While the label of 'histrionic personality disorder' continues to be used by the profession (Rapinesi et al., 2012), many of the problematic assumptions that relate to hysteria are carried forward in another controversial diagnosis, considered the 'new' female malady (Becker, 2009, p. 24; Wirth-Cauchon, 2001): 'borderline personality disorder' (BPD). BPD is another diagnosis that is predominantly applied to women[7] (APA, 2013; Berger, 2014). It is one of the most used diagnoses in the profession (Wirth-Cauchon, 2001), making up 15–25 per cent of psychiatric cases only four years after its introduction to the DSM (Gunderson & Zanarini, 1987). Despite its popularity, it is problematically vague and contradictory (Wirth-Cauchon, 2001), and it pathologizes behaviours that are commonly associated with femininity (Warner & Wilkins, 2003). Consequently, there are many parallels to psychiatric constructions of 'hysteria' (Jimenez, 1997; Shaw & Proctor, 2005).

Stern (1938) first used the term 'borderline' to refer to patients between the diagnoses of 'neurotic' and 'psychotic' (Shaw & Proctor, 2005),[8] but it was not introduced as a diagnostic category until the third edition of the DSM in 1980 (APA, 1980). Stern (1957) believed the 'disorder' to be characterized by a 'love hunger', a term borrowed from Levy's (1939) work on 'maternal overprotection'.[9] This was something that he considered to be apparent in all cases and was characterized as general insecurity, helplessness and an immense need for emotional support (Stern, 1957, p. 348). He theorized that the cause of this 'hunger' was trauma that occurred in childhood; revising Freud's argument that childhood sexual abuse was mere fantasy (Stern, 1945).[10] The result, according to Stern (1957), was an 'emotional infantilism' (p. 348), an immaturity and over-emotionality that is common in psychiatric constructions of women. This continued in psychoanalytic perspectives into the 1960s and 1970s, with 'developmental arrest' theories (Cary, 1972; Masterson, 1971; Pines, 1984) being popular explanations for the 'disorder' (Becker, 2009). The framing of women as 'overly' emotional, lacking in self-control, and undeveloped within a context of colonization and capitalism also links to discourses of the *uncivilized* (McVeigh & Rolston, 2009; Mills, 2014), which is further supported by the need for women to be polite and compliant or risk being diagnosed (Ussher, 2013), and that the over-representation of women in the diagnosis of BPD can disappear when issues of race and class are taken into account (Grant et al., 2008).

When the DSM adopted the term, it defined those with the 'disorder' as having an 'unstable mood', 'inappropriate, intense anger', a 'lack of control', unstable relationships, fears of abandonment and suicidal thoughts or actions (APA, 1980, p. 321). Originally, the DSM also had a version of the diagnosis for children and adolescents called 'identity disorder', which was quite different in terms of criteria, but centred on distress caused by uncertainty regarding identity (such as sexual orientation, career choice and friendships) (APA, 1980; 1987). This disorder was removed from the DSM when the fourth edition was published in 1994.

Since BPD's introduction to the DSM in 1980, the APA (1980, 1987, 1994, 2013) has consistently acknowledged that it is most often applied to women (in 75 per cent of cases). The DSM version of the diagnosis reaffirmed prior conceptualizations of a fear of abandonment and of being alone, but also emphasized the role of 'inappropriate' and 'uncontrolled' anger, as well as women feeling that they are 'bad' and 'evil'. This further consolidates the construction of 'mad' individuals as 'dangerous' and something to be feared, a problematic and controversial claim (Allen & Nairn, 1997; Wahl, 1997). It also pathologizes women for actions that would be considered 'normal' for most men[11] (in the sense of expressing anger), although the evaluation of such anger as being 'inappropriate' and 'uncontrolled' brings it back into psychiatry's realm of 'irrational' and 'unreasonable' femininity (see Tosh, 2015). This is in addition to a long list of behaviours that coincide with those associated with idealized femininity (such as 'shopping sprees': APA, 1987, p. 346), much like those of hysteria or histrionic personality disorder. Other behaviours in the criteria are within the realm of the 'normal' experience of women, such as 'casual sex', 'binge eating' and 'extreme sarcasm' (APA, 1987, p. 346). The DSM diagnosis of BPD has remained relatively consistent and the focus on an over-emotionality continues.

Feminist critiques have highlighted how the diagnosis pathologizes women, particularly those who have experienced violence and abuse. Like hysteria, the diagnosis has been criticized for its contradictory criteria, meaning that regardless of how women behave, they are easily diagnosed (Wirth-Cauchon, 2000). For example, Shaw and Proctor (2005) show how women who express anger are deemed to be not conforming to their prescribed gender role, but when they repress anger and self-harm they are punished for conforming too much. Consequently, psychiatry positions 'normal' women as never angry, especially when they have plenty to be angry about, such as enduring and widespread violence and abuse. As many diagnosed with BPD have experiences of childhood sexual abuse (Shaw & Proctor, 2005), the categorization of anger as 'inappropriate' not only denies the experience of abuse, but is the basis of a diagnosis. In this way, abuse survivors become psychiatrized as their experiences of abuse, and the consequences of it, are used to pathologize *them* (Warner & Wilkins, 2003).[12] This is also due to the commonality between 'symptoms' of childhood sexual abuse and those listed as criteria for BPD (Warner & Wilkins, 2003), such as suicide attempts (Berger, 2014).

Therefore, instead of examining the impact of abuse, or of understanding behaviours as ways of coping and surviving in unsafe and violent contexts, the individual perspective of psychiatry decontextualizes them, and without context, the behaviour appears 'abnormal' or 'irrational' (Warner & Wilkins, 2003, p. 174). This could also explain the reduced impact of gender when race and class are considered, as victimization and oppression are central to this diagnosis. The impact of intergenerational trauma experienced by Aboriginal communities (e.g. Menzies, 2007) are also likely to overlap with the 'symptoms' outlined for BPD, which would explain the over-representation of Aboriginal men in diagnoses of BPD (Grant et al., 2008).

The diagnosis is also used to frame women as 'dangerous' (Harrison et al., 2015) and 'out of control' that is then used to justify their commitment in high-secure psychiatric wards (Warner & Wilkins, 2003, p. 167). This produces another form of violence for survivors: that of sanism. Their experiences of sexual abuse become untrustworthy and discredited as they are framed as 'mentally ill'. The popularity of the diagnosis within psychiatry, and the high rates of diagnostic prevalence, indicate the continuing dominance of the medical model in explaining (and explaining away) sexual violence and its consequences (Shaw & Proctor, 2005). Therefore, despite the presence of childhood sexual abuse experiences in accounts of BPD, the act of diagnosis prevents discussion of the issue, hiding it away in high-secure psychiatric wards (Warner & Wilkins, 2003), as well as pathologizing feminists and others who campaign against violence. For instance, the latest DSM edition states that those with BPD 'may suddenly change from the role of a needy supplicant for help to that of a righteous avenger of past mistreatment' (APA, 2013, p. 664), making it sound as though being a righteous avenger is a bad thing.

Masochism

In addition to the constructions of hysteria and borderline personality disorder, where highly generalized accounts of femininity and women are pathologized, psychiatry, psychology and psychoanalysis also produced narratives of women as 'naturally' masochistic. The term 'masochism' was coined in the late 19th century after the author Sacher-Masoch (1836–95), much to his displeasure (Deleuze, 2004). Sacher-Masoch's (2014) most famous work was *Venus in Furs* originally published in 1870 in German (*Venus im Pelz*), and described the relationship between Wanda and Severin who wilfully enter into a slave/master arrangement. Severin describes his feelings towards Wanda as love to the point of madness. In response to Wanda's invitation, 'Do you want to be my slave?'[13] Severin responds, 'There is no equality in love . . . Whenever it is a matter of choice for me of ruling or being ruled, it seems much more satisfactory to me to be the slave of a beautiful woman' (Sacher-Masoch, 2014 [1870], p. 20). Krafft-Ebing (1892) declared that Sacher-Masoch's works were the inspiration for naming 'masochism' as a perversion and he initially defined it as the 'association of passively endured cruelty and violence with lust' (p. 89). The diagnosis was positioned in opposition to 'sadism', where the pleasure was framed as resulting from inflicting pain, suffering and humiliation on another. These two psychiatric categories were considered to have varying degrees of intensity, ranging from the relatively 'normal', to the 'symbolic' and including 'severe maltreatment' (Krafft-Ebing, 1892, p. 149). The concept was taken up by the DSM and listed as a form of 'sexual deviation' (APA, 1968), and later as a 'paraphilia' (APA, 1980).

A common thread throughout early psychiatric literature was the association between femininity and masochism, with masochism (in its most extreme form) representing a pathological form of feminine love. As Krafft-Ebing (1892) explained, 'Owing to her passive *rôle* in procreation and long existent social conditions, ideas of subjection are, in women, normally connected with the idea of sexual relations' (p. 137). This connection between passivity and sexuality was framed as a result of 'nature' extending to 'an instinctive inclination to voluntary subordination to man' which was 'often accepted with secret satisfaction' (p. 138). This positioning of women as naturally passive and (secretly) desiring domination by male partners continued in the writings of Ellis, who highlighted their complementary structure:

> We thus see that there are here two separate groups of feelings: one, in the masculine line, which delights in displaying force and often inflicts pain or the simulacrum of pain; the other, in the feminine line, which delights in submitting to that force, and even finds pleasure in a slight amount of pain, or the idea of pain, when, associated with the experience of love. We see, also, that these two groups of feelings are complementary. Within the limits consistent with normal and healthy life, what men are impelled to give women love to receive.
>
> (Ellis, 1903, p. 104)

Influenced by Krafft-Ebing, Ellis, Schrenck-Notzing (Grossman, 1986) and others (e.g. Moll, 1899), Freud (1949 [1905]) described sadism and masochism as "the most important of the perversions" and developed these concepts further in 'A Child is Being Beaten' (Freud, 1922) and 'The Economic Problem of Masochism' (Freud, 1924). He theorized that masochism was connected to 'thanatos', the death instinct (Freud, 1962 [1930]), which due to its passive nature, was also considered to be feminine. Freud argued that masochism was sadism turned inward toward the self, what he considered to be 'secondary masochism'. Primary (or 'erotogenic') masochism was framed as the general association of pleasure and pain, which separated into two further versions: feminine and moral masochism. Feminine masochism was 'an expression of the feminine nature' in that 'they place the subject in a characteristically female situation; they signify, that is, being castrated, or copulated with, or giving birth to a baby' (Freud, 1924, p. 162).

The neo-Freudian, Karen Horney, summarized psychoanalytic theories of masochism as follows:

> What the woman secretly desires in intercourse is rape and violence, or in the mental sphere, humiliation. The process of childbirth gives her an unconscious masochistic satisfaction . . . Furthermore, as far as men indulge in masochistic fantasies or performances, these represent an expression of their desire to play the female role.
>
> (Horney, 1973 [1935], p. 215)

Therefore, this term did not describe female sexuality, but a feminine expression of sexuality that could be experienced by any gender (Grossman, 1986). Nevertheless, women's sexuality and personality were closely associated with the concept in generalized terms. As Krafft-Ebing (1892) stated, 'Many young women like nothing better than to kneel before their husbands' (p. 138). Therefore, despite being framed as pathological and perverse, early psychological writings embedded the concept of masochism firmly in gendered norms of heterosexuality, with only the most extreme versions being classed as requiring a diagnosis. Passivity was classed as the 'normal' female role, and thus only bordered on the pathological when 'severe maltreatment' was endured or when men engaged in such activities.

However, there were also attempts to produce separate concepts related to masochistic personalities. Freud's (1924) concept of moral masochism was the furthest removed from sexuality, with strong connections to guilt for some perceived wrongdoing that deserved punishment. Freud (1924) stated that what was central to the diagnosis was suffering, not the person who inflicted the pain or humiliation (p. 165).[14] The concept was taken forward by Reich (1933), who developed the psychoanalytic theory of masochism to include character structures that were considered responses to a sexually repressive society. This further consolidated a version of masochism as a (feminine) personality type. Reich argued that masochistic individuals not only experienced pleasure from pain, but had also learnt that pleasure (i.e. love) itself was painful (Fuller, 1986).

It was this psychoanalytic concept that went on to influence the development of 'self-defeating personality disorder' or 'masochistic personality disorder' (Fuller, 1986), which was included in the *DSM-III* (APA, 1980) under 'other personality disorders' and the *DSM-III-R* (APA, 1987) under diagnoses in need of further research. The DSM described this disorder as 'The person may often avoid or undermine pleasurable experiences, be drawn to situations or relationships in which he or she will suffer, and prevent others from helping him or her' (APA, 1987, p. 371). It was criticized by feminists due to the potential for misuse and the misdiagnosis of women, particularly those within abusive relationships (Caplan & Gans, 1991; Ritchie, 1989).

While 'masochistic personality disorder' ultimately did not make it into the DSM, debates continue within the profession regarding whether masochism and sadism are dangerous 'paraphilias' or 'normal' (Baumeister & Butler, 1997; Moser, 2011; Moser & Kleinplatz, 2006; Shindel & Moser, 2011). This is in addition to criticisms from within BDSM and kink communities that these diagnoses pathologize sexual diversity (Langdridge & Barker, 2013). Nevertheless, masochism remains in the *DSM-5* as 'sexual masochism disorder' (APA, 2013), defined as 'recurrent and intense sexual arousal from the act of being humiliated, beaten, bound, or otherwise made to suffer', in addition to distress or 'impairment in social, occupational, or other important areas of functioning' (p. 694).

There are numerous problems with a psychiatric concept that promotes a pathology based on pleasure in pain, then frames this as 'naturally' feminine, in addition to generalizing it as an 'innate and unchanging' personality type. Criticisms from feminist perspectives have been frequent, but they have also lacked consensus. Chancer (2000) summarizes the feminist conflict regarding sadomasochism as between those who view it as part of a patriarchal hierarchy and those who consider it to be a sexuality that should be able to be expressed and experienced without condemnation.

These disagreements are partly due to the range of meanings of the term 'masochism', of which psychiatric discourse is only one, and one that is far removed from BDSM and kink communities. For instance, Caplan (2005) has comprehensively outlined her objections to a concept that women are naturally masochistic in terms of their personality, as this has been misused by therapists and other professionals to blame women for their own victimization. She quotes from one woman: 'I had been in therapy for eight years, and every week, after I told him how unhappy I was feeling, my therapist would nod wisely and say, "Do you see how you bring your misery on yourself?"' (Caplan, 2005, p. xiii). Its connection to women who have experienced domestic abuse was of concern to feminists, as it framed their victimization as a result of internal abnormalities (or 'failures') on behalf of the woman (Wetzel, 1991, p. 16).

Some feminists, then, viewed masochism as solely a psychiatric concept used to justify the abuse of women and rejected it outright: 'The word is an oxymoron, a myth; no one feels pleasure in pain. The concept has been discredited for some years as a pejorative, discriminatory term that had been applied mainly to women and other subordinate groups' (Wetzel, 1991, p. 17).

However, this viewpoint and its complete denial masked women who engaged in masochism as a part of consensual BDSM and kink communities.

Therefore, responding to psychiatric oppression resulted in the silencing of another (invisible or not considered) group. Viewing this issue in terms of binaries, of two opposing perspectives, risked further oppression when attempting to challenge psychiatric constructions of femininity.

Conclusions

In addition to framing women's personalities as overly emotional (and thus more likely to 'over'-react to situations), as untrustworthy (in terms of their accusations of abuse and sexual violence), they were also positioned as enjoying their suffering. Altogether, this creates a protective narrative against accusations of abuse, patriarchy and oppression, as when women challenge their inequality or violence they can be labelled as 'over-reacting', 'hormonal' (see Caplan et al., 1992; Swann, 1997; Ussher, 2003), or being 'hysterical', as well as queries regarding if such abuses are a result of their imagination, and even when such abuses are evident, women are then accused of enjoying the abuse they suffered in the first place. Each diagnosis (in addition to many others not covered in this chapter) functions to detract attention away from violence against women and gendered inequality through the maintenance of the status quo and the discrediting of women's voices through their label as being 'mentally ill', and consequently, the intersection of sexism and sanism. The final aspect of this process of the psychiatrization of women's oppression is the diagnosis of depression, which individualizes the consequences or distress experienced by women living in patriarchal society (see Ussher, 2010). This is in addition to other axes of oppression, such as racism, where women of colour are diagnosed and treated without consideration of the broader social context that impacts upon their well-being.

As women are frequently diagnosed and pathologized when they conform to norms of femininity, *and* when they breach the boundaries of their gendered roles, we could think of this contradiction as the pathologization of femininity and gender nonconformity as separate but related concepts. This is supported by evidence of the pathologization of men who are considered to be feminine, as well as the diagnosis of transgender and gender-nonconforming people with disorders typically associated with women and femininity, including those discussed in this chapter (Williams, 2012; Grant et al., 2011; McCann & Sharek, 2014). As Ussher (1992) stated, 'As madness itself is synonymous with femininity, those . . . who wholeheartedly embrace the gender role assigned to them, or those who reject it, are at high risk of being diagnosed as mad' (p. 167). Showalter concluded:

> Whilst the name of the symbolic female disorder may change from one historical period to the next, the gender asymmetry of the representational tradition remains constant. Thus madness, *even when experienced by men*, is metaphorically and symbolically represented as feminine.
>
> (Showalter, 1987, p. 4, my emphasis)

Therefore, rather than consider this a 'double-bind' (Chesler, 1997), of the pathologization of women whether or not they conform to expectations of femininity, we could think of this as the pathologization of femininity, *in addition to* the pathologization of gender nonconformity (the focus of the next chapter). This enables us to conceptualize more clearly the intersecting constructions and oppressions in play as gender-conforming women are pathologized as feminine, while those who do not conform are pathologized for their nonconformity. As a result, anyone who expresses femininity is pathologized (Wetzel, 1991), and only gender-conforming masculinity is positioned as the 'norm'.

Notes

1 While I include trans women in my use of the term 'woman', psychiatry most often assumes a cisgender woman when discussing these diagnoses, but they are also applied to transgender and gender-nonconforming individuals (Williams, 2012; Blanchard, 1993; Grant et al., 2011; McCann & Sharek, 2014).

2 Although the name 'Brigit' was used to refer to goddesses more generally in pagan Ireland.

3 While there is uncertainty about Tituba's ethnicity, her story was used to further fears regarding witchcraft and black women, as well as Aboriginal women.

4 For instance, the assumption that all women's bodies have wombs, and that there are only two genders; two assumptions that are invalidated through the experiences of intersex and transgender individuals.

5 An issue that was revived during the 1970s and 1980s with the introduction of the diagnosis 'false memory syndrome' (Shaw & Proctor, 2005), which also positioned women's experiences of sexual abuse as unreliable and untrustworthy (see Haaken, 1994, 1996, 2000; Haaken & Reavey, 2009).

6 Although, while psychoanalytic psychiatry was popular in North America, it was 'not quite as Freud had intended' but was 'more moralistic' (Becker, 2009, p. 23).

7 The *DSM-IV* (APA, 1994) states that 75 per cent of those diagnosed are women.

8 Although Stern coined the term 'borderline' in this context, it was popularized by Knight in 1953 in his chapter 'Borderline states' (Becker, 2009).

9 Framed as a parenting problem resulting in 'spoiled' children (Levy, 1939).

10 Stern argued that trauma (e.g. separation or desertion) by a mother had more impact – thus drawing on the 'mother-blaming' narrative identified in many areas that excuse men from harmful behaviour (e.g. Howe, 2009).

11 This is also impacted on by issues related to race and class, where the violence perpetrated by 'white' men is viewed as justified or less of a problem, than those of other ethnic and racial subject positions (Ferber, 2007; Katz, 2003; Mehta, 2014).

12 This is further compounded as BPD supersedes post-traumatic stress disorder (PTSD) in clinical settings, repositioning the issue as an internal and individual pathology (Shaw & Proctor, 2005), although PTSD is also used to medicalize women's problems (Becker, 2000).

13 Demaj (2014) notes how role-playing sexual power relationships cannot escape their historical and cultural context, such as within race play. Thus the term 'slave' used in the context of erotica draws on racial discourses, but also has the potential to subvert them.

14 Note also the significant discrepancy between psychoanalytic theories of masochism and those from outside of the 'psy-complex' (Rose, 1985). For instance, in response to this quotation from Freud, Noyes (1997) stated, 'We know that this is not true. Whenever our culture has imagined the masochist turning his cheek to receive a blow, it has been absolutely essential that the blow is dealt by the right kind of person in the right kind of setting. Leopold von Sacher-Masoch would have been horrified at the idea of his dominatrix administering punishment without the necessary fur coat' (p. 140).

References

Allen, R., & Nairn, R. G. (1997). Media depictions of mental illness: An analysis of the use of dangerousness. *Australian and New Zealand Journal of Psychiatry, 31*(3), 375–81.

APA (American Psychiatric Association) (1952). *Diagnostic and statistical manual of mental disorders first edition (DSM-I)*. Washington, DC: Author.

APA (American Psychiatric Association) (1968). *Diagnostic and statistical manual of mental disorders second edition (DSM-II)*. Washington, DC: Author.

APA (American Psychiatric Association) (1980). *Diagnostic and statistical manual of mental disorders, third edition (DSM-III)*. Washington, DC: Author.

APA (American Psychiatric Association) (1987). *Diagnostic and statistical manual of mental disorders, third edition revised (DSM-III-R)*. Washington, DC: Author.

APA (American Psychiatric Association) (1994). *Diagnostic and statistical manual of mental disorders fourth edition (DSM-IV)*. Washington, DC: Author.

APA (American Psychiatric Association) (2000). *Diagnostic and statistical manual of mental disorders, fourth edition text revision (DSM-IV-TR)*. Washington DC: Author.

APA (American Psychiatric Association) (2013). *Diagnostic and statistical manual of mental disorders fifth edition (DSM-5)*. Washington DC: Author.

Arnold, C. (2008). *Bedlam: London and its mad*. London: Simon and Schuster.

Baumeister, R., & Butler, J. (1997). Sexual masochism: Deviance without pathology. In D. Laws & W. O'Donohue (Eds), *Sexual deviance: Theory, assessment, and treatment* (pp. 225–39). New York: Guilford Press.

Becker, D. (2000). When she was bad: Borderline personality disorder in a posttraumatic age. *American Journal of Orthopsychiatry, 70*(4), 422–32.

Becker, D. (2009). *Through the looking glass: Women and borderline personality disorder*. Oxford: Westview Press.

Berger, B. (2014). Power, selfhood, and identity: A feminist critique of borderline personality disorder. In L. Doran, K. Berringer, J. Mancino, & C. Quinlivan (Eds), *Advocates' forum* (pp. 1–8). Chicago, IL: University of Chicago Press.

Bernheimer, C., & Kahane, C. (1990). *In Dora's case: Freud—hysteria—feminism*. New York: Columbia University Press.

Billig, M. (1999). *Freudian repression: Conversation creating the unconscious*. Cambridge: Cambridge University Press.

Bitel, L. M. (1998). *Land of women: Tales of sex and gender from early Ireland*. Ithaca, NY: Cornell University Press.

Blanchard, R. (1993). Varieties of autogynephilia and their relationship to gender dysphoria. *Archives of Sexual Behavior, 22*(3), 241–51.

Brennan, T. (2002). *Between feminism and psychoanalysis*. London: Routledge.

Breuer, J., & Freud, S. (1895). *Studies in hysteria*. New York: Basic Books.

Briquet, P. (1859). *Traité clinique et thérapeutique de l'hystérie*. J.-B. Baillière et Fils.

Buhle, M. J., & Buhle, M. J. (2009). *Feminism and its discontents: A century of struggle with psychoanalysis*. Boston, MA: Harvard University Press.

Caffrey, M. (2000). Complementary power: Men and women of the Lenni Lanape. *American Indian Quarterly, 24*(1), 44–63.

Caplan, P. J. (2005). *The myth of women's masochism*. Lincoln: iUniverse.

Caplan, P. J., & Gans, M. (1991). Is there empirical justification for the category of 'self-defeating personality disorder'? *Feminism & Psychology, 1*(2), 263–78.

Caplan, P. J., McCurdy-Myers, J., & Gans, M. (1992). Should 'premenstrual syndrome' be called a psychiatric abnormality? *Feminism & Psychology, 2*(1), 27–44.

Carroll, C. (1990). The construction of gender and the cultural and political other in *The Faerie Queene* and *A View of the Present State of Ireland*: The critics, the context, and the case of Radigund. *Criticism, 32*(3), 163–92.

Cary, G. L. (1972). The borderline condition: A structural-dynamic viewpoint. *Psychoanalytic Review, 59*(1), 33–54.

Cermele, J. A., Daniels, S., & Anderson, K. L. (2001). Defining normal: Constructions of race and gender in the *DSM-IV* casebook. *Feminism & Psychology, 11*(2), 229–47.

Chancer, L. S. (2000). From pornography to sadomasochism: Reconciling feminist differences. *Annals of the American Academy of Political and Social Science, 571*(1), 77–88.

Charcot, J. M. (1887). *Leçons du mardi à la Salpêtrière*. Paris: Progres Medical.

Charcot, J. M., & Freud, S. (1886). *Neue vorlesungen über die krankheiten des nervensystems, insbesondere über Hysterie*. Leipzig: Toeplitz & Deuticke.

Chesler, P. (1997). *Women and madness: Revised and updated*. New York: Four Walls Eight Windows.

Chodorow, N. J. (1989). *Feminism and psychoanalytic theory*. London: Yale University Press.

Crualaoich, G. (1995). Non-sovereignty Queen aspects of the Otherworld female in Irish hag legends: The case of Cailleach Bhearra. In *Sounds from the supernatural: Papers presented at the Nordic-Celtic legend symposium*. (pp. 147–62). Dublin: The Folklore of Ireland Society.

Cusack, C. (2007). Brigit: Goddess, Saint, 'Holy Woman', and bone of contention. In V. Barker & F. Laura (Eds), *On a panegyrical note: Studies in honour of Garry W. Trompf*. (pp. 75–97). Sydney: University of Sydney.

Deleuze, G. (2004). Coldness and cruelty. In G. Deleuze & L. von Sacher-Masosch (Eds), *Masochism: Coldness and cruelty & Venus in Furs* (pp. 15–123). New York: Zone Books.

Demaj, A. (2014). Touching race through play: Sadomasochism, phenomenology, and the intertwining of race and sexuality. *Annual Review of Critical Psychology, 11*, 97–111.

Dickason, O., & McNab, D. T. (2008). *Canada's First Nations: A history of Founding Peoples from earliest times*. Don Mills, Ont: Oxford University Press.

Didi-Huberman, G. (2004). *Invention of hysteria: Charcot and the photographic iconography of the Salpêtrière*. Cambridge, MA: MIT Press.

Ehrenreich, B., & English, D. (1973). *Witches, midwives, and nurses: A history of women healers*. New York: The Feminist Press.

Ehrenreich, B., & English, D. (2013). *For her own good: Two centuries of the experts' advice to women*. New York: Knopf Doubleday Publishing Group.

Ellis, H. (1903). *Studies in the psychology of sex, Volume III: Analysis of the sexual impulse; Love and pain; The sexual impulse in women*. Philadelphia, PA: Davis Company.

Fast, E., & Collin-Vezina, D. (2010). Historical trauma, race-based trauma and resilience of Indigenous Peoples: A Literature review. *First Peoples Child & Family Review, 5*(1), 126–36.

Ferber, A. L. (2007). The construction of black masculinity white supremacy now and then. *Journal of Sport & Social Issues, 31*(1), 11–24.
Fhloinn, B. N. (2005). The book of the Cailleach – Stories of the wise-woman healer. *Folk Life, 44*(1), 146–7.
Freud, S. (1905). *Three essays on the theory of sexuality.* London: Imago Publishing.
Freud, S. (1922). A child is being beaten. *Journal of Nervous and Mental Disease, 56*(4), 405–6.
Freud, S. (1924). The economic problem of masochism. *Standard Edition, 19,* 157–70.
Freud, S. (1930). *Civilization and its discontents.* New York: Norton & Company Inc.
Friedan, B. (2010 [1963]). *The feminine mystique.* New York: W. W. Norton & Company.
Fuller, K. (1986). Masochistic personality disorder: A diagnosis under consideration. *Jefferson Journal of Psychiatry, 4*(2), 7–21.
Gill, R. (2003). From sexual objectification to sexual subjectification: The resexualisation of women's bodies in the media. *Feminist Media Studies, 3*(1), 100–106.
Gill, R. (2008). Empowerment/sexism: Figuring female sexual agency in contemporary advertising. *Feminism & Psychology, 18*(1), 35–60.
Gould, C. (2011). Why the histrionic personality disorder should not be in the DSM: A new taxonomic and moral analysis. *IJFAB: International Journal of Feminist Approaches to Bioethics, 4*(1), 26–40.
Grant, B., Chou, P., Goldstein, R., Huang, B., Stinson, F., Saha, T., . . . Ruan, J. (2008). Prevalence, correlates, disability, and comorbidity of *DSM-IV* borderline personality disorder: Results from the wave 2 national epidemiologic survey on alcohol and related conditions. *Journal of Clinical Psychiatry, 69*(4), 533–45.
Grant, J. E., Flynn, M., Odlaug, B. L., & Schreiber, L. R. N. (2011). Personality disorders in gay, lesbian, bisexual and transgender chemically dependent patients. *The American Journal on Addictions/American Academy of Psychiatrists in Alcoholism and Addictions, 20*(5), 405–11.
Grossman, W. (1986). Notes on masochism: A discussion of the history and development of a psychoanalytic concept. *Psychoanalysis Quarterly, 55,* 379–413.
Gunderson, J. G., & Zanarini, M. C. (1987). Current overview of the borderline diagnosis. *Journal of Clinical Psychiatry, 48,* 5–11.
Haaken, J. (1994). Sexual abuse, recovered memory, and therapeutic practice. *Social Text, 40,* 115–45.
Haaken, J. (1996). The recovery of memory, fantasy, and desire: Feminist approaches to sexual abuse and psychic trauma. *Signs,* 1069–94.
Haaken, J. (2000). *Pillar of salt: Gender, memory, and the perils of looking back.* New Brunswick, NJ: Rutgers University Press.
Haaken, J., & Reavey, P. (2009). *Memory matters: Contexts for understanding sexual abuse recollections.* London: Routledge.
Harrison, M. A., Murphy, E. A., Ho, L. Y., Bowers, T. G., & Flaherty, C. V. (2015). Female serial killers in the United States: Means, motives, and makings. *Journal of Forensic Psychiatry & Psychology, 26*(3), 383–406.
Horney, K. (1935). The problem of feminine masochism. In K. Horney (Ed.), *Feminine psychology* (pp. 214–33). New York: Norton & Company Inc.
Howard, J. A. J. (2011). *Spirited into America: Narratives of possession, 1650–1850.* Purdue University: http://gradworks.umi.com/35/07/3507244.html (accessed 20 November 2015).
Howe, A. (2009). *Sex, violence and crime: Foucault and the 'man' question.* London: Routledge.
Hunter, D. (1983). Hysteria, psychoanalysis, and feminism: The case of Anna O. *Feminist Studies, 9*(3), 464–88.

Jimenez, M. A. (1997). Gender and psychiatry: Psychiatric conceptions of mental disorders in women, 1960-1994. *Affilia, 12*(2), 154–175.

Kanani, N. (2011). Race and madness: Locating the experiences of racialized people with psychiatric histories in Canada and the United States. *Critical Disability Discourse, 3*, 1–14.

Katz, J. (2003). Advertising and the construction of violent white masculinity: From Eminem to Clinique for men. In G. Dines & J. Humez (Eds), *Gender, race, and class in media: A text-reader* (pp. 349–58). London: SAGE Publications.

Krafft-Ebing, R. (1892). *Psychopathia sexualis with especial reference to contrary sexual instinct: A medico-legal study*. Philadelphia, PA: F. A. Davis Co. Publishers.

Langdridge, D., & Barker, M. J. (Eds). (2013). *Safe, sane and consensual: Contemporary perspectives on sadomasochism*. New York: Palgrave Macmillan.

Levy, D. (1939). Maternal overprotection. *Psychiatry: Interpersonal and Biological Processes, 2*(4), 563–97.

Loewenthal, K., & Cinnirella, M. (2003). Religious issues in ethnic minority mental health with special reference to schizophrenia in Afro-Caribbeans in Britain: A systematic review. In D. Ndegwa & D. Olajide (Eds), *Main issues in mental health and race*. (pp. 108–34). Aldershot: Ashgate.

Mai, F. M. and Merskey H. (1980). Briquet's treatise on hysteria: A synopsis and commentary. *Archives of General Psychiatry, 37*(12), 1401–5.

Masson, J. M. (2012). *Against therapy: Emotional tyranny and the myth of psychological healing*. Untreed Reads.

Masterson, J. F. (1971). Treatment of the adolescent with borderline syndrome: A problem in separation-individuation. *Bulletin of the Menninger Clinic, 35*(1), 5–18.

McCann, E., & Sharek, E. (2014). Survey of lesbian, gay, bisexual, and transgender people's experiences of mental health services in Ireland. *International Journal of Mental Health Nursing, 23*, 118–27.

McMillan, T. (1994). Black magic: Witchcraft, race, and resistance in colonial New England. *Journal of Black Studies, 25*(1), 99–117.

McVeigh, R., & Rolston, B. (2009). Civilising the Irish. *Race & Class, 51*(1), 2–28.

Mehta, H. (2014). 'Violent' Aboriginals and 'benign' white men: White's alternative representation of the encounter in Voss. In C. Driesen & B. Ashcroft (Eds), *Patrick White Centenary: The legacy of a prodigal son*. (pp. 241–56). Newcastle upon Tyne: Cambridge Scholars Publishing.

Menzies, P. (2007). Understanding Aboriginal intergenerational trauma from a social work perspective. *Canadian Journal of Native Studies, 2*, 367–92.

Metzl, J. (2011). *The protest psychosis: How schizophrenia became a black disease*. Boston, MA: Beacon Press.

Metzl, J. M. (2003). Selling sanity through gender: The psychodynamics of psychotropic advertising. *Journal of Medical Humanities, 24*(1–2), 79–103.

Mills, C. (2014). *Decolonizing global mental health: The psychiatrization of the majority world*. London: Routledge.

Mitchell, J. (1974). *Psychoanalysis and feminism* (Vol. xxiii). Oxford: Pantheon.

Mitchell, W. (1875). *Rest in the treatment of nervous disease*. New York: G. P. Putnam's Sons.

Mitchell, W. (1904). The evolution of the rest treatment. *Journal of Nervous and Mental Disease, 31*(6), 368–73.

Mitchell, W. (1908). The treatment by rest, seclusion, etc., in relation to psychotherapy. *JAMA, 25*, 2033–7.

Moll, A. (1899). *Die konträre sexualempfindung*. Berlin: Fischer's Medicinische Buchhandlung.

Moser, C. (2011). Yet another paraphilia definition fails. *Archives of Sexual Behavior, 40*(3), 483–5.

Moser, C., & Kleinplatz, P. (2006). *DSM-IV-TR* and the paraphilias: An argument for removal. *Journal of Psychology & Human Sexuality, 17*(3–4), 91–109.

Moss, J. (1999). Postmodernizing the Salem witchcraze: Maryse Conde's I, Tituba, Black witch of Salem. *Colby Quarterly, 35*(1), 5–17.

Ndegwa, D., & Olajide, D. (Eds). (2003). *Main issues in mental health and race*. Burlington, VT: Ashgate.

Noyes, J. K. (1997). *The mastery of submission: Inventions of masochism*. Ithaca, NY: Cornell University Press.

Oosterhuis, H. (2012). Sexual modernity in the works of Richard von Krafft-Ebing and Albert Moll. *Medical History, 56*, 133–55.

Ó Siochrú, M. (2008). *God's executioner: Oliver Cromwell and the conquest of Ireland*. London: Faber & Faber.

Pines, M. (1984). Group analytic psychotherapy and the borderline patient. *Analytic Psychotherapy & Psychopathology, 1*(1), 57–70.

Rapinesi, C., Serata, D., Del Casale, A., Simonetti, A., Milioni, M., Mazzarini, L., . . . Girardi, P. (2012). Successful and rapid response to electroconvulsive therapy of a suicidal patient with comorbid bipolar I disorder and histrionic personality disorder: *Journal of ECT, 28*(1), 57–8.

Reeds-Gibson, P. (2004). Histrionic personality. In P. Caplan & L. Cosgrove (Eds), *Bias in psychiatric diagnosis* (pp. 201–6). Oxford: Rowman & Littlefield.

Reich, W. (1933). *Character analysis* (3rd edition). New York: Farrar, Straus & Giroux.

Ritchie, K. (1989). The little woman meets son of *DSM-III*. *Journal of Medicine and Philosophy, 14*(6), 695–708.

Robinson, C. M., & Spivey, S. E. (2007). The politics of masculinity and the ex-gay movement. *Gender & Society, 21*(5), 650–75.

Rose, N. (1985). *The psychological complex: Psychology, politics and society in England, 1869–1939*. London: Routledge

Sacher-Masoch, L. von. (2014 [1870]). *Venus in furs*. B&R Samizdat Express.

Sharkey, S. (1994). *Ireland and the iconography of rape: Colonisation, constraint and gender*. London: University of North London

Shaw, C., & Proctor, G. (2005). Women at the margins: A critique of the diagnosis of borderline personality disorder. *Feminism & Psychology, 15*(4), 483–90.

Shindel, A., & Moser, C. (2011). Why are the paraphilias mental disorders? *Journal of Sexual Medicine, 8*(3), 927–9.

Showalter, E. (1987). *The female malady: Women, madness and English culture, 1830–1980*. London: Virago Press Ltd.

Siddiqui, S., Lacroix, K., & Dhar, A. (2014). Faith healing in India: The cultural quotient of the critical. *Disability and the Global South, 1*(2), 285–301.

Smith, D., Varcoe, C., & Edwards, N. (2005). Turning around the intergenerational impact of residential schools on Aboriginal people: Implications for health policy and practice. *Canadian Journal of Nursing Research, 37*(4), 38–60.

Sprenger, J., & Kraemer, H. (1496). *Malleus maleficarum*. Nuremberg.

Stark, J. (2013). Unequal communities: Exploring the relationship between colonialism, patriarchy and the marginalization of Aboriginal women. *Footnotes, 6*: https://journal.lib.uoguelph.ca/index.php/footnotes/article/view/2383 (accessed 20 November 2015).

Stern, A. (1938). Borderline group of neuroses. *Psychoanalytic Quarterly*, 7, 467–89.

Stern, A. (1945). Psychoanalytic therapy in the borderline neuroses. *Psychoanalytic Quarterly, 14*, 190–98.

Stern, A. (1957). The transference in the borderline group of neuroses. *Journal of the American Psychoanalytic Association., 5*, 348–50.

Stevenson, W. (1989). Rebirth of women warriors. *Saskatchewan Indian* (March), 15.

Strmiska, M. (2003). The evils of Christianization: A Pagan perspective on European history. In T. Waddell (Ed.), *Cultural expressions of evil and wickedness: Wrath, sex, crime*. Amsterdam: Rodopi.

Swann, C. (1997). Reading the bleeding body: Discourses of premenstrual syndrome. In J. Ussher (Ed.), *Body talk: The material and discursive regulation of sexuality, madness and reproduction* (pp. 176–98). London: Routledge.

Szasz, T. (1997). *The manufacture of madness: A comparative study of the inquisition and the mental health movement*. Syracuse, NY: Syracuse University Press.

Szasz, T. (2007). *The medicalization of everyday life*. Syracuse, NY: Syracuse University Press.

Tiefer, L. (2009). *Sex is not a natural act and other essays*. New York: Westview Press.

Tosh, J. (2015). *Perverse psychology: The pathologization of sexual violence and transgenderism*. London: Routledge.

Ussher, J. (1992). *Women's madness: Misogyny or mental illness?*. Amherst: University of Massachusetts Press.

Ussher, J. (2003). The role of premenstrual dysphoric disorder in the subjectification of women. *Journal of Medical Humanities, 24*(1–2), 131–46.

Ussher, J. (2010). Are we medicalizing women's misery? A critical review of women's higher rates of reported depression. *Feminism & Psychology, 20*(1), 9–35.

Ussher, J. (2011). *The madness of women: Myth and experience*. London: Routledge.

Ussher, J. (2013). Diagnosing difficult women and pathologising femininity: Gender bias in psychiatric nosology. *Feminism & Psychology, 23*(1), 63–9.

Valenti, J. (2009). *The purity myth: How America's obsession with virginity is hurting young women*. Berkeley, CA: Seal Press.

Wahl, O. F. (1997). *Media madness: Public images of mental illness*. New Brunswick, NJ: Rutgers University Press.

Warner, S., & Wilkins, T. (2003). Diagnosing distress and reproducing disorder: Women, child sexual abuse and 'borderline personality disorder'. In P. Reavey & S. Warner (Eds), *New feminist stories of child sexual abuse: Sexual scripts and dangerous dialogues* (pp. 167–86). London: Routledge.

Wetzel, J. (1991). Universal mental health classification systems: Reclaiming women's experience. *Affilia, 6*, 8–31.

Whaley, A. L. (2004). Ethnicity/race, paranoia, and hospitalization for mental health problems among men. *American Journal of Public Health, 94*(1), 78–81.

Williams, A. R. (2012). Transsexualism, personality disorders, and spinal cord injury. *Journal of Gay & Lesbian Mental Health, 16*(1), 56–65.

Wirth-Cauchon, J. (2000). A dangerous symbolic mobility: Narratives of borderline personality disorder. In D. Fee (Ed.), *Pathology and the postmodern: Mental illness as discourse and experience* (pp. 141–63). London: SAGE Publications.

Wirth-Cauchon, J. (2001). *Women and borderline personality disorder: Symptoms and stories*. New York: Rutgers University Press.

Chapter 3

Psychiatric constructions of transgender identities and gender nonconformity

Psychiatric diagnoses related to gender identity have undergone much change and speculation. Unlike the previous chapter, where many long-standing diagnoses pathologized different aspects of normative femininity (e.g. emotionality) and experiences of patriarchal oppression (e.g. victims of domestic abuse and sexual violence), the history of psychiatric constructions of gender nonconformity traces the erratic development of a single concept from two points of view. The pathologization of gender nonconformity is divided into a fetishized behaviour (cross-dressing) and an identity 'disorder' (transgender or non-binary identities). There are numerous terms used to pathologize gender-nonconforming, cross-dressing and transgender people, but rather than representing distinct diagnoses, they often replace a label that has come before. This changeability is a result of professional disagreement, public protest and a lack of consensus on whether gender nonconformity is related to sexual desire or identity. It has also been, in part, influenced by the de-medicalization of homosexuality (Conrad & Angell, 2004), and the psychiatric profession's interest in intersex individuals (Tosh, 2013), due to the problematic assumption that sexuality, sex and gender identity are inseparable and interchangeable. This complex terrain is made all the more confusing by the wide range of people with diverse sexual orientations and gender identities subsumed under the same diagnostic label. This chapter outlines this array of diagnostic terms and the psychological theories that scaffold them. It offers a historically situated account of transgender people from a psychiatric perspective. As a result, I critique a fickle psychiatric concept, not those to whom it is applied.

Before psychiatry

Present understandings of gender and gender identity may appear universal and timeless, but actually represent a particular moment within a particular culture (Bolich & Bolich, 2007). In historical documents, there have been a wide range of terms applied to those who defy gender norms, such as 'men dressing as women' or 'women dressing as men'. The specifics of these individual cases, and their personal gender experiences are not identifiable by records that have been produced by others, so it is not possible for us to know how they would have described themselves (Tosh, 2015, pp. 77–8). This illustrates one of many difficulties that are encountered when researching the history of gender-nonconforming and transgender people (Bolich & Bolich, 2007). For example, the concepts and terms we currently use (which continue to change and diversify) did not begin to take shape until the mid-20th century, when increasing attention was given to medical advancement in body-modification procedures (Boag, 2005). As Bolich states:

> To apply today's incomplete and sometimes controversial labels to people of the past may help make them feel accessible to us but comes at a cost: in their own context such labels were not used and the meaning today attached to them may or may not have existed then.
>
> (Bolich & Bolich, 2007, p. 15)

Consequently, historians tend to focus on described actions (such as cross-dressing) rather than unknowable identities or modern categories of people (Whittington, 2014). In addition, when feminists began challenging the exclusion of women from historical accounts by highlighting the role of women in history, they inadvertently erased the histories of gender-nonconforming and transgender people by viewing history through the lens of a gender binary. When using examples of 'women' cross-dressing as 'men', it was often assumed that these individuals *were* women, without reflection that this may not have been the case (Boag, 2005). This assumption, that cross-dressing 'women' were in fact women, is deeply embedded in what Garber (2011) calls the 'progress narrative'. Garber (2011) explains that instances of cross-dressing are 'explained away' and normalized through a narrative that assumes (all) women dressed as men to open doors for employment and a wide range of opportunities otherwise closed off to them. It rationalizes the behaviour within a patriarchal context and maintains the gender binary by ignoring those who refute it (Garber, 2011); it also concurs with other narratives of 'progress', such as colonial discourse that positions alternatives to the gender binary as part of a chaotic and 'barbaric' past (el-Malik, 2014; Morgensen, 2012; Robinson, 2012). The progress narrative overlooks the resulting disadvantages that cross-dressing can result in, such as social exclusion, forced relocation and the consequences of being 'outed' (Boag, 2005). It has pervaded historical analyses due to the lack of original accounts produced by those who cross-dressed, in addition to interpretations made by those who find the idea of transgender people 'unimaginable' (Garber, 2011), which has resulted in their actions and identities being assumed by others for a different purpose and in a different time.

The confusion that results from conflating diverse communities (e.g. women challenging rigid gender roles, cross-dressing individuals, and transgender people) is further exacerbated by the wide variation with regards to the expression, acceptance and representation of gender nonconformity within different historical periods and across cultures. Information regarding gender nonconformity is also inconsistent: 'in one era our knowledge of a particular gender's gender-crossing behaviour may be much richer, only to find a much different situation in studying another era' (Bolich & Bolich, 2007, p. 15). This makes generalizations or summaries a nearly impossible task (Tosh, 2015, p. 78; Whittington, 2014); therefore I provide only a few examples to illustrate the diversity and scope of cross-dressing.

Playing with gender roles was (and is) a component of a variety of religious rituals and festivals. Within Christianity, despite the condemnation of cross-dressing more generally, it was a part of 'Mumming' during Christmas where people would dress as a different gender. Similarly, dressing in the style of a different gender was a part of Wiccan celebrations, such as at the beginning of the new Celtic year on 31 October (Bullough & Bullough, 1993). Hinduism, Buddhism and Islam also refer to cross-dressing in different forms of spirituality and worship (Bolich & Bolich, 2007), as do a wide range of indigenous religions:

> Africa is a continent rich in indigenous religions as well as major world religions introduced through conquest and colonization. Often the result of the meetings between indigenous traditions and imported religions is a creative mixture . . . many indigenous religions make place for transgender realities and utilize crossdressing behaviour.
>
> (Bolich, 2009, p. 371)

These temporary transgressions of gender roles were accompanied by more permanent nonconformity, such as 'cross-dressing shamans' (Bullough & Bullough, 1993, p. 25) and those within a variety of cultures where more than two gender categories were part of the 'norm' (Bolich & Bolich, 2007; Cameron, 2005; Tafoya, 2003). There are also examples where the gender binary was less authoritative, such as the 'one-sex' model of the Middle Ages that, despite rigid gender roles, considered the biology of the sexes to be a part of the same anatomy, whereby the vagina was thought to be an 'internal penis' (Laqueur, 1992), something Whittington (2014) argued was potentially a more progressive theory than current understandings of sexed bodies.

There are many more examples beyond these few descriptions, but there was inconsistency in how these gender transgressions were expressed within society, as well as how they were received. Temporary gender transgressions as a part of a festival or within theatre were less likely to receive hostility, whereas long-term nonconformity was more likely to be considered a problem, particularly for gender-nonconforming femininity. This was due to the perception of women and femininity as being inferior to men and masculinity: 'the definitions of masculine and feminine seem to have taken their meaning as polar opposites: if men are strong, women are weak; if men are steadfast, women are fickle; if men are dominant, women are subordinate' (Bullough & Bullough, 1993, p. 174).

Due to masculinity being considered superior, those who were deemed 'cross-dressing women' moved up the social hierarchy, whereas those thought to be 'cross-dressing men' were seen to be moving down the social hierarchy (Bullough, 1982; Torjesen, 2004). The former transgression appeared to be a more rational move, and led to less instances of hostility. Consequently, there are numerous stories of cross-dressing female saints, or of medieval holy women transforming into men (Anson, 1974), but none of cross-dressing men (Bullough, 1982; Whittington, 2014). Due to an inability to see the value of women and femininity, and the general association of masculinity with sexuality and aggression, medieval theories centred around the assumption that individuals would only choose this lower social status to achieve access to women for the purposes of sex:

> . . . the implication remains, however, that the only reason a man might don female garb and live in a convent was to gain sexual satisfaction from the nuns. A woman who dressed as a man and lived in a monastery, however, was assumed to be innocent of any such intentions.
>
> (Bullough, 1982, p. 46)

The hostility directed towards those who did not conform to gender norms, then, were deeply embedded within societal understandings and perceptions of women and femininity (Bullough, 1982; Bullough & Bullough, 1993). This condemnation of gender-nonconforming femininity (within a context of devalued femininity more generally) continued within the 16th and 17th centuries where public occurrences decreased. During the 19th century, women began to challenge their position of subordination, making successful moves in their acknowledgement as people within their own right, rather than through their relationship with a man. This included achieving the right to vote, but resulted in changes in how masculinity was considered in response to the gains of the 19th century women's movement. These included a change in dress, away from lace and frills to what was deemed a more 'masculine' and 'practical' look, as well as an emphasis on the importance of sport in the evaluation of a 'real man' through physical strength and dominance (Bullough & Bullough, 1993). This increasing polarization of the sexes led to fewer experiences of cross-gendered behaviour and less tolerance for those who did, particularly men. When men did show an interest in femininity or interests considered feminine, they were often ostracized and victimized (Bullough & Bullough, 1993; Tosh, 2015, pp. 78–9).

Due to changes in social norms regarding styles of dress and gender roles, tracing the origin of cross-dressing is a problematic if not impossible endeavour, but what is known, is that cross-dressing and gender nonconformity have a long history across the world, with ancient texts referring to the practice for millennia (Bolich & Bolich, 2007).

Perversion and paraphilias

In the 19th century, sexuality began to be redefined in terms of normality and pathology by the increasingly influential profession of psychiatry (Foucault, 1979). Key to this process of reconstruction was Krafft-Ebing's (1892) sexology text entitled *Psychopathia Sexualis*. Krafft-Ebing is described by some as a 'founding father of scientific sexology' (Oosterhuis, 2000, p. 47) and by others as providing the 'first and most influential' classification of perversions (Schaffner, 2011, p. 45). Using the terms 'sexual inversion' or 'contrary sexual instinct', Krafft-Ebing (1892) categorized homosexuality as either an acquired sexual interest or present from birth, with the former consisting of varying degrees of 'severity'. These were: an attraction to the same-sex (degree 1); 'eviration', the development of a feminine personality (degree 2); 'metamorphis sexualis paranoica', described as when a man would feel as if they were a woman (degree 3), or they believed that they were a woman (degree 4) (Tosh, 2015, p. 62). Therefore, psychiatry initially framed homosexuality and gender nonconformity as a continuum, with declarations of a transgender identity not only being positioned as a more 'severe' form of homosexuality, but also as a 'delusion' (Krafft-Ebing, 1892).[1] As homosexuality was combined with transgender identities at this time and considered a form of sexual deviance, psychiatry positioned gender nonconformity as a pathological sexual desire under the category of 'perversion' (meaning 'abnormal' 'sexual ideas', Krafft-Ebing, 1892, p. 56). Psychiatry continues to do so under the current term 'paraphilia', which means 'abnormal' 'love' (Moser, 2001; Tosh, 2015). In addition to the already described 'metamorphosis sexualis paranoica', cross-dressing and gender nonconformity have been controversially associated with several diagnoses related to sexuality, including the highly contested 'transvestism' and 'autogynephilia'.

Transvestism

In *Psychopathia Sexualis*, Krafft-Ebing (1892) described 'fetichism of female attire' as a perversion, referring to men who fixated on women's clothing. Originally the interest in women's clothing was not considered 'abnormal', but the limited focus concerned psychiatrists, the reason being, it was argued, that men 'should' be attracted to women in general, not just their clothing. Krafft-Ebing (1892) theorized that 'this limited sexual interest, within its narrower limits, is usually expressed with a correspondingly greater and abnormal intensity' (p. 153). He defined a 'fetich' as 'objects, or parts, or simply peculiarities of objects, which, by virtue of associative relations to an intense feeling, or to a personality or idea that awakens deep interest, exert a kind of charm' (p. 17). He described case studies of men engaging in sexual activity only when women were dressed in a particular way, but also of those considered to be 'men',[2] wearing women's underwear during sexual activity (e.g. petticoats and corsets).

The term was not solely applied to sexual desire, but to an intense fascination toward something deemed undeserving of such an interest (or an 'unreasonable' interest). Krafft-Ebing borrowed the term from Müller (1874), who used it in his studies of religion. Thus, Krafft-Ebing (1892) also described a 'religious fetichism' as a 'deluded' belief in idols possessing 'divine attributes' (p. 17), whereas 'erotic fetichism' was applied to qualities of an individual or object that resulted in sexual pleasure. The term, from the medieval Portuguese *feitiço* (Long, 2004), was used in the late 19th and early 20th centuries by those promoting Christianity to describe African religious artefacts, such as household items 'believed to contain the spirit of the family protector' (Ffoulkes, 1909, p. 387), or as a general term to refer to African gods (Farrow, 1926). It was used in these writings to justify the propagation of Christianity amongst those considered 'savage', arguing that it was the superior religion (e.g. Farrow, 1926). Therefore, we again observe the complex interweaving of colonial discourse within psychiatry and the dissuasion of gender nonconformity.

This theory of cross-dressing as a sexual desire was taken up by Hirschfeld (2006 [1910]) in *The Transvestites: The Erotic Drive to Cross-Dress*. He argued that theories regarding fetishism[3] were inadequate in explaining the phenomenon, concluding that 'the transvestites themselves . . . are surely as dissatisfied with this explanation as with the tracing back of their feminine drive to homosexuality' (p. 30). Rather than an intense focus on a particular clothing item (i.e. fetishism), or the psychoanalytic perspective that dressing as a socially subordinate gender was for the purposes of humiliation and self punishment (i.e. masochism), Hirschfeld countered that the underlying motivation for transvestism was 'the wish for effemination' (p. 32), though this was limited to cross-dressing. He concluded that 'No matter how much transvestite men feel like women when dressed in women's clothing and women feel like men when dressed in men's clothing, they still remain aware that in reality it is not so', ultimately agreeing with Krafft-Ebing (1892) that sexual metamorphosis was a delusion. He did, however, move away from a rigid gender binary, instead proposing a theory of sexual intermediaries where gender (both mentally and physically) existed as a continuum with 'absolute' men and women at either extreme. 'Absolute' individuals represented those who had both the anatomy and personality expected for a person of that gender identity (or 'cisgender' as we would call them today) (Tosh, 2015, p. 80).

The DSM's first and second editions listed 'transvestism' under the deviations of sexuality section (APA, 1952, 1968), and it moved away from Hirshfeld's (2006 [1910]) definition by focusing solely on heterosexual men (or those defined as men by psychiatrists) (Blanchard, 1990). The third edition of the DSM introduced the term 'paraphilia', and listed 'transvestism' under this newly named category. It was differentiated from the diagnosis of 'fetishism' as based on the sole focus of women's clothing (APA, 1980). It was defined thus: 'Transvestism phenomena range from occasional solitary wearing of female clothes to extensive involvement in a transvestic subculture. Usually more than one article of women's clothing is involved, and the man may dress entirely as a woman' (APA, 1980, p. 269).

Its association to eroticism and psychopathology has been repeatedly emphasized within psychiatric texts, such as its name change to 'transvestic fetishism' in 1987 (APA, 1987), and subsequently 'transvestic disorder' with 'fetishism' (APA, 2013). This is, in part, influenced by Blanchard's (1989, 2005) work that has attracted much criticism (Daley & Mulé, 2014; Moser, 2009, 2010, 2011; Serano, 2009, 2010; Veale, Clarke & Lomax, 2011; Winters, 2006, 2008).

Autogynephilia

Autogynephilia[4] is a controversial and highly criticised concept (Moser, 2010, 2011; Serano, 2010) that was introduced by Blanchard (1989). He described the term as referring to heterosexual men who were 'erotically aroused by the thought or image of themselves as women' (Blanchard, 2005, p. 439). Blanchard (1993) divided the concept into four categories: 'transvestic' (cross-dressing), behavioural (expressing femininity), physiologic (feminine bodily changes such as pregnancy or menstruation) and anatomic (wanting body-modification procedures). Therefore, the concept includes those who cross-dress or have fetishes regarding women's clothing (i.e. those under the psychiatric category of 'transvestism'), as well as transgender people who pursue body-modification procedures (Blanchard, 1993). As Blanchard rejected self-determined gender identities, his use of the phrase 'heterosexual men' actually includes a wide range of gender identities and sexual orientations. For example, in a 2013 interview, Blanchard gave the following description of his understanding of transgender identities: 'I think that a transsexual should be considered as whatever their biological sex is plus the fact that they are transsexuals' (Blanchard, 2013, para. 21). Similarly, Lawrence, who has continued Blanchard's work in this area, also rejects self-determined gender identities: 'One MtF transsexual type consists of males who have a life-long history of female-typical interests, behaviours, and personality characteristics. From earliest childhood, these individuals behaved liked girls, identified with girls, and often proclaimed themselves to *be* girls' (Lawrence, 2012, p. 1).

While Blanchard focuses on 'biological sex' and thus physical characteristics such as genitalia, Lawrence misgenders those who have identified as women. The broad scope of the diagnosis is unsurprising, then, when the conceptualization of 'normality' is viewed as so narrow. For instance, the centrality of heterosexuality and assumptions of heterosexual marriage as a universal 'norm', are deeply embedded in writings around autogynephilia. Blanchard (1993) stated, ' . . . an autogynephile's desire to unite in the flesh with his feminine self-image corresponds to a heterosexual's desire to unite in marriage with a female partner' (p. 244), and 'Using the analogy of heterosexual marriage, [Blanchard] observed that husbands often continue to experience a deep emotional connection to their wives, even after their initial intense sexual attraction has diminished or completely disappeared' (Lawrence, 2004, p.81). He also stated that the experience of gender dysphoria would result in the 'inevitable dissolution of . . . marriage', which not only assumes that heterosexual marriage is 'normal', but also that transgender individuals cannot have a successful one (Blanchard, 1993). This concurs with Iantaffi and Bockting's (2011) research that found that heterosexuality was deemed the only 'legitimate' and 'non-pathological' option for transgender people (p. 367). Again, this is unsurprising when key figures in the defining of gender 'normality' describe a 'gold standard' of sexuality as follows:

> . . . normal sexuality is whatever is related to reproduction. Now you have everything else. I would distinguish between behaviors which are anomalous and benign vs. those that are malignant. So homosexuality would be not normal but benign. Whereas something like serious dangerous sadism would be a malignant variation.
>
> (Blanchard, 2013, para. 39)

In addition to the heteronormative assumptions embedded in the concept, there is an overt focus on the pathologization of femininity; both 'transvestism' and 'autogynephilia' are considered issues solely for (heterosexual) men/'men' (Zucker & Blanchard, 1997). Blanchard (2013) goes further and states that the opposing diagnosis ('autoandrophilia', an arousal at the thought of being a man) does not exist. However, Moser (2009) found that over 90 per cent of gender-conforming women would fit the definition of 'autogynephilia' and were aroused at the thought of themselves as women. He concluded that it would be unsurprising to find that some transgender individuals were aroused at the thought of themselves as women, as it appeared to be a more frequent occurrence generally in people of a range of gender identities.

Such conflicting research is to be expected, as there are numerous issues in the assessment of autogynephilia and its underlying assumptions. For instance, Blanchard (1993) assessed for 'autogynephilic ideation' based on the answer to the question, 'Which of the following pictures of yourself has been most strongly associated with sexual arousal?' and selecting one of the following three options, 'as a nude female', 'as a female dressed only in underwear, or foundation garments (for example, a corset)', or 'as a fully clothed female'. As the research focused predominantly on trans women, then viewing themselves in their underwear, or nude, would 'normally' be associated with arousal, as nudity and lingerie (particularly the fetishized item of a 'corset' given in the example) are highly associated with sexual activity and the lead-up to sexual activity. Moreover, trans women exist in a culture that expects them to be attractive, and that sexualizes women's clothing, and women *in* clothing; therefore, arousal when imagining themselves in clothing (or seeing themselves as 'sexy' and 'attractive') would also be 'normal'.

Autogynephilia is also highly criticized for its framing of gender-nonconforming, cross-dressing and transgender identities as a paraphilia.

Blanchard (1993, 2005) and Lawrence (2004, 2012) have both connected 'autogynephilia' with transgender people, arguing that their motivation to pursue body-modification procedures is sexual. There has been an adamant rejection of this theory from transgender communities, but Blanchard and Lawrence continued to promote it, framing those that disagree with their perspective as in 'denial' about their sexual motivations or as 'liars' (see Blanchard, 2013, para. 19). Therefore, in addition to overriding their gender identities, psychiatric professionals refuse to acknowledge personal descriptions of subjectivity, embodied experiences of gender, and motivations for body modification. This is another example of sanism silencing those framed as 'mentally ill': when those in a position of power, such as a medical professional, can redefine someone's experience and their voice of dissent as part of an 'illness'.

While Lawrence (2004, 2012) links autogynephilia with 'love', the diagnosis has also reaffirmed the long-standing construction of gender nonconformity with 'perversion'. For example, Bailey's (2003) controversial book *The man who would be queen: The science of gender-bending and transsexualism* stated that paraphilias tended to coincide, and he linked 'autogynephilia' with 'sadism', 'masochism' and 'autoerotic asphyxia',[5] as do others (e.g. Lawrence, 2004). Thus, we see the continued framing of gender nonconformity as a sexual 'perversion' within psychiatric discourse, tied to sexual activities that are often thought of as 'monstrous' or frightening (Douard, 2007; Jewkes & Wykes, 2012). However, the counter to this construction risks the creation of a two-tiered classification of 'real' and 'illegitimate' transgender people based on whether they consider their gender nonconformity as a result of a gender or sexual identity (Baril & Trevenen, 2014).

Resolute rejections of cross-dressing as connected to sexuality, and of other forms of sexual interest (such as sadism or masochism), however, also have the potential to further pathologize or oppress minority groups, such as those from consensual BDSM and kink communities. Psychiatry's observation of those who describe sexual excitement at cross-dressing is likely to be a consequence of the problem of subsuming many different groups under broad categories. That is to say, the psychiatric category of 'transvestism' will include those who cross-dress in a non-sexualised way as well as those who experience fetishism as a part of a consensual BDSM or kink culture (Kleinplatz & Moser, 2014; Richards & Barker, 2013). The conflation of erotic interests in cross-dressing, with those who cross-dress in a non-erotic way, or transgender people, functions to justify the fetishization of one group of people, based on the existence of another group of already pathologized people (those in BDSM or kink communities). This is a common problem or confusion, as many terms used within sexual subcultures derive from psychiatric discourse, including sadism, masochism and fetishism (Tosh, 2015).

Despite the widespread criticism and disagreement with the association of cross-dressing and transgender people with sexual deviance (Conway, 2003;

Winters, 2008), autogynephilia was included in the fourth edition of the DSM, as a link between transvestic fetishism and gender identity disorder (Zucker & Bradley, 2004). It remains in the current *DSM-5* (APA, 2013) and is a point of contention amongst cross-dressing, gender-nonconforming and transgender communities (Meyer-Bahlburg, 2010).

Gender identity

Counter to the long-standing conflation of transgender identities with homosexuality and 'perversion', from the early 20th century, psychiatric texts began to describe individuals as cross-dressing and gender nonconforming due to their gender identity. This began with the diagnosis of transsexualism, due to developments in medical technologies and body-modification procedures, as well as increasing awareness of individuals who pursued such surgeries (Bullough & Bullough, 1993).

Transsexualism

The term 'transsexualism' was first used by Caudwell (2006 [1949]) in his work entitled *Psychopathia transexualis* (Drescher, 2010). Harry Benjamin advanced the popularity of the term in his presentation in 1953 (Ekins & King, 2001) and his subsequent publication *The transsexual phenomenon* (Benjamin, 1966). Hirschfeld (1923) also referred to 'psychic transsexualism' ('seelisher transsexualismus'), but this had a different meaning from how the term was generally taken up (Drescher, 2010). Therefore, Caudwell (2006 [1949]) is often credited with the introduction of 'transsexualism', although his work was pathologizing and ultimately sought a cure in the form of preventative education. Caudwell defined 'transsexualism' as, 'individuals who wish to be members of the sex to which they do not properly belong. Their condition usually arises from a poor hereditary background and a highly unfavourable childhood environment' (pp. 40–41).

Benjamin's presentations and book were inspired by Christine Jorgensen's body-modification surgery in 1952 and the subsequent surge in media interest. Benjamin (1954) described cross-dressing, transvestism and transsexualism as varying degrees of gender nonconformity. At the less 'severe' end was sporadic cross-dressing, then transvestism, which he considered to be a desire to live as another gender, and then the most 'severe' or 'genuine' transvestism, was when individuals wanted to become a different gender through body-modification surgery (or who wanted their gender identity and physical body to be congruent). Therefore, Benjamin's work continued this demarcation of the subtle and complex differences between a variety of expressions of gender and gender identity. Benjamin (1954) concluded that psychotherapy was 'a waste of time' for transsexual individuals (p. 51), and recommended hormonal intervention, conversion surgery and psychotherapy for guidance (Tosh, 2015, pp. 80–81).

During the 1960s, American psychoanalyst Stoller popularized the theory of gender as being made up of a gender role (a public and social expression of gender) and gender identity (a subjective and psychological aspect). The concept of gender role was attributed to John Money (Green, 2008; Money, 1994) and taken up by queer and feminist theorists (Stryker & Whittle, 2006; see Chapters 4 and 5). There was also the concept of 'sex', which Stoller framed as biological. Therefore it was possible to have a 'male' body, with a 'female' gender identity with a feminine gender role. Green (2008) described Stoller as one of the 'sexological kings'[6] for his role in developing gender clinics that provided sex-reassignment treatments and his introduction of the concept of gender identity to psychoanalytic and psychiatric theorizing. However, his work was also criticized for its pathologization of gender nonconformity (Beemyn, 2013; Monro, 2000), as well as his attempts at preventing transsexualism by treating gender-nonconforming youth. For example, Stoller (1968) described childhood transsexualism as a 'potentially malignant personality disorder' (p. 193). The cause of the 'disorder' was theorized to be the child's mother, thus Stoller introduced the mother-blaming narrative that is common in accounts of gender nonconformity. This narrative outlined that a distant relationship with a father failed to protect sons from the 'malignant effect of his mother's excessive closeness' (Stoller, 1968, p. 204). After concluding that mothers' 'constant cuddling' was the primary cause, he proposed that the most effective treatment for transsexualism was intervention in childhood to avoid 'their demands for sex transformation procedures' (Stoller, 1968, p. 206).

The diagnosis did not appear in the DSM until 1980, when two new terms emerged: 'transsexualism' and 'childhood gender identity disorder'. The difference between 'transsexualism' and 'transvestic fetishism' was stated to be the lack of sexual pleasure, as well as the desire to become or live as the opposite sex that was described as an essential feature of transsexualism (APA, 1980). The childhood diagnosis opened the door for preventative treatments, which developed out of the failure of therapies to stop gender-nonconforming behaviour among adolescents and adults diagnosed as 'transsexual' (Money & Green, 1969; Rekers, 1977).

Gender identity disorder

In 1994, the American Psychiatric Association (APA) combined two diagnoses ('transsexualism' and 'gender identity disorder nontranssexual type') into 'gender identity disorder in adolescents or adults'.[7] This matched the diagnosis with the childhood version[8] that had existed since the *DSM-III* (APA, 1980). This new diagnosis altered the psychiatric construction from a disordered desire to be the opposite sex, to an internal 'incongruence between anatomic sex and gender identity' (APA, 1980, p. 261). For children, the diagnosis included the following criteria: 'A repeatedly stated desire to be, or insistence that he or she is, the other sex', in addition to wearing clothing and participating in activities stereotypical of 'the other sex' (APA, 1994, p. 537). This moved the concept even further away from the eroticized construction of 'transvestism'. However, these changes were very controversial (Bryant, 2006; Hird, 2003) and there remains much professional disagreement regarding the diagnosis, as well as public protest (Tosh, 2011, 2015). As Baril and Trevenen (2014) outlined, there are those who see the diagnosis as a valid psychiatric category (Zucker, 2008), those who wish to reform the diagnosis to more accurately reflect their experience of gender-related distress and to maintain access to medical support (Winters, 2006, 2009), and those who promote a complete removal of the diagnosis from the DSM (Burke, 1996; Isay, 1997).

The introduction of 'childhood gender identity disorder' in the *DSM-III* was heavily influenced by increasing research into 'gender-variant' or 'feminine' boys in the 1960s (Bryant, 2006), such as Green's work on 'sissies' and 'tomboys', culminating in his book *The 'sissy boy syndrome' and the development of homosexuality* in 1987. Thus, as with the diagnoses of transvestism and autogynephilia, psychology and psychiatry were predominantly concerned with those who expressed femininity: '"tomboy" – a romping, boisterous, boyish young girl; "sissy" – an effeminate boy or man, a timid or cowardly person. Thus for a boy to be called "sissy" can be devastating. It pierces a boy's self-image at its most vulnerable point' (Green, 1979, p. 1).

This concern over femininity was tied to the assumption that feminine 'boys' would be homosexual later in life, and it was argued by some in the profession that parents had a right to be concerned and a right to intervene, despite the declassification of homosexuality as a mental illness years earlier (APA, 1973). For example, Green (1979) stated that parents had a right to be concerned due to 'feminine boys' being more likely to grow up to be 'sexually atypical adults' (p. 1), although he also stated that it was 'debatable' whether such therapies should be done. Similarly, Rekers (1977) stated, 'Intervention on deviant sex-role development in childhood may be the only effective manner of treating (i.e. preventing) serious forms of sexual deviance in adulthood' (p. 562). Consequently, Green's (1979) studies of a girl-like syndrome (p. 1) in homosexual men showed that the development of the gender identity disorder diagnosis was not exclusively based on transsexualism or transvestism.

In addition to research on adult homosexual men and 'feminine boys', the gender identity disorder diagnosis also developed from research on intersex children, particularly the work of John Money (e.g. Money, Hampson & Hampson, 1957). This work focused on the role of medical professionals and psychologists assigning a gender to a child, and encouraging families to raise their child in the gender assigned. For example, if a child was born with genitalia that did not conform to medical categories of 'male' or 'female',[9] then doctors would choose a gender based on what would be easier to construct via surgery. This early guesswork on the part of professionals, in addition to extensive genital surgery and physical examinations, has been highly criticized since then, for its failure to account for the existence of intersex people in their own right (rather than trying to force them to fit into pre-assigned medical categories), as well as carrying out what have been termed non-consensual treatments, some of which have been described as abusive (David, 1994; Ehrenreich & Barr, 2005; Kessler, 2002; Tosh, 2013).

A significant case, known as the John/Joan case, was not of an intersex child, but of an accident during a circumcision procedure where a young boy's penis was left severely damaged. Money and Ehrhardt (1972) recommended that the child be raised as a girl following genital surgery. Based on his experience with intersex children, and what was later described as a 'successful' change of John to Joan (Money, 1975), this account of a change in gender identity opened the door for gender conversion therapies in childhood. This was an extremely unfortunate course of events, as later such therapies were discredited through documented returns to the original gender identity after treatment, as well as reports of suicide that families linked to such therapies (Colapinto, 2000; 'David Reimer, 38, Subject of the John/Joan Case,' 2004; Diamond & Sigmundson, 1997). From the 1950s onwards, however, Money's work was very influential. This was both in the treatment of intersex children as well as his work on transgender and gender-nonconforming youth.

Discussions regarding gender at this time centred around the dilemma of nature versus nurture. While feminists challenged the use of naturalistic and biological discourse to justify the discrimination and oppression of women (Bleier, 1984; Lambert, 1978; Sayers, 1982), Money and his colleagues distinguished between a biological sex, and a combination of gender role and gender identity. In a paradigm shift away from theories that linked gendered behaviour to biology (e.g. Archer, 1976; Gray, 1971), Money promoted a theory of gender identity and gender role as influenced by the environment and thus not as rigid or innate as had been previously thought:

> The foregoing three matched pairs of hermaphrodites, and many others like them, concordant for diagnosis and discordant for gender identity, wreck the assumption that gender identity as male or female is preordained by the sex (XX or XY) chromosomes. Clearly it is not.
>
> (Money & Ehrhardt, 1972, p. 161)

As a result, gender identity became framed as a fluid and malleable construct that could be changed in childhood during a 'critical period' of development (before 18 months). Money argued that children learned which gender role they were supposed to embrace and express through 'imprinting', that involved observing a parent and then mimicking that behaviour (Money, Hampson & Hampson, 1957). Thus, children learn their gendered behaviour from social interaction with their parents, he argued, and he compared the experience to that of learning languages. A failure to do so, would result in an 'unfinished' gender identity, i.e. one that was not predominantly feminine or masculine (Money & Ehrhardt, 1972). The problem with this conceptualization was that it was taken up within the profession as evidence that gender identity was as changeable as socially and culturally constructed gender roles, despite Money's emphasis on a 'critical window' of development, as well as his research on biological determinants of gender (see Chapter 4).

Despite the criticisms of the theory (Hausman, 2000; Kessler, 1990; Rogers & Walsh, 1982; Sloop, 2000), it remains influential within psychology (and feminism), with similar definitions of gender identity and gender role replicated in a wide range of clinical literature, such as:

> Gender identity can be defined as a child's recognition or awareness that he or she is a member of one sex and not the other . . . Gender role can be defined in relation to those behaviours, attitudes, and personality traits that a society, in a given culture and historical period, designates as masculine and feminine.
>
> (Zucker, 1990, p. 4)

In its over 30-year existence, 'gender identity disorder' accumulated an extensive amount of criticism and generated professional and public debate regarding homosexuality, transgender people and ethics of psychiatric treatment (Bryant, 2006, 2008; Burke, 1996; Hegarty, 2009; Hird, 2003; Langer & Martin, 2004; Lev, 2006; Menvielle & Tuerk, 2002; Tosh, 2015; Winters, 2009; Wren, 2002). It was replaced with 'gender dysphoria' in 2013 with the release of the *DSM-5* (APA, 2013).

Gender dysphoria

In 2010, the American Psychiatric Association released proposals for the fifth edition of the DSM. Initially it included a possible name change for the diagnosis of 'gender identity disorder' of 'gender incongruence' but settled on 'gender dysphoria' prior to publication (APA, 2013), although the next edition of the *International Classification of Diseases* (ICD) is due to use 'gender incongruence' (Drescher, 2013). The term 'gender dysphoria' was first introduced by Fisk (1973, 1978, 1974) in his work at the Stanford University gender clinic:

> Chromosomal make-up, sex of assignment and rearing, external and internal genital morphology, pre-natal and post-natal endocrinologic factors, as well as behaviour, are all seemingly interrelated within the concept of the gender. A dictionary definition of dysphoria includes dissatisfaction, anxiety, restlessness and discomfort.
>
> (Fisk, 1974, p. 387)

Rather than developing from research, or for the purposes of the DSM, Fisk's term derived from clinical interventions and dissatisfaction with the narrow definition of transsexualism, which seemed to limit the amount of people that he could help (Fisk, 1974). By introducing the broader term of 'gender dysphoria syndrome', which had numerous subcategories that included transsexualism, transvestism and so on, Fisk was able to recommend surgical intervention for a more diverse group of people. Fisk considered psychotherapy ineffective with trans people, finding that surgical interventions reduced suicide attempts and depression (Fisk, 1974, 1978).

Its meaning has since changed from Fisk's initial desire for a broader, more flexible and liberal term to be used for the purposes of extending surgical intervention and medical support, to something more similar to prior conceptualizations of transsexualism, as 'discontent with one's biological sex, the desire to possess the body of the opposite sex, and also to be regarded by others as a member of the opposite sex' (Blanchard, 1990, p. 56). Whereas Fisk's work included 'effeminate homosexuals' and transvestism as part of a 'spectrum' of 'gender disorders' (Fisk, 1974), the current *DSM-5* (APA, 2013) diagnosis focuses specifically on gender nonconformity: 'a marked incongruence between one's experienced/expressed gender and assigned gender' (p. 452). However, others have also put forward the idea that gender 'disorders' are more of a continuum rather than strict categories, such as Zucker (1990) who stated that children with 'gender identity disorder' ranged from those who wished to be a different gender (something he classed as 'gender confusion', although this frames trans people as untrustworthy in their knowledge about their identity) to those who believed they were another gender (what he classed as the 'extreme end' of the continuum).

In many texts, prior to the name change in 2013, 'gender dysphoria' was framed as a less 'severe' form of transsexualism (e.g. APA, 1994) or as a sporadic experience of gendered distress, rather than the long-standing history of gender nonconformity that was associated with transsexualism (e.g. Blanchard, 1990). There was, however, a continued interest in how 'gender dysphoria' was tied to sexual orientation, with researchers insistent on categorizing people based on their assigned gender, and the gender of their sexual interest. For example, Blanchard described 'homosexual' 'men' as the majority of cases that were seen by psychiatry, which not only continued psychiatry's focus on femininity, but also the misgendering of people as well as mislabelling their sexuality:

> It should be noted that the DSM type labels, heterosexual, homosexual, and so on, do not change according to the individual's current surgical status or cross-gender convictions. Thus, a surgical[ly] reassigned male-to-female transsexual living as the lesbian lover of a biological female would still be classified as a heterosexual transsexual.
>
> (Blanchard, 1990, p. 57)

Thus, Blanchard's (1990) 'homosexual' 'men', were in fact, lesbian trans women, whereas 'homosexual' 'women' (i.e. heterosexual trans men) were described as disliking playing with dolls or being dressed as 'pretty little girls', instead having a preference for blue jeans (p. 80). A fondness for athletics and fixing cars were listed as part of the history of the 'disordered' individual. Asexual and bisexual individuals were also studied, but considered less prevalent.

'Gender dysphoria', then, is the latest in a long and complicated history of the pathologization of gender nonconformity that has included and been influenced by the pathologization and mistreatment of homosexual, intersex, and BDSM and kink individuals. While this latest name change could have reflected a broader term, as well as emphasizing the distress felt by those pursuing body-modification procedures, it continues to frame gender nonconformity as pathological and enables the continuation of unethical therapies used on trans children with the aim of 'preventing' transsexualism (e.g. Zucker & Bradley, 1995, 2004).

Gender conversion therapy

> One position has been called reparative or conversion therapy since it aims to convert the child back to a stereotypically gendered child, encouraging them to conform to the gender expectations of their birth sex, thus 'repairing' the gender nonconformity . . . .
>
> (Hill et al., 2010, p. 7)

While the introduction of the transsexualism diagnosis was based on the development of body-modification procedures and gender identity clinics to provide such surgeries, the introduction of 'gender identity disorder in childhood' was based on research that focused on 'feminine boys' and intersex children. At this time, it had been explicitly stated that therapies aimed at converting an individual's sexual orientation and gender identity had been unsuccessful with adult 'patients' (e.g. Bancroft, 1974; Davison, 1976). The conclusion was that therapies should target gender-nonconforming children, which in some cases would be a means of 'preventing homosexuality' (e.g. Acosta, 1975; Zuger, 1966), transvestism (Rekers, 1977) and transsexualism (Stoller, 1968; Zucker & Bradley, 2004). Therefore, the aim of these therapies was to change the individual, to deny their gender identity and to get them to conform to the gender binary – or as Stoller (1968) states, 'the goal of treatment should be to make the child feel he is a male and want to be a masculine boy' (p. 206).

A range of methods fall under this title of 'conversion therapies', although few use the term to describe their work due to its negative connotations and prohibition by several professional organizations (Hill et al. 2010). Rekers used behavioural therapy such as advising parents to reward masculine behaviour and punish feminine behaviours. This included high levels of monitoring, with professionals and parents observing the child's behaviour intensely and providing a response depending on their play, dress, or actions (Pyne, 2014). Punishments included physical discipline (e.g. 'swatting') by parents, in some cases (Rekers, 1977). Reker's approach was criticized for numerous reasons, but it also lost favour in the scientific community due to the motivation for therapy being 'Christian values' and morality. It was also criticized by the family of one of his earlier cases (known as 'Kraig'). Despite its reported 'success', 'Kraig' stated that he felt ashamed and his family attributed his suicide in 2003 to the treatments he underwent in childhood (Bronstein & Joseph, 2011; Burke, 1996).

Others preferred to justify their work based on the difficulties of being homosexual in an 'unaccepting culture' and the invasive procedures required for body modification (Zucker, 1990). Stoller, for example, used psychoanalytic interventions aimed at readdressing the mother-child relations, due to his theory that gender nonconformity was caused by an excessive closeness with the mother. Green (1979) also worked with the parents, firstly 'sensitizing' them to the 'problems' of a gender-nonconforming child. Zucker (2008) mentions this also, that is, the importance of getting parents to see their child as a 'problem', of 'shifting their position' from one of 'tolerance' for gender nonconformity (p. 361). Unfortunately, families supportive of their gender-nonconforming child are seen as a barrier to successful therapy rather than a strength within gender conversion approaches. Within these psychotherapies, it is common for the child's gender-nonconforming behaviours to be restricted, so this includes restrictions on cross-dressing, cross-gender role play, being encouraged to play with 'same-sex' peers and to see the benefits of being the gender assigned to them at birth (Green, 1979; Zucker & Bradley, 2004; Zucker, 1990, 2008).

Therefore, initially the diagnosis was used as a means to intervene in the prevention of homosexuality, as well as transsexualism. While the former has since been overtly challenged, with admissions that this is no longer considered ethical practice (Zucker et al., 2012), the prevention of transsexualism as a treatment aim has been much more difficult to address. The prevention of transsexualism is still promoted as a justification of therapy by current members of the APA (e.g. Zucker & Bradley, 2004; Zucker, 2008). While there were calls against the pathologization of gender nonconformity and of treatments aimed at encouraging gender conformity, these were dismissed by those working in the profession as radical perspectives that would never be accepted. For example, Reker (1977) stated:

> One might draw the inference from the papers by Winkler and Mordyke et al. that transsexualism, transvestism, and homosexual-orientation disturbances are deviant or undesirable only in the eyes of a skewed society with distorted and antiquated social standards. But we strongly reject that position . . . .
>
> (Reker, 1977, p. 563)

And Zucker has stated, 'It would seem that preventing transsexualism is a goal that will never gather systematic opposition' (1985, p. 116).[10]

However, there have been increasing reports of suicide as a result of 'conversion therapies' (CBC News, 2015; Csanady, 2015; Fox & Rothman, 2015; Horner, 2003; Laemmle, 2013; Pyne, 2015; 'David Reimer, 38, Subject of the John/Joan Case', 2004). This is in addition to the criticisms of gender conversion therapies targeting children, which have been vociferous and extensive from academics and activists alike (Ansara & Hegarty, 2012; Burke, 1996; Hird, 2003; Lev, 2006; Pyne, 2014; Rosenberg, 2002; Tosh, 2011, 2015; Winters, 2009), resulting in the professional disavowal of the treatments as well as its criminalization in several provinces in Canada. Paradoxically, the most influential individuals who pathologize gender nonconformity in childhood (Ansara & Hegarty, 2012), who were directly involved in the *DSM-5* revisions for sexual and gender identity 'disorders' (Zucker, 2015; Zucker & Duschinsky, 2015), are no longer able to use their approach to therapy in Ontario without potentially breaking the law (Cross, 2015; Ling, 2015), and their gender identity clinic was closed following a 'damning' external review (Tosh, in press). These recent changes in law regarding therapies that aim to change someone's gender identity or expression, show that once again, psychiatry has been on the wrong side of history.

Gender affirmative therapies

> Affirmative psychotherapy positively affirms identity without promoting a particular perspective.
>
> (Embaye, 2006, p. 53)

Following a diagnosis of transsexualism or gender dysphoria, surgical and hormonal interventions can be recommended for adults (Gooren, 2005; Wierckx et al., 2011) and hormones for adolescents (e.g. puberty suppressants) (Cohen-Kettenis et al., 2008). While there can be much resistance to this approach from those not supportive of transgender people, and multiple barriers to support due to the pathologization of transgender identities (Garner, 2014), access to medical services has been found to reduce depression and suicide attempts in trans populations (De Cuypere et al., 2006; Fisk, 1973, 1978; Murad et al., 2010; Pauly, 1973), but is not the 'cure-all' as gender-nonconforming individuals can still experience emotional distress as a result of discrimination, parental rejection and social isolation, with suicide rates for trans women remaining higher than cisgender populations even after surgery (Asscheman et al., 2011, p. 640; Dhejne et al., 2011). However, more research on this area is needed as explanations of why suicide attempts are so high are lacking, as are accurate data on actual suicides, and current research is predominantly based on (unrepresentative) clinical samples (De Cuypere et al., 2005).

Suicide and suicide attempts are a known issue in trans communities, with research indicating that around 40 per cent of trans people try to end their life prior to receiving medical support (Goldblum et al., 2012; Haas, Rodgers & Herman, 2014; Reyes, 2014; Wermuth, 2015), rising to 60 per cent when medical care is refused (Haas, Rodgers & Herman, 2014). Moreover, despite fears of surgical 'regret', dissatisfaction with the results of surgery or regret are rare (Cohen-Kettenis et al., 2011; Pfafflin & Junge, 1998), (in around 1–2 per cent of cases, most often by those assigned male at birth who have not had a life-long identification as trans: Dhejne et al., 2014; Gooren, 2011). Research also shows that therapies that support the gender identity of the person (instead of trying to 'convert' them to a gender deemed more socially appropriate by a professional) have also been found to dramatically reduce suicide risk, particularly when they are supported by families where in some cases reported suicide attempts have been reduced by 93 per cent (Travers et al., 2012). Therefore, the very support that conversion therapies try to dissuade is actually one of the most important components to minimizing the distress of trans people.

Unfortunately, medical support is not always readily available. There are numerous hurdles that trans people are made to overcome to be deemed eligible, hurdles that are designed by psychiatrists and other medical professionals, which is in addition to 'anti-transgender bias' and financial difficulties (Haas et al., 2014). This includes the 'real-life test', where people are required to live as 'the other gender' for a minimum of twelve months prior to being referred for surgery (Clemmensen, 1990; Petersen & Dickey, 1995). This process can include directions from psychiatrists on how best to 'pass' as another gender, and thus can result in stereotypical presentations of gender based on the view of the psychiatrist rather than the gender identity of the individual wanting support. It can also lead to ridicule and the risk of assault (Denny, 1992). There are other criteria that require huge life changes that can also be distressing, such as divorce. Some services require individuals to be either single or divorced prior to being referred for medical services (Clemmensen, 1990; Petersen & Dickey, 1995). In addition to these required life changes, the assessment by a psychiatrist is another difficult endeavour that requires trans people to perform as the ideal patient for referral. Fisk (1973) described this issue as a consequence of having an almost impossibly narrow criterion for eligibility based on the diagnosis of transsexualism, and therefore many people presented as the 'perfect' patient to get access to the much needed support. As Lev stated:

> It is easy to accuse such clients of 'conning' and 'game-playing', but the nature of the system as it has been developed 'requires' the person who desires medical treatments to have a consistent autobiography . . . How can anything resembling psychotherapy take place within this kind of system?
>
> (Lev, 2013, p. 215)

As a result of this, Fisk (1973) broadened his criteria, as previously discussed. However, it also created a discourse of 'deceit', where trans people were framed as untrustworthy and untruthful. Fisk (1973) reflected on this and was uncomfortable in his role as 'interrogator' rather than therapist; unfortunately, this is not always the case, and many psychiatrists and psychologists continue to view trans people as 'deceivers' rather than address their narrow (and near-impossible) expectations for access to treatment.

For children, rather than therapies that aim to change the child, affirmative approaches work with families to help them to support their gender-nonconforming child, and promote love and acceptance (Wren, 2002). Menvielle and Tuerk's 'leading edge of interventions' addresses how to support transgender children in a wide range of ways such as helping parents to support their child through bullying and harassment, to be advocates for their child, educating others in the life of the child and 'creating a safe space' (Hill et al., 2010, p.10).

Affirmative therapies draw on a diverse range of approaches, such as group therapies for parents (Hill et al. 2010), training for schools on trans issues and the prevention of violence (Lev, 2013), psychotherapy for the child and parents, art therapy (Schnebelt, 2015) and family therapy to support those who experience cisgenderism (the oppression of gender-nonconforming people) (Blumer, Ansara & Watson, 2013). Hidalgo et al. (2013) define their affirmative approach with gender-nonconforming children as embracing gender diversity across cultures, understanding gender as a complex mix of social, biological and cultural aspects, and condemning transphobia, homophobia and sexism. Like others from this perspective, they acknowledge the gender identity that the child describes in therapy, as well as rejecting the pathologizing discourse of framing gender dysphoria as a mental 'illness'. As Lev (2013) suggested, 'I encourage everyone to practice your therapy as if there was no *DSM-5* diagnosis for Gender Dysphoria, and at the same time I caution you to be very conscious of the reality of gender dysphoria' (p. 295).

Conclusions

> There has been some comment about the transsexual being difficult to deal with, manipulative, exploitative, hysterical etc. Let me just remind you that the exploitation and manipulation can be a characteristic of the researcher as well.
>
> (Pauly, 1973, p. 49)

Since the late 19th century, psychiatry has held the authoritative position in defining and describing trans people, positioning them as 'mentally ill' and deciding what therapeutic approaches should be available. This silencing of trans people, through their diagnosis as 'transsexual', 'transvestite', 'autogynephile' and 'gender dysphoric' means that their voice is not trusted in a sanist society. This is in addition to the discourse of deceit, promoted by psychiatry and produced by a system upheld by medical institutions, which means that trans people are rarely heard, but often studied. The wealth of literature in this topic area, in addition to the many changing terms and labels shows a vast interest in the topic of gender nonconformity, in the defining of the careers of a minority of influential (cisgender) men. As Pauly (1973) stated, we should be concerned at the prioritizing of research and career progression over the lives of trans people and the distress experienced from gender dysphoria.

In addition to these systems that create barriers and make access to support difficult, and sometimes impossible, trans people are framed as 'mentally ill' for their gender nonconformity. This intersection of sanism and cisgenderism results in an extremely narrow definition of gender 'normality'. It is notable, however, how this 'norm' excludes femininity. In the previous chapter, it was shown how psychiatry framed women and femininity as pathological in many different ways. In this chapter, there is a common thread as psychiatry shows a predominant interest in gender-nonconforming femininity (e.g. Blanchard, 1990; Green, 1987). Therefore, while gender-conforming women are pathologized for their expression of femininity (and therefore experience both sanism and sexism), trans women are pathologized for their femininity *and* their nonconformity (thus, they experience sanism, sexism *and* cisgenderism). This is in addition to gender-nonconforming women and trans men who are pathologized for their nonconformity, due to expressions of masculinity (and so experience sanism, and for trans men, also cisgenderism). The fact that trans women are often diagnosed with many of the terms described in the previous chapter (such as masochism, hysteria, borderline personality disorder), shows that the psychiatric construction of femininity and gender nonconformity is an issue for all women, gender conforming or not. Moreover, trans men describe experiences of marriage and pregnancy as a result of social pressure to participate in these social rites and institutions (Blanchard, 1990), which are also pushed on gender-conforming women. The participation in unwanted sex and pregnancy has the potential to be extremely distressing if an individual's body is incongruent with their gender identity. Therefore, rather than challenge the pathologization of women and the pathologization of trans people, which separates interrelated concepts and issues, countering psychiatry's constructions of femininity *and* gender nonconformity tackles the underlying and common issue. The campaigns of gender-conforming women, gender-nonconforming men and women, and trans people have many areas of mutual interest and concern. While feminist and transgender scholars and activists have critiqued and protested psychiatry on many occasions, the alliance between feminist and transgender perspectives has been anything but simple.

Notes

1 Culturally established as a sin and a crime (Halperin, 2000), the framing of homosexuality as a pathological sexuality was initially met with gratitude, as those previously labelled 'evil' or 'monsters' came to be thought of as 'sick' and in need to treatment and sympathy (Oosterhuis, 2000). However, the label of 'pervert' and the harsh interventions that ensued, including electric shocks and pharmaceuticals to induce vomiting all aimed at 'converting' homosexual individuals to heterosexuality (e.g. MacCulloch and Feldman, 1967; Freund, 1960), soon revealed the problems with this new (and unsympathetic) discourse.

2 But their gender identities are unknown to us.

3 The spelling changed from 'fetichism' to 'fetishism' in the early 20th century.
4 This was based on a concept described by Hirschfeld (2006 [1910]) called 'automonosexualism' (Winters, 2006).
5 Restricting air to the lungs during sexual activity.
6 The others being John Money and Harry Benjamin (Green, 2008).
7 While transsexualism was no longer a diagnostic category, the *DSM-IV* (APA, 1994) defined it as 'severe gender dysphoria' (p. 771) often resulting in the desire for sex reassignment surgery or hormonal treatment.
8 'Gender identity disorder of adolescence or adulthood nontranssexual type' (GIDAANT) only featured briefly in the *DSM-III-R*, describing a gender-nonconforming individual (particularly related to cross-dressing) who did not wish to change their biological sex. Fundamentally, it was a non-eroticised version of transvestism. GID also experienced a brief episode in the 'Disorders Usually Diagnosed in Childhood' section of the *DSM-III-R*, but was quickly reinstated as a 'sexual and gender identity' disorder in the *DSM-IV* with adult and child versions (although transvestism remained under the paraphilias section).
9 Such as a clitoris larger than 0.9cm or a penis smaller than 2.5cm (Kessler, 2002).
10 These contradictions were highlighted by Jake Pyne (2015) in his article entitled, 'Fix society. Please' after the final words of transgender teen Leelah Acorn.

References

Acosta, F. (1975). Etiology and treatment of homosexuality: A review. *Archives of Sexual Behavior, 4*(1), 9–29.

APA (American Psychiatric Association) (1952). *Diagnostic and statistical manual of mental disorders first edition (DSM-I)*. Washington, DC: Author.

APA (American Psychiatric Association) (1968). *Diagnostic and statistical manual of mental disorders second edition (DSM-II)*. Washington, DC: Author.

APA (American Psychiatric Association) (1973). Position Statement on homosexuality and sexual orientation disturbance: Proposed change in *DSM-II*. Washington, DC: Author: www.psychiatryonline.com/DSMPDF/DSM-II_Homosexuality_Revision.pdf; no longer available.

APA (American Psychiatric Association) (1980). *Diagnostic and statistical manual of mental disorders, third edition (DSM-III)*. Washington, DC: Author.

APA (American Psychiatric Association) (1987). *Diagnostic and statistical manual of mental disorders, third edition revised*. Washington, DC: Author.

APA (American Psychiatric Association) (1994). *Diagnostic and statistical manual of mental disorders fourth edition (DSM-IV)*. Washington, DC: Author.

APA (American Psychiatric Association) (2013). *Diagnostic and statistical manual of mental disorders fifth edition (DSM-5)*. Washington, DC: Author.

Ansara, G., & Hegarty, P. (2012). Cisgenderism in psychology: Pathologising and misgendering children from 1999 to 2008. *Psychology & Sexuality, 3*(2), 137–60.

Anson, J. (1974). The female transvestite in Early Monasticism: The origin and development of a motif. *Medieval and Renaissance Studies, 5*(1), 1–32.

Archer, J. (1976). Biological explanations of psychological sex differences. In B. B. Lloyd & J. Archer (Eds), *Exploring sex differences* (pp. xi, 280). Oxford: Academic Press.

Asscheman, H., Giltay, E. J., Megens, J. A. J., Ronde, W. (Pim) de, Trotsenburg, M. A. A. van, & Gooren, L. J. G. (2011). A long-term follow-up study of mortality in transsexuals receiving treatment with cross-sex hormones. *European Journal of Endocrinology, 164*(4), 635–42.

Bailey, J. M. (2003). *The man who would be queen: The science of gender-bending and transsexualism.* Washington, DC: Joseph Henry Press.

Bancroft, J. (1974). *Deviant sexual behaviour: Modification and assessment.* Oxford: Oxford University Press.

Baril, A., & Trevenen, K. (2014). Exploring ableism and cisnormativity in the conceptualization of identity and sexuality 'disorders'. *Annual Review of Critical Psychology, 11*, 389–416.

Beemyn, G. (2013). A presence in the past: A transgender historiography. *Journal of Women's History, 25*(4), 113–21.

Benjamin, H. (1954). Transsexualism and transvestism as psychosomatic and somatopsychic syndromes. *American Journal of Psychotherapy, 8*(2), 219.

Benjamin, H. (1966). *The transsexual phenomenon.* Boston, MA: Human Outreach & Achievement Institute.

Blanchard, R. (1989). The concept of autogynephilia and the typology of male gender dysphoria. *Journal of Nervous and Mental Disease, 177*(10), 616–23.

Blanchard, R. (1990). Gender identity disorders in adult men. In R. Blanchard & B. Steiner (Eds), *Clinical management of gender identity disorders in children and adults.* (pp. 47–76). Washington, DC: American Psychiatric Press, Inc.

Blanchard, R. (1993). Varieties of autogynephilia and their relationship to gender dysphoria. *Archives of Sexual Behavior, 22*(3), 241–51.

Blanchard, R. (2005). Early history of the concept of autogynephilia. *Archives of Sexual Behavior, 34*(4), 439–46.

Blanchard, R. (2013). How the psychiatrist who co-wrote the manual on sex talks about sex. *Motherboard*: http://motherboard.vice.com/blog/heres-how-the-guy-who-wrote-the-manual-on-sex-talks-about-sex#ixzz2SSORkDVM (accessed 20 November 2015).

Bleier, R. (1984). *Science and gender: A critique of biology and its theories on women.* New York: Pergamon Press.

Blumer, M. L. C., Ansara, Y. G., & Watson, C. M. (2013). Cisgenderism in family therapy: How everyday clinical practices can delegitimize people's gender self-designations. *Journal of Family Psychotherapy, 24*(4), 267–85.

Boag, P. (2005). Go west young man, go east young women: Searching for the trans in western gender history. *The Western Historical Quarterly, 36*(4), 477–97.

Bolich, P. D. G. G. (2007). *Transgender history & geography: Crossdressing in context*: http://www.maletka.eu/download-pdf-transgender-history-geography-crossdressing-in-context-book-by-lulucom.pdf (accessed 21 November 2015).

Bolich, P. D. G. G. (2009). *Crossdressing in context, vol. 4: Transgender & religion*: http://radio.blogvictory.com/crossdressing-in-context-vol-4-transgender-religion-by-ph-d-g-g-bolich/ (accessed 21 November 2015).

Bronstein, S., & Joseph, J. (2011). Therapy to change feminine boy created a troubled man, family says. *CNN*: http://edition.cnn.com/2011/US/06/07/sissy.boy.experiment/ (accessed 21 November 2015).

Bryant, K. (2006). Making gender identity disorder of childhood: Historical lessons for contemporary debates. *Sexuality Research & Social Policy, 3*(3), 23–39.

Bryant, K. (2008). In defense of gay children? 'Progay' homophobia and the production of homonormativity. *Sexualities, 11*(4), 455–75.

Bullough, V. (1982). Transvestism in the Middle Ages. In V. Bullough & J. Brundage (Eds), *Sexual practices and the Medieval Church.* (pp. 43–54). Buffalo, NY: Prometheus Books.

Bullough, V., & Bullough, B. (1993). *Cross dressing, sex, and gender.* Philadelphia: University of Pennsylvania Press.

Burke, P. (1996). *Gender shock: Exploding the myths of male and female.* New York: Anchor Books.

Cameron, M. (2005). Two-spirited Aboriginal people: Continuing cultural appropriation by non-Aboriginal society. *Canadian Woman Studies, 24*, 123–7.

Caudwell, D. (2006 [1949]). Psychopathia transsexualis. In S. Stryker & S. Whittle (Eds), *The transgender studies reader* (pp. 40–44). New York: Routledge.

CBC News (2015). LGBT conversion therapy ineffective and harmful, critics say: http://www.cbc.ca/1.3101838 (accessed 21 November 2015).

Clemmensen, L. (1990). The 'real-life test' for surgical candidates. In R. Blanchard & B. Steiner (Eds), *Clinical management of gender identity disorders in children and adults.* (pp. 119–36). Washington, DC: American Psychiatric Association.

Cohen-Kettenis, P. T., Delemarre-van de Waal, H. A., & Gooren, L. J. G. (2008). The treatment of adolescent transsexuals: Changing insights. *Journal of Sexual Medicine, 5*(8), 1892–7.

Cohen-Kettenis, P., Schagen, S., Steensma, T., de Vries, A., & Delemarre-van de Waal, H. (2011). Puberty suppression in a gender-dysphoric adolescent: A 22-year follow-up. *Archives of Sexual Behavior, 40*(4), 843–7.

Colapinto, J. (2000). *As nature made him: The boy who was raised as a girl.* New York: HarperCollins Publishers.

Conrad, P., & Angell, A. (2004). Homosexuality and remedicalization. *Society, 41*(5), 32–9.

Conway, L. (2003). An investigative report into the publication of J. Michael Bailey's book on transsexualism by the National Academies: http://ai.eecs.umich.edu/people/conway/TS/LynnsReviewOfBaileysBook2.html (accessed 21 November 2015).

Cross, J. S. (2015). Outcry prompts CAMH to review its controversial treatment of trans youth: http://metronews.ca/news/toronto/1315743/outcry-prompts-camh-to-review-its-controversial-treatment-of-trans-youth/ (accessed 21 November 2015).

Csanady, A. (2015). 'I never realized that I could be happy': Committee hears harrowing accounts of conversion therapy: http://news.nationalpost.com/news/canada/canadian-politics/i-never-realized-that-i-could-be-happy-committee-hears-harrowing-accounts-of-conversion-therapy (accessed 21 November 2015).

Daley, A., & Mulé, N. J. (2014). LGBTQs and the *DSM-5*: A critical queer response. *Journal of Homosexuality, 61*(9), 1288–312.

David. (1994). I am not alone! *Hermaphrodites with Attitude, 1*(1), 4–5.

'David Reimer, 38, Subject of the John/Joan Case.' (2004, 12 May). *The New York Times*: http://www.nytimes.com/2004/05/12/us/david-reimer-38-subject-of-the-john-joan-case.html (accessed 21 November 2015).

Davison, G. (1976). Homosexuality: The ethical challenge. *Journal of Consulting and Clinical Psychology, 44*, 157–62.

De Cuypere, G., Elaut, E., Heylens, G., Van Maele, G., Selvaggi, G., T'Sjoen, G. . . . Monstrey, S. (2006). Long-term follow up: Psychosocial outcome of Belgian transsexuals after sex reassignment surgery. *Sexologies, 15*(2), 126–33.

De Cuypere, G., T'Sjoen, G., Beerten, R., Selvaggi, G., De Sutter, P., Hoebeke, P., . . . Rubens, R. (2005). Sexual and physical health after sex reassignment surgery. *Archives of Sexual Behavior, 34*(6), 679–90.

Denny, D. (1992). The politics of diagnosis and a diagnosis of politics: The university-affiliated gender clinics, and how they failed to meet the needs of transsexual people. *Chrysalis Quarterly, 1*(3), 9–20.

Dhejne, C., Lichtenstein, P., Boman, M., Johansson, A. L. V., Långström, N., & Landén, M. (2011). Long-term follow-up of transsexual persons undergoing sex reassignment surgery: Cohort study in Sweden. *PLoS ONE, 6*(2), e16885.

Dhejne, C., Öberg, K., Arver, S., & Landén, M. (2014). An analysis of all applications for sex reassignment surgery in Sweden, 1960–2010: Prevalence, Incidence, and Regrets. *Archives of Sexual Behavior, 43*(8), 1535–45.

Diamond, M., & Sigmundson, H. (1997). Sex reassignment at birth: Long-term review and clinical implications. *Archives of Pediatrics & Adolescent Medicine, 151*(3), 298–304.

Douard, J. (2007). Loathing the sinner, medicalizing the sin: Why sexually violent predator statutes are unjust. *International Journal of Law and Psychiatry, 30*(1), 36–48.

Drescher, J. (2010). Transsexualism, gender identity disorder and the DSM. *Journal of Gay & Lesbian Mental Health, 14*(2), 109–22.

Drescher, J. (2013). Controversies in gender diagnoses. *LGBT Health, 1*(1), 10–14.

Ehrenreich, B., & Barr, M. (2005). Intersex surgery, female genital cutting, and the selective condemnation of 'cultural practices'. *Harvard Civil Rights-Civil Liberties Law Review, 40*, 71–140.

Ekins, R., & King, D. (2001). Pioneers of transgendering: The popular sexology of David O. Caudwell. *International Journal of Transgenderism, 5*(2).

el-Malik, S. S. (2014). Rattling the binary: Symbolic power, gender, and embodied colonial legacies. *Politics, Groups, and Identities, 2*(1), 1–16.

Embaye, N. (2006). Affirmative psychotherapy with bisexual transgender people. *Journal of Bisexuality, 6*(1–2), 51–63.

Farrow, S. S. (1926). *Faith, fancies and fetish or Yoruba paganism: Some account of the religious beliefs of the West African Negroes.* Society for Promoting Christian Knowledge.

Ffoulkes, A. (1909). Borgya and Abirwa: Or, the latest fetich on the Gold Coast. *Journal of the Royal African Society, 8*(32), 387–97.

Fisk, N. (1973). Gender dysphoria syndrome (the how, what, and why of a disease). In *Proceedings of the second interdisciplinary symposium on gender dysphoria syndrome* (pp. 7–14). Palo Alto, CA: Stanford University Press.

Fisk, N. (1974). Editorial: Gender dysphoria syndrome – the conceptualization that liberalizes indications for total gender reorientation and implies a broadly based multi-dimensional rehabilitative regimen. *Western Journal of Medicine, 120*(5), 386–91.

Fisk, N. (1978). Five spectacular results. *Archives of Sexual Behavior, 7*(4), 351–69.

Foucault, M. (1979). *The history of sexuality.* London: Allen Lane.

Fox, F., & Rothman, L. (2015). Leelah Alcorn's suicide: Conversion therapy is child abuse. *Time*: http://time.com/3655718/leelah-alcorn-suicide-transgender-therapy/ (accessed 15 November 2015).

Freund, K. (1960). Some problems in the treatment of homosexuality. In H. J. Eysenck (Ed.), *Behaviour therapy and the neuroses* (pp. 312–14). New York: Pergamon Press.

Garber, M. B. (2011). *Vested interests: Cross-dressing and cultural anxiety.* London: Psychology Press.

Garner, T. (2014). Chest surgeries of a different 'nature'. *Annual Review of Critical Psychology, 11*, 337–56.

Goldblum, P., Testa, R. J., Pflum, S., Hendricks, M. L., Bradford, J., & Bongar, B. (2012). The relationship between gender-based victimization and suicide attempts in transgender people. *Professional Psychology: Research and Practice, 43*(5), 468–75.

Gooren, L. (2005). Hormone treatment of the adult transsexual patient. *Hormone Research, 64*(2), 31–6.

Gooren, L. (2011). Care of transsexual persons. *New England Journal of Medicine, 364*(13), 1251–7.

Gray, J. A. (1971). Sex differences in emotional behaviour in mammals including man: Endocrine bases. *Acta Psychologica, 35*(1), 29–46.

Green, R. (1979). 'Sissies' and 'tomboys'. *SIECUS Report*, 7(3), 1–15.

Green, R. (1987). *The 'sissy boy syndrome' and the development of homosexuality*. New Haven, CT: Yale University Press.

Green, R. (2008). The three kings: Harry Benjamin, John Money, Robert Stoller. *Archives of Sexual Behavior, 38*(4), 610–13.

Haas, A., Rodgers, P., & Herman, J. (2014). *Suicide attempts among transgender and gender non-conforming adults: Findings of the National Transgender Discrimination Survey*. New York: American Foundation for Suicide Prevention.

Halperin, D. (2000). How to do the history of homosexuality. *GLQ: A Journal of Lesbian and Gay Studies, 6*(1), 87–123.

Hausman, B. L. (2000). Do boys have to be boys? Gender, narrativity, and the John/Joan Case. *NWSA Journal, 12*(3), 114–38.

Hegarty, P. (2009). Toward an LGBT-informed paradigm for children who break gender norms: Comment on Drummond et al. (2008) and Rieger et al. (2008). *Developmental Psychology, 45*(4), 895–900.

Hidalgo, M. A., Ehrensaft, D., Tishelman, A. C., Clark, L. F., Garofalo, R., Rosenthal, S. M., . . . Olson, J. (2013). The gender affirmative model: What we know and what we aim to learn. *Human Development, 56*(5), 285–90.

Hill, D. B., Menvielle, E., Sica, K. M., & Johnson, A. (2010). An affirmative intervention for families with gender variant children: Parental ratings of child mental health and gender. *Journal of Sex & Marital Therapy, 36*(1), 6–23.

Hird, M. J. (2003). A typical gender identity conference? Some disturbing reports from the therapeutic front lines. *Feminism & Psychology, 13*(2), 181–99.

Hirschfeld, M. (1923). Die intersexuelle konstitution. *Jahrbuch Fuer Sexuelle Zwischenstufen, 23*, 3–27.

Hirschfeld, M. (2006 [1910]). The transvestites: The erotic drive to cross-dress. In S. Stryker & S. Whittle (Eds), *The transgender studies reader* (pp. 28–39). New York: Routledge.

Horner, J. (2003). Undoing the damage: Working with LGBT clients in post-conversion therapy. *Columbia Social Work Review, 1*, 8–16.

Iantaffi, A., & Bockting, W. O. (2011). Views from both sides of the bridge? Gender, sexual legitimacy and transgender people's experiences of relationships. *Culture, Health & Sexuality, 13*(3), 355–70.

Isay, R. (1997). Remove gender identity disorder from the DSM. *Psychiatric News, 32*(22), 9.

Jewkes, Y., & Wykes, M. (2012). Reconstructing the sexual abuse of children: 'cyber-paeds', panic and power. *Sexualities, 15*(8), 934–52.

Kessler, S. (1990). The medical construction of gender: Case management of intersexed infants. *Signs, 16*(1), 3–26.

Kessler, S. (2002). *Lessons from the intersexed*. New Brunswick, NJ: Scholarly Book Services Inc.

Kleinplatz, P., & Moser, C. (2014). *Sadomasochism: Powerful pleasures*. London: Routledge.

Krafft-Ebing, R. (1892). *Psychopathia sexualis with especial reference to contrary sexual instinct: A medico-legal study*. Philadelphia, PA: F. A. Davis Co. Publishers.

Laemmle, J. (2013). California's conversion: A ban on minor conversion therapy and the effect on other States. *Indiana Journal of Law and Social Equality, 2*(1), 248–70.

Lambert, H. (1978). Biology and equality: A perspective on sex differences. *Signs, 4*(1), 97–117.

Langer, S. J., & Martin, J. I. (2004). How dresses can make you mentally ill: Examining gender identity disorder in children. *Child and Adolescent Social Work Journal, 21*(1), 5–23.
Laqueur, T. W. (1992). *Making sex: Body and gender from the Greeks to Freud*. Cambridge, MA: Harvard University Press.
Lawrence, A. (2004). Autogynephilia: A paraphilic model of gender identity disorder. In U. Leli & J. Drescher (Eds), *Transgender subjectivities: A clinician's guide*. (pp. 69–87). Binghamton, NY: Haworth Medical Press.
Lawrence, A. (2012). *Men trapped in men's bodies: Narratives of autogynephilic transsexualism*. Springer Science & Business Media.
Lev, A. I. (2006). Disordering gender identity: Gender identity disorder in the *DSM-IV-TR*. *Journal of Psychology & Human Sexuality, 17*(3–4), 35–69.
Lev, A. I. (2013). *Transgender emergence: Therapeutic guidelines for working with gender-variant people and their families*. London: Routledge.
Ling, J. (2015). Canada's most populous province just banned conversion therapy for LGBTQ youth: https://news.vice.com/article/canadas-most-populous-province-just-banned-conversion-therapy-for-lgbtq-youth (accessed 21 November 2015).
Long, C.H. (2004). A postcolonial meaning of religion: Some reflections from the indigenous world. In J. Olupona (Ed.), *Beyond primitivism: Indigenous religious traditions and modernity* (pp. 89–98). London: Routledge.
MacCulloch, M., & Feldman, M. (1967). Aversion therapy in management of homosexuals. *British Medical Journal, 4*, 51–2.
Menvielle, E., & Tuerk, C. (2002). A support group for parents of gender-nonconforming boys. *Journal of the American Academy of Child & Adolescent Psychiatry, 41*(8), 1010–13.
Meyer-Bahlburg, H. F. L. (2010). From mental disorder to iatrogenic hypogonadism: Dilemmas in conceptualizing gender identity variants as psychiatric conditions. *Archives of Sexual Behavior, 39*(2), 461–76.
Money, J. (1975). Ablatio penis: Normal male infant sex-reassigned as a girl. *Archives of Sexual Behavior, 4*(1), 65–71.
Money, J. (1994). The concept of gender identity disorder in childhood and adolescence after 39 years. *Journal of Sex & Marital Therapy, 20*(3), 163–77.
Money, J., & Ehrhardt, A. (1972). *Man and woman, boy and girl: Differentiation and dimorphism of gender identity from conception to maturity* (Vol. xiv). Oxford: Johns Hopkins University Press.
Money, J., & Green, R. (1969). *Transsexualism and sex reassignment*. Oxford: Johns Hopkins University Press.
Money, J., Hampson, J., & Hampson, J. (1957). Imprinting and the establishment of gender role. *A.M.A. Archives of Neurology & Psychiatry*, 77(3), 333–6.
Monro, S. (2000). Theorizing transgender diversity: Towards a social model of health. *Sexual and Relationship Therapy, 15*(1), 33–45.
Morgensen, S. L. (2012). Theorising gender, sexuality and settler colonialism: An introduction. *Settler Colonial Studies, 2*(2), 2–22.
Moser, C. (2001). Paraphilia: A critique of a confused concept. In P. Kleinplatz (Ed.), *New directions in sex therapy: Innovations and alternatives* (pp. 91–108). Hove: Accelerated Development.
Moser, C. (2009). Autogynephilia in women. *Journal of Homosexuality, 56*(5), 539–47.
Moser, C. (2010). Blanchard's autogynephilia theory: A critique. *Journal of Homosexuality, 57*(6), 790–809.
Moser, C. (2011). Yet another paraphilia definition fails. *Archives of Sexual Behavior, 40*(3), 483–85.

Müller, F. M. (1874). *Lectures on the science of religion*. Scribner, Armstrong, and Company.

Murad, M. H., Elamin, M. B., Garcia, M. Z., Mullan, R. J., Murad, A., Erwin, P. J., & Montori, V. M. (2010). Hormonal therapy and sex reassignment: A systematic review and meta-analysis of quality of life and psychosocial outcomes. *Clinical Endocrinology, 72*(2), 214–31.

Oosterhuis, H. (2000). *Stepchildren of nature: Krafft-Ebing, psychiatry, and the making of sexual identity*. Chicago, IL: University of Chicago Press.

Pauly, I. (1973). Female transsexualism. In *Proceedings of the second interdisciplinary symposium on gender dysphoria syndrome*. (pp. 49–55). Palo Alto, CA: Stanford University Press.

Petersen, M. E., & Dickey, R. (1995). Surgical sex reassignment: A comparative survey of International centers. *Archives of Sexual Behavior, 24*(2), 135–56.

Pfäfflin, F., & Junge, A. (1998). *Sex reassignment: Thirty years of international follow-up studies after sex reassignment surgery a comprehensive review, 1961–1991*: http://web.archive.org/web/20070503090247/http://www.symposion.com/ijt/pfaefflin/1000.htm (accessed 21 November 2015).

Pyne, J. (2014). The governance of gender non-conforming children: A dangerous enclosure. *Annual Review of Critical Psychology, 11*, 79–96.

Pyne, J. (2015). 'Fix society. Please': https://nowtoronto.com/news/leelah-alcorn-fix-society-not-trans-people/ (accessed 21 November 2015).

Rekers, G. A. (1977). Atypical gender development and psychosocial adjustment. *Journal of Applied Behavior Analysis, 10*(3), 559–71.

Reyes, E. A. (2014, January 28). Transgender study looks at 'exceptionally high' suicide-attempt rate. *Los Angeles Times*: http://articles.latimes.com/2014/jan/28/local/la-me-ln-suicide-attempts-alarming-transgender-20140127 (accessed 21 November 2015).

Richards, C., & Barker, M. J. (2013). *Sexuality and gender for mental health professionals: A practical guide*. London: SAGE Publications.

Robinson, M. (2012). Two-spirited sexuality and white universality. *Journal of Postcolonial Networks*, 1–5.

Rogers, L., & Walsh, J. (1982). Shortcomings of the psychomedical research of John Money and co-workers into sex differences in behavior: Social and political implications. *Sex Roles, 8*(3), 269–81.

Rosenberg, M. (2002). Children with gender identity issues and their parents in individual and group treatment. *Journal of the American Academy of Child & Adolescent Psychiatry, 41*(5), 619–21.

Sayers, J. (1982). *Biological politics: Feminist and anti-feminist perspectives*. London: Tavistock.

Schaffner, A. K. (2011). *Modernism and perversion: Sexual deviance in sexology and literature, 1850–1930*. London: Palgrave Macmillan.

Schnebelt, B. (2015). *Art therapy considerations with transgender individuals*. Los Angeles, CA: Loyola Marymount University.

Serano, J. (2009). Psychology, sexualization and trans-invalidations. Presented at the 8th Annual Philadelphia Trans-Health Conference.

Serano, J. (2010). The case against autogynephilia. *International Journal of Transgenderism, 12*(3), 176–87.

Sloop, J. M. (2000). 'A van with a bar and a bed': Ritualized gender norms in the John/Joan case. *Text and Performance Quarterly, 20*(2), 130–49.

Stoller, R. J. M. D. (1968). Male childhood transsexualism. *Journal of the American Academy of Child Psychiatry, 7*(2), 193–209.

Stryker, S., & Whittle, S. (2006). *The transgender studies reader.* London: Taylor & Francis.

Tafoya, T. (2003). Native gay and lesbian issues: The two-spirited. In L. Garnets & D. Kimmel (Eds), *Psychological perspectives on lesbian, gay, and bisexual experiences* (pp. 401–9). New York: Columbia University Press.

Torjesen, K. (2004). Martyrs, ascetics, and gnostics: Gender-crossing in early Christianity. In S. Ramet (Ed.), *Gender reversals and gender cultures: Anthropolgical and historical perspectives* (pp. 79–91). London: Routledge.

Tosh, J. (2011). 'Zuck off!' A commentary on the protest against Ken Zucker and his 'treatment' of childhood gender identity disorder. *Psychology of Women Section Review, 13*(1), 10–16.

Tosh, J. (2013). The (in)visibility of childhood sexual abuse: Psychiatric theorizing of transgenderism and intersexuality. *Intersectionalities: A Global Journal of Social Work Analysis, Research, Polity, and Practice, 2*(1), 71–87.

Tosh, J. (2015). *Perverse psychology: The pathologization of sexual violence and transgenderism.* London: Routledge.

Tosh, J. (In press). 'Zuck Off!' Part II: Trans feminist activism and the end of gender conversion therapy. *Psychology of Women Section Review.*

Travers, R., Bauer, G., Pyne, J., Bradley, K., Gale, L., & Papdimitriou, M. (2012). *Impacts of strong parental support for trans youth: A report prepared for Children's Aid Society of Toronto and Delisle Youth Services.* Trans Pulse Project: http://transpulseproject.ca/wp-content/uploads/2012/10/Impacts-of-Strong-Parental-Support-for-Trans-Youth-vFINAL.pdf (accessed 21 November 2015).

Veale, J., Clarke, D., & Lomax, T. (2011). Male to female transsexuals' impressions of Blanchard's autogynephilia theory. *International Journal of Transgenderism, 13*(3), 131–9.

Wermuth, S. (2015). Delayed transgender treatments causing self-harm, suicide – UK watchdog: http://rt.com/uk/260441-nhs-transgender-patient-care/ (accessed 21 November 2015).

Whittington, K. (2014). Medieval. *TSQ: Transgender Studies Quarterly, 1*(1-2), 125–129.

Wierckx, K., Van Caenegem, E., Elaut, E., Dedecker, D., Van de Peer, F., Toye, K., . . . T'Sjoen, G. (2011). Quality of life and sexual health after sex reassignment surgery in transsexual men. *Journal of Sexual Medicine, 8*(12), 3379–88.

Winters, K. (2006). Gender dissonance. *Journal of Psychology & Human Sexuality, 17*(3-4), 71–89.

Winters, K. (2008). Autogynephilia: The infallible derogatory hypothesis, Part 1: https://gidreform.wordpress.com/2008/11/10/autogynephilia-the-infallible-derogatory-hypothesis-part-1/ (accessed 21 November 2015).

Winters, K. (2009). *Gender madness in American psychiatry: Essays from the struggle for dignity.* Dillon, CO: BookSurge Publishing.

Wren, B. (2002). 'I can accept my child is transsexual but if I ever see him in a dress I'll hit him': Dilemmas in parenting a transgendered adolescent. *Clinical Child Psychology and Psychiatry, 7*(3), 377–97.

Zucker, K. (1985). Cross-gender identified children. In B. Steiner (Ed.), *Gender dysphoria: Development, research, management* (pp. 75–174). New York: Plenum Press.

Zucker, K. (1990). Gender identity disorders in children: Clinical descriptions and natural history. In R. Blanchard & B. W. Steiner (Eds), *Clinical management of gender identity disorders in children and adults.* (pp. 1–24). Washington, DC: American Psychiatric Press.

Zucker, K. (2008). Children with gender identity disorder: Is there best practice? *Neuropsychiatrie de L'enfance et de L'adolescence, 56*, 358–64.

Zucker, K. (2015). The *DSM-5* diagnostic criteria for gender dysphoria. In C. Trombetta, G. Liguori, & M. Bertolotto (Eds), *Management of gender dysphoria* (pp. 33–7). Milan: Springer Milan.

Zucker, K., & Blanchard, R. (1997). Transvestis fetishism: Psychopathology and theory. In R. Laws & W. O'Donohue (Eds), *Sexual deviance: Theory, assessment, and treatment*, pp. 253–79. New York: Guilford Press.

Zucker, K., & Bradley, S. (1995). *Gender identity disorder and psychosexual problems in children and adolescents*. New York: Guilford Press.

Zucker, K., & Bradley, S. (2004). Gender identity and psychosexual disorders. In J. Wiener & M. Dulcan (Eds), *The American Psychiatric Publishing Textbook of Child and Adolescent Psychiatry*. (pp. 813–35). Washington DC: American Psychiatric Publishing.

Zucker, K., & Duschinsky, R. (2015). Dilemmas encountered by the Sexual and Gender Identity Disorders Work Group for *DSM-5*: An interview with Kenneth J. Zucker. *Psychology & Sexuality*, 7(1), 1–11.

Zucker, K., Wood, H., Singh, D., & Bradley, S. (2012). A developmental, biopsychosocial model for the treatment of children with gender identity disorder. *Journal of Homosexuality*, *59*(3), 369–97.

Zuger, B. (1966). Effeminate behavior present in boys from early childhood. *The Journal of Pediatrics*, *69*(6), 1098–107.

Chapter 4

Feminist constructions of gender dysphoria and transgender people

In Chapters 2 and 3, I outlined psychiatric constructions of women, transgender and gender-nonconforming individuals. In this chapter, I examine how gender identity and gender dysphoria have been framed within feminist discourse, which includes constructions of these same groups of individuals (i.e. women, transgender and gender nonconforming). While I used feminist perspectives to critique psychiatry in Chapter 2, I now place feminism under analysis. I describe controversial texts produced during the 1970s and 1980s that continue to influence more recent feminist work (e.g. Gottschalk, 2009; Nicki, 2006; Sweeney, 2004). This includes perspectives that draw on the pathologization of trans people uncritically; by this, I mean an uncritical approach to psychiatric narratives. For example, Jeffreys (2014a) talks about approaches that are 'critical of transgenderism', and Raymond (1979) is described as being critical of 'patriarchal medicine', but I argue that these fail to be *critical of psychiatry* in their repetition of a problematic narrative that frames trans people as pathological. As a result, those feminist perspectives that refuse to acknowledge trans people actually repeat long-standing psychiatric narratives, some from over a century ago, as well as discourses that have existed from medieval times within colonial and patriarchal accounts of religion (see Chapter 3). Therefore, rather than represent a 'radical' form of feminism, this perspective demonstrates a conservative approach within authoritative discourses, such as psychiatry; where psychiatry has physically, socially and emotionally harmed women, feminists, gender nonconformists, lesbians and many others (Brown, 1989; Burke, 1996; LeFrançois & Diamond, 2014; Showalter, 1987; Stevens & Hall, 1991).

Feminism

Feminism is broad and diverse, with many definitions and meanings. General definitions of 'gender equality' and 'women's rights' overlook its complexity. This is in addition to negative media coverage of some of the more marginal views, which produces a limited picture of a far-reaching movement (e.g. Faludi, 2009; Vint, 2007). Consequently, those unsupportive of feminism have often made their judgement without engaging with the many feminisms that are embraced by all kinds of people. This wide-ranging, contradictory and ever-changing movement for social justice includes a vast array of feminisms, such as liberal (Marilley, 1996), black (hooks, 1989), lesbian (Kitzinger & Perkins, 1993), radical (Daly, 1978), eco (Gaard, 2011), trans (Salamon, 2008), socialist (Haraway, 2002), Indigenous (Smith, 2005), cyber (Braidotti, 2003), and more – from campaigns to end pornography (Norden, 1990), to feminist porn (Penley et al., 2013); from arguments that heterosexual sex should promote a culture of consent to reduce violence against women (Friedman & Valenti, 2008), to those who question if it is even possible for a women to consent to sex within a patriarchal culture (Dworkin, 2006); from those who view transsexual people as a threat to lesbianism (Raymond, 1979), to transsexual lesbian feminists (Stryker, 2013). Feminism cannot be summarized simply, other than to state that it offers as many contradictions as it does solutions. This is its weakness and its strength. In representing such a wide variety of views, it can tackle numerous issues from a range of perspectives, and it embraces debate and complexity. However, it also means that some of the perspectives will impede the progress of others, and it can lead to a replication of the dominant hierarchies that exist in patriarchal and cisgenderist cultures.

It is important, however, not to reify these feminist categories or to imply that these groupings are in some way essentialized.[1] I use these terms to illustrate the diversity of feminist positions, but I consider each category as equally diverse (Tosh, 2013a). The boundaries between these discursive feminist groups are not rigid, nor do they mean that any one individual can only identify with one group at any given time (Bevacqua, 2000, 2008). For example, it would be entirely possible to have a radical feminist perspective on some issues, such as Connell and Wilson's (1974) perspective on rape, but disagree with Raymond's (1979) radical position on transsexualism and take a more trans-feminist stance on this specific issue (see Chapter 5). As Sorisio (2003) states, 'I consider feminism a quest that we continually redefine, rather than a doctrine that seeks to confine me' (p. 136). It is a 'transformative' project (Lombardo & Verloo, 2009) where the 'perceived unity and homogeneity are replaced by dialogues' (Yuval-Davis, 1997, p. 131).

Feminism is often divided into waves, both chronologically and ideologically (Jervis, 2006). 'First wave', 'second wave' and 'third wave' usually refer to the mid-19th century until the early 20th century, the 1960s until the 1980s, and 1992 onwards, respectively (Burgess-Proctor, 2006; Dicker & Piepmeier, 2003). Analyses of transsexualism are often associated with the second wave of feminism, although it also features in more trans-positive third-wave perspectives. However, defining these movements in three distinct 'waves' often denotes generalized summaries of the movements' actions and positions on issues related to gender. As has been identified by many critical of the wave metaphor (e.g. Hoeflinger, 2008; Jervis, 2006), these generalizations reduce the movements to a few achievements or political positions and mask the variety of perspectives and people who identified as being 'feminist' at these times in history.

As with the categories of feminist positions, the 'waves' have equally fluid ideological boundaries. There are many 'third wavers' who also strongly identify with concepts and positions classed as 'second wave', and there are 'second wavers' who have pioneered aspects considered central to a 'third-wave' ethos. For example, Brown's (1962) *Sex and the single woman* and her subsequent position as editor of *Cosmopolitan* magazine, embraced new media and an individualized and feminized form of female empowerment that resonated with many from a third-wave perspective (e.g. Walker, 1992). While the wave metaphor can conceal differences within movements and divide different generations of feminists (Jervis, 2006), I use the term only to denote a moment in time and aim never to convey feminism in a way that implies unity/coherence or stability. As Campbell stated in 1973:

> Whatever the phrase 'women's liberation' means, it cannot as yet, be used to refer to a cohesive historical political movement. No clearly defined programme or set of policies unifies the small, frequently transitory groups that compose it, nor is there much evidence of organizational unity and cooperation.
>
> (Campbell, 1973, pp. 198–9)

The relationships between feminism, transgender people and psychology have been equally varied. There have been those supportive of trans issues, some are trans feminists, and there are those who have been hostile towards trans people. Therefore, the situation is more complex that a trans and feminist binary, or a simple pro or against stance. Instead, it is a complex interweaving of collaboration and mutuality as well as disagreement and protest.

Feminism and gender identity

Revisions for the third edition of the DSM (APA, 1980, 1987) coincided with the second wave of feminism. This was a key time in the definition of gender and sexual 'normality' within psychiatry, which occurred alongside feminist challenges to narrow and rigid definitions of gender. This resulted in the feminist uptake of several theories from psychology and psychiatry that developed at this time, such as John Money's work on gender identity (see Chapter 3). This theory aligned well with feminist critiques of biological perspectives that justified discrimination against women based on arguments that women were physically 'inferior', or that they were 'naturally' better suited to certain roles (Sayers, 1982). However, this overlooked the development of the psychological theories, from reparative therapies for homosexual individuals (harmful therapies that aimed to 'convert' homosexual individuals to heterosexuality, e.g. Zuger, 1966), the non-consensual practices employed on intersex children (Ehrenreich & Barr, 2005), and the use of the theory to justify harmful gender conversion therapies in the psychiatric treatment of trans and gender-nonconforming children (see Chapters 3 and 5). While 'barely a ripple' (Green, 1979, p. 1) of feminist influence had reached psychiatry, psychiatric theories regarding the diagnoses of transsexualism and gender identity disorder (APA, 1980, 1994, 2000) influenced feminist thought.

From nature to nurture

While psychologists debated and researched gender differences with aims to prevent homosexuality and transsexualism, and to encourage gender conformity to assigned gender roles, feminism had a keen interest in these developments to challenge the long-standing arguments that women had a subordinate place in society due to their innate/natural physical and intellectual inferiority (Fausto-Sterling, 2008; Shields, 1982). This resulted in scepticism of biological discourse, due to its gross misuse in the oppression of women. Consequently, when Money began publishing the 'success' of the John/Joan case (see Chapter 3) arguing that gender identity was malleable, feminists heralded this as scientific evidence that women were not innately inferior and that femininity was not an inevitable or necessary role for women to embrace. For instance, Warren (1985) author of *Gendercide: The implications of sex selection* repeated Money's findings unquestioningly:

> Some infants are born with ambiguous genitals and may be assigned to the 'wrong' sex, and reared as boys when their chromosomal sex is female or vice versa. It is known that in such cases the sex of assignment, that is the sex according to which an individual is reared, is a much more powerful determinant of that person's gender identity and character structure than either the chromosomal structure or the hormonal environment. Thus, a genetic male reared as a female will generally develop a character considered to be well within the normal 'feminine' range.
>
> (Warren, 1982, p. 176)

She also cited Stoller (1974) as further evidence for feminist arguments, despite his mother-blaming narrative that 'too much mother' was the cause of homosexuality and gender nonconformity. Based on these works, Warren concluded that 'whatever effects sexual biology may prove to have upon human behaviour, they clearly can be overridden by social influences' (1982, p. 176). Even celebrated pioneers of feminism and feminist psychology[2] drew on Money and Stoller's work to support their arguments for gender equality, such as Kate Millet, who stated in *Sexual politics*:

> Stoller later makes emphatic the distinction that sex is biological, gender psychological, and therefore cultural . . . In the absence of complete evidence, I agree in general with Money, and the Hampsons who show in their large series of intersexed patients that gender role is determined by

> postnatal forces, regardless of the anatomy and physiology of the external genitalia . . . Psychosexually . . . there is no differentiation between the sexes at birth. Psychosexual personality is therefore postnatal and learned.
>
> (Millett, 2000 [1969], pp. 30–31)

Weisstein, author of one of the first critiques of the sexism within psychology *Psychology constructs the female* (1971), described Money's work on intersex children to show that the 'trait' of anger was not biologically male (Weisstein, 2003, pp. 408–9). Therefore, despite being critical of psychology's sexism, some feminist psychologists adopted the individualized and internal view of psychology to challenge rigid gender norms, by focusing on psychological objects, concepts constructed *by* psychology to describe human experience, such as the emotion of anger. This redirected feminist work from social constraints on women, to gendered notions of emotionality, which were then used to argue that gender and gender identity was malleable. This was without consideration of the conceptual move from gendered psychological objects (i.e. emotion) to gender identity and cultural norms of gender. It also reinterpreted Money's work, which posited that gender *was* influenced by biology in the form of prenatal hormones and emphasized a critical period in early childhood before gender identity became more permanent (Money & Ehrhardt, 1972).

Critics of Money, however, highlighted this emphasis on biological determinism and the problems of holding Money up as an example of liberalism:

> A perceptive reader of books or articles in which Money and co-workers summarize their research . . . notices obvious contradictions in thought; occasionally, evidence for the importance of cultural factors is mentioned, but the theme soon returns to one of belief in the overriding importance of biological determinants . . . .
>
> (Rogers, 1983, p. 1109)

Rogers (1983) also drew attention to Money and Tucker's (1975) position that the gender binary was necessary for society. Thus, despite arguing that gender was malleable, Money promoted the view that this apparent malleability should be used to rear intersex children in the gender role decided upon by medical professionals and therefore reaffirmed the gender binary rather than refuting it (Carrera, DePalma & Lameiras, 2012).

Unfortunately, many were so eager to incorporate Money's position into their arguments against the oppression of women, that they overlooked its widely discredited position within psychology. This was a result of the publication of David's (aka 'John/Joan') own account of the therapy (Colapinto, 2000), which included descriptions of traumatizing practices such as being made to engage in what Money termed 'sexual rehearsal play'[3] with his brother. Based on research from rhesus monkeys, Money defined such 'play' as 'pelvic rocking or thrusting movements against the body of a partner' (Money, 1986a, pp. 16–17) that he believed began in childhood (at around five years old) and was considered necessary for 'normal' heterosexual development. Money was also determined to change David's views on his genitalia, as Butler described:

> Money tried to talk to her about getting a real vagina, and she refused; in fact, she went screaming from the room. Money had her view sexually graphic pictures of vaginas. Money even went so far as to show Brenda pictures of women giving birth . . . .
>
> (Butler, 2001, pp. 58–9)

Not only does this quote show the kind of practices on which Money's theory was derived, but also how feminist analysis of it tended to coincide with psychiatric definitions of gender. That is, if the psychiatrist labelled a child a girl, then within feminist texts 'she' was often considered a girl, and only when the surrounding medical systems changed the child, 'she' then 'became' a 'boy'. This misgendering is common within psychology (Ansara & Hegarty, 2012), and overrides the child's own gender identity. Therefore, in this description of a child whose gender could not be changed, the article retains a construction of gender (identity) as changeable.

Arguments from within feminism that drew on Money's work did so at the expense of its problematic source as well as those aspects that contradicted feminist challenges to oppression. Ultimately, it failed to address the discrediting and disrepute of the theory. Drawing on problematic theories and concepts from within psychology to challenge sexism, and the conflation of psychological objects with gender, was also particularly evident in feminist texts promoting the concept of psychological androgyny.

Psychological androgyny

Bem introduced the concept of 'psychological androgyny' in 1981, drawing on empiricist approaches within psychology and the increasing research interest in gender and sex roles (Bem, 1981, 1995). She developed the Bem Sex Role Inventory (BSRI), which was innovative at the time within psychology for its positioning of masculinity and femininity as separate character traits, and thus an individual could possess both (or neither) at the same time. This countered much psychological work that assumed masculinity and femininity were opposing phenomena on opposite ends of a continuum (Barker & Richards, 2015). Bem's research (e.g. Bem & Lewis, 1975) found that individuals who combined aspects of both masculinity and femininity performed better, or were more successful, in a greater range of situations. However, others showed how this 'success' was actually due to the expression of masculinity rather than androgyny, with Bem later stating that reviews of her work identified this issue: 'In other words, it is psychological masculinity – *not androgyny* – that is associated with mental health in both sexes' (Bem, 1986, p. 190, my emphasis).

This outcome is somewhat unsurprising, as psychology frames 'normality' in the image of a (white) gender-conforming man, and thus expressions of masculinity would be expected to score more highly on psychological tests; this outcome also concurs with results that show feminine women as scoring the most poorly (Bem & Lewis, 1975). To conclude that androgyny is better for 'mental health' puts too much faith in psychological surveys and 'mental health' than either concept deserves. Nevertheless, the concept of androgyny was taken up within feminism and psychology (e.g. Gilbert, 1981; White, 1979; Wiggins & Holzmuller, 1981) and it continues to be cited in support of trans and non-binary identities (Kłonkowska, 2014). This is despite criticisms of both the concept and inventory (Hagger-Johnson, 2015), as well as some feminists arguing that the concept was only ever a metaphor (Warren, 1982).

Warren described the origin of the term as follows:

> The term 'androgyny' derives from the Greek words for male and female, and suggests a state intermediate between masculinity and femininity. To many feminists androgyny has come to represent escape from the prison of gender – that is, from socially enforced preconceptions of ways in which women and men ought to differ in their psychology and behaviour. Androgyny, in this feminist sense, has nothing to do with physical hermaphroditism . . . What the feminist androgynists (i.e. advocates of androgyny) recommend, rather, is psychological androgyny, the combination in a single person, of either sex, of so-called feminine and masculine character traits.
>
> (Warren, 1982, p. 170)

However, Harris (1974) highlighted how feminist proponents of the concept failed to acknowledge the problematic and oppressive history tied to the word, with 'androgyne' and 'hermaphrodite'[4] having been used to incite fear and prejudice against those who did not conform to heterosexual and cisgender 'norms'. Moreover, it was also argued that positioning a feminine and masculine combination as the 'ideal' perpetuated heteronormativity by rendering feminine/feminine and masculine/masculine combinations as unthinkable (Stimpson, 1974). Again, we see the use of psychological and psychiatric concepts regarding intersex (and homosexual) individuals being used to develop feminist theory on conceptualizations of gender that explicitly excluded them.

This response to an oppressive and rigid gender binary argued for a blending of the components, but it also positioned androgyny as 'vastly preferable' to masculine or feminine characters and the 'feminist ideal' (Warren, 1982, p. 170). As a result, conformity and femininity were framed in negative terms, such as being less 'complete' or less 'competent' (Warren, 1982, p. 173). Warren (1982) described this as the 'strong, rational, unemotional male on the one hand or the weak, emotional, irrational female on the other' (p. 170). Therefore, it was taken up in some feminist work as an ideal gender expression and potentially produced another harmful 'norm' or standard of gender to live up to. Trebilcot (1977) called this kind of idealized androgyny, 'monoandrogyny'. She proposed an alternative of 'polyandrogyny', to refer to individuals defining their own gender identity as feminine, masculine, or androgynous, without feeling the need to conform to an ideal.

This androgynous 'ideal', as well as the conclusion that unbalanced scores on the BSRI were representative of a less mature and less competent character (Warren, 1982), showed an undervaluation of femininity and masculinity. However, critiques of both were common within feminism at this time (e.g. Friedan, 2010 [1963]), such as Brownmiller's book, *Femininity*, where she explained that she did not wear skirts:

> Because I don't like this artificial gender distinction. Because I don't wish to start shaving my legs again. Because I don't want to return to the expense and aggravation of nylons. Because I will not reacquaint myself with the discomfort of feminine shoes.
>
> (Brownmiller, 1984, p. 81)

She concluded that 'the extremes of femininity are harmful only – only! – to women themselves in the form of a self-imposed masochism (restraint, inhibition, self-denial, a wasteful use of thought and time) that is deliberately mistaken for "true nature"' (p. 236). However, this describes an oppressive patriarchal and sanist society that promotes and enforces gender 'norms'. Thus, the problem is not expressing femininity per se, but of having to express femininity within a culture of conformity, of not being allowed to express other variations of gender that may be more congruent with your gender identity or gender expression. Thus, femininity is not the issue being described, but compulsory femininity:

> I'll be the first to admit that the expectation that all girls and women are, or should be, conventionally feminine marginalizes and injures many people. Those who are androgynous, or tomboys, or butches, or on the trans-masculine spectrum face disdain for their gender nonconformity. And many women who perhaps are naturally feminine are routinely made to feel embarrassed, ashamed, unworthy, and disempowered, because they do not quite meet society's practically unattainable standards of beauty. But the problem here is not femininity, but expectations. What we as feminists should be challenging is compulsory femininity rather than femininity itself.
>
> (Serano, 2012, pp. 182–3)

On the other hand, there were those who rejected the concept of androgyny outright, due to a denunciation of masculinity (Daly, 1978). Those from a feminist-separatist perspective valued an essentialized understanding of femininity and women, and therefore considered the concept of androgyny an 'abomination'.

The devaluation of gender-conforming femininity was used to uphold justifications for gender conversion therapies. For example, Rekers (1977) stated, 'Bem's research . . . would support our objective of attempting to treat sex-role rigidity (extremely feminine behaviour in boys) because her findings suggest that rigid femininity has negative correlates' (p. 559), and, argued that because Bem's work showed the negative impact of rigid femininity on women, the same could be said for femininity expressed by men. Feminist promotion of the idea that someone from a predominantly feminine gender identity could be encouraged to express masculine 'traits' (and vice versa) colluded with the psychological discourse that aimed to prevent homosexuality and transsexualism. This was in addition to Bem's gender schema theory that combined cognitive and social learning theory, that also framed gender roles as learned and therefore malleable: 'Thus, like social learning theory, gender schema theory assumes that sex typing is a learned phenomenon and hence that it is neither inevitable nor unmodifiable' (Bem, 1986, p. 186). Regardless of the intention of the author, whether for gender equality or conformity, the construction of gender as changeable and as an area appropriate for psychological intervention, resulted in the perpetuation of therapies aimed at changing children's identities and behaviours to conform to a gender binary. Moreover, while the concept was considered a temporary measure towards the abandonment of gender categories entirely (Warren, 1982), it maintained the gender binary and its associated stereotypes by continuing to divide behaviours and expressions in dichotomous and gendered terms. For instance, Harris (1974) stated:

> We cannot discuss the myth, in psychological terms, without resorting to sexist polarizations for the definition of identity ('My intellect is my masculine self; my intuition, my feminine self"); simply from a linguistic point of view, the myth is self-defeating.
>
> (Harris, 1974, p. 171)

Bem (1995) acknowledged this limitation in her later work, instead arguing for the proliferation of many possible genders. While the concept made the possibility of non-binary identities understandable to a profession deeply embedded in the maintenance of the gender binary (Barker & Richards, 2015), the concept of psychological androgyny was also part of a discourse that enabled conversion therapies to thrive.

The problem, then, of drawing on psychological discourse and the psychologizing of gender 'traits', was that it focused on psychological objects such as empathy and rationality, which were disconnected from embodied gender, or social context and culture. While psychology used the theory to promote femininity or masculinity as the ideal/norm, feminism promoted a combination of femininity and masculinity as the ideal/norm. It put gender firmly in the jurisdiction of psychology under the guise of liberation.

Gender as socially constructed

> There is no gender identity behind the expressions of gender; that identity is performatively constituted by the very 'expressions' that are said to be its results.
>
> (Butler, 1990, p. 25)

In this move away from a biologically determined understanding of gender to an emphasis on social influences and the learning of roles, there were also those who put forward a more relativist argument that gender was socially constructed. In other words, they argued that the concept of gender was something that people produced and maintained (as opposed to biological), and applied to bodies (rather than being embodied), behaviours and all manner of things, from clothing to colours. Most notable within feminist perspectives was the work of Judith Butler (1990), and her book *Gender trouble*. A highly celebrated book in feminism and queer studies for its proposition that gender was performative:

> . . . she was challenging the feminist critique of sex as produced by discourse, the sex-gender divide, and the idea of compulsory heterosexuality as ineffective strategies. Gender, sex, sexuality all became performances. The idea of gender, sex, and sexuality as free floating is one of the main tenets of queer theory.
>
> (Gherovici, 2011, pp. 114–15)

However, the work drew criticism from transgender scholars and activists (see Chapter 5). This was due to her theory that gender was a performance rather than an internal characteristic or tied to sexed bodies and genitalia. While the separating of biological anatomies with gender identity supported much of trans and intersex experiences, her argument that gender was 'neither a noun nor a set of attributes' but 'always a doing' (Butler, 1990, p. 25) was thought to undermine those who had been denied the option to have their gender recognized and acknowledged (e.g. trans, non-binary, intersex people). Also, her work was often taken up by others to assume that gender was *only* a performance (Serano, 2007). Her framing of a fixed or core gender as a 'fiction' mirrored and extended psychological discourse that already destabilized the concept of gender, but in doing so had the potential to undermine people's embodied and subjective experiences:

> As a consequence, gender cannot be understood as a role which either expresses or disguises an interior 'self', whether that 'self' is conceived as sexed or not. As performance which is performative, gender is an 'act', broadly construed, which constructs the social fiction of its own psychological interiority.
>
> (Butler, 1988, p. 528)

Butler's perspective on the topic has changed over time, and in 2014 she admitted that she had not considered the experiences of trans people sufficiently in her theorizing of gender in *Gender trouble*. She stated that when writing the book, 'I did not think well enough about trans issues' and that 'I did not mean to argue that gender is fluid and changeable (mine certainly is not)'(Butler & Williams, 2014, para. 42). Butler further explained that her intention at the time was to open the possibilities of gender and to counter or challenge those discourses that pathologize, criminalize and encourage victimization and discrimination.

In her recent comments, Butler states that she does not consider gender a 'choice', but notes the limitations both of social constructionism and language more generally in addressing the tensions and inequalities between those labels that are assigned to individuals, and those that people assign to themselves. She also ops out of the common nature/nurture debates about sex and gender, offering an alternative approach to the problem: that knowing the origin (or 'cause' in psychological terms) of gender and sex is unnecessary because 'we are all ethically bound to recognize another person's declared or enacted sense of sex and/or gender' and that this recognition is essential for their well-being (Butler & Williams, 2014, para. 20). Like Steinem's recent recantation and apology for prior writings, and her conclusion that 'As feminists know, power over our own minds and bodies comes first' (Steinem, 2013, para. 11), Butler argues that 'one should be free to determine the course of one's gendered life' (Butler & Williams, 2014, para. 4).[5]

However, Butler's work on transgender and intersex identities was also troubling. When discussing the John/Joan case, she commented on the changing of pronouns during her article (changing from 'she' to 'he' when describing David). She stated that, for a period of time David 'was' Brenda (Butler, 2001), but David did not identify as a 'girl', but was told he was one within a context of medical non-consent. The attempt to complicate gender by using what was perceived to be an 'anomaly' or 'interesting case' to reflect on the gender of those who do not undergo such treatments, showed how the role of medical and psychiatric authority in the assigning of gender had been overlooked. David's pronoun should not change within the article, as his gender identity did not change, it was the acceptance of his gender by others that changed, their viewpoints and decisions changed, but David was always David. Butler also analyses him more so than the systems that surround him. Firstly acknowledging and recognizing his identity and his knowledge, and then questioning it, interrogating it, and analysing him for the purposes of gender theory:

> To do justice to David is, certainly, to take him at his word, and to call him by his chosen name, but how are we to understand his word and his name? Is this the word he creates? Is the word that he receives?
>
> (Butler, 2001, p. 69)

This is highly problematic, as it parallels the wealth of psychiatric case studies that similarly analysed the behaviour and word of intersex and trans children (although David was neither), it called their experience and knowledge into question. It continues the placement of gender nonconformists under the gaze of psychiatry, and also, the gaze of feminism.

There are other parallels between this feminist study of gender and psychological approaches to gender therapies. Butler's study of cross-dressers, drag queens and transvestism in an attempt to understand gender, and to conclude that sex, gender performance and gender identity are separate but related concepts (Gherovici, 2011), mirrors Money's (1985) studies on cross-dressing, drag queens (what he called 'gynemimesis'), transvestism and transsexualism to conclude gender role and gender identity are 'sides of the same coin' (p. 71) with sex a further separate but related category. While psychology framed gender (or sex) roles[6] as a learned behaviour that was expressed or performed in response to social and cultural cues (Bem, 1981; Money, Hampson & Hampson, 1957), with gender identity being a 'private' expression of the public role (Money, 1991), feminism framed gender performance as a socially constructed phenomenon that was acted out publicly and an internal representation was created through this performance. While there are also key differences in the theories, such as Money's inclusion of biological determinism and a minimizing of agency, and Butler's aim of broadening and expanding gender possibilities rather than coercing individuals to conform to a gender binary, the common discourse of gender as malleable, as developed within a social context, shows that rather than Money's work representing a liberal and progressive stance, it was feminism that verged on the replication of conservative and problematic discourses from within psychological theory. Feminism's mirroring of psychological discourse is disconcerting (or 'troubling'), as both promoted this conceptualization of gender, which has been so influential in the disciplines that the existence of trans people potentially undermines the key concepts within them. It is unsurprising then, that the disciplines that have been the most hostile towards trans people are psychiatry, psychology and feminism.

Radical feminism

> rad·i·cal
>
> *n.*
>
> 1 A person who holds or follows strong convictions or extreme principles; extremist.
>
> 2 A person who advocates fundamental political, economic, and social reforms by direct and often uncompromising methods.[7]

These dual meanings of 'radical', of wanting social revolution and of being extreme, well describe the radical feminist movement. What began as a movement that challenged patriarchy and sexism (Willis, 1984, p. 91), also became associated with views that were positioned as 'extreme'. So, while there are many who describe themselves as radical feminists, who believe that an overhaul of society is needed to stop gendered oppression, within this group are some who argue for separatism between men and women, and state that any form of genital touching is inherently 'sexist' (Willis, 1984). Critical of feminist psychology, and of the focus on 'sex roles' rather than foregrounding gendered oppression (Kitzinger, 1990), radical feminism promoted a different view of gender. Considered by many to be unrepresentative of feminism, and 'a minority view . . . out on some weird edge' (Willis, 1984, p. 103), this group became strongly associated with a particular hostility toward transgender people (sometimes referred to a 'trans-exclusionary radical feminism' or 'TERF'). Despite being positioned as a minority view within the movement, and a lack of literature since the 1970s (Jeffreys, 2012, 2014a), it was as influential as it was controversial (Stryker & Whittle, 2013), with long-standing consequences that continue to impact feminism and the lives of trans people.

Questioning gender

At a time when feminism was challenging and questioning gender roles, it also began to consider the concept of gender in relation to the increasing visibility of trans people. For example, in the mid-1970s, Dr Renée Richards, a professional tennis player, sued the United States Tennis Association (USTA) for refusing to let her compete in women's tennis, which attracted media attention in relation to her gender identity and name change. Feminists began to ask

> . . . is a biological male who has had hormone treatments and genital surgery, and undergone cosmetic and behavioural changes so that he can successfully 'pass' as a woman – who claims that he was all along a woman, anyway – really then a woman?
>
> (Yudkin, 1978, p. 97)

We can see that the very questions posed by Yudkin reveal her answer, by referring to Renee as a 'biological male' and 'he'. She goes on to say that there are many ways to define 'male' and 'female' that can produce different answers to her question –whether based on chromosomes, observable sex characteristics, genitalia and other gendered organs and so on. After problematizing the definition, she considers if transsexual individuals can be considered women and asks 'How are *we* to decide?' (Yudkin 1978, p. 98, my emphasis). In addition to the overt separation between 'us' and 'them' (positioning trans people as Other), privilege is illustrated by the superiority of a group who get to 'decide', and thus define 'gender' or 'woman', much like how psychology defines 'normal' gender (see Chapter 3). Therefore, while the questioning of gender and gender roles was comprehensive at the time, the questioning in relation to transgender identities was relatively superficial, as this branch of radical lesbian-feminism already had a fairly unyielding definition of gender.

In her well-known and highly contested work of 1979, *The transsexual empire: The making of a she-male*, Raymond stated, 'Ultimately, women must ask if transsexually constructed lesbian-feminists are our peers. Are they equal to us? Questions of equality often center on proportional equality, such as "equal pay for equal work," or "equal rights to health care"' (Raymond, 2006, p. 141). In addition to showing the tendency for feminists to assume the privilege of deciding who is equal and who is not, she goes on to say that work and health care are not the way to determine the answer to her question. In doing so, she ignores areas where discrimination of trans people and inequality are undeniable (Garner, 2014; Grant et al., 2010; Lev, 2006), but reinforces this version of radical feminism's definition of 'woman', which remains in use by some groups today: that a woman must have a complete life history of being a woman, in other words, she must have been a woman (i.e. with female genitalia) since birth:

> We know that we are women who are born with female chromosomes and anatomy, and that whether or not we were socialized to be so-called normal women, patriarchy has treated and will treat us as women. Transsexuals have not had this same history. No man can have the history of being born and located in this culture as a woman. He can have his history of wishing to be a woman and of acting like a woman, but this gender experience is that of a transsexual, not of a woman.
>
> (Raymond, 2006, p. 139)

By ignoring the experiences of oppression of trans women, and focusing solely on the problem of sexism, Raymond overlooked the societal devaluation of femininity and those that express it (regardless of gender). In addition to promoting a very narrow definition of 'woman', she assumed that there was only one way to be a woman. It also resulted in the meticulous and deliberate use of language to include/exclude certain people, making the terms used to describe trans people a key site for oppression and liberation. For example, Raymond (2006) described trans people as 'the transsexually constructed lesbian-feminist' who was 'a man, and not a woman' (p. 133). Daly (1978), Raymond's thesis supervisor, described trans people as 'pseudofemale' (1978, p. 68), and Jeffreys (2014b) uses the phrase 'men who transgender', rejecting their gender identity and using the term as a verb rather than a noun on the basis that 'no change in biology takes place' (p. 43). By framing trans women as 'constructed', 'pseudo' and not biologically female, in addition to the requirement that women be women from birth, radical feminism defined 'woman' as 'real' through biology as well as experience of sexism.

In contrast to this definition of 'woman', gender was thought of as something that was not 'real', it was constructed and forced on women by patriarchy. Some theorized this as a combination of sex (e.g. biology), gender (e.g. psychology) and sex roles (e.g. social) (Yudkin, 1978), again replicating psychological perspectives from the 1950s onwards. On the one hand, this view that trans women needed a biologically female body was repeated as the reason why trans women were not women, but at other times this biological foundation was weakened in theorizing that showed even biological sex was a constructed concept, particularly when intersex individuals were considered (e.g. Yudkin, 1978, p. 98).

Consequently, a significant portion of feminist thought argued that what was needed in society, or what the social revolution would require, was an abolition of gender (Jeffreys, 2005), that is, rejecting that people have a gender at all (Jeffreys, 2014b). It was theorized that removing the categorizations of gender and sex would remove the inequality. However, this represented a form of 'universal social constructionism'[8] (Hacking, 1999) or 'conservative relativism'[9] (Parker, 1998), where it was thought that there was nothing beyond discourse or 'nothing outside the text' (Wilkinson, 1997, p. 184) and that simply changing the way concepts were constructed would lead to social change. There are many problems with this approach, not least the neglect of structural inequality, materiality and embodiment (Cromby & Nightingale, 1999), but events such as the depathologization of homosexuality illustrate that when a term is redefined, the social inequalities do not disappear (Conrad & Angell, 2004), much in the same way that arguments of 'colour blindness' fail to address racism (Bonilla-Silva, 2006; Carr, 1997) by 'negating racial inequality' (Gallagher, 2003, p. 22).

Moreover, some radical feminists argue that, as gender is a social construction, so too is 'transgenderism'. They conclude that if gender is abolished, then transgender people will no longer exist (Jeffreys, 2014a; Yudkin, 1978), reaffirming Raymond's (1979) theory that transgenderism was caused by patriarchy and gender stereotypes (Riddell, 2006). Butler stated that Raymond's and Jeffrey's use of 'constructionism' was badly misunderstood and oppressive, and failed to consider how people embrace or reject constructions as well as embodied and lived experiences beyond discourse (Butler & Williams, 2014). As Hacking (1999) has argued, just because a concept is socially constructed does not mean that it does not exist. For example, the concept of rape is constructed within legal, psychiatric and popular discourse (to name a few), but that does not mean that the violence is not 'real' (Tosh, 2013a). Nevertheless, these radical feminist perspectives were popularized within feminism, and had very real consequences for trans women. For instance, the stance that 'real' women needed to have been born a woman (i.e. be assigned female at birth) and live as a woman since birth (and therefore had experienced sexism) became criteria for the use of feminist services, such as rape crisis centres. As a consequence, trans women have been refused access to these services, despite the need for such support for trans victims and survivors of rape (Elliot, 2012; Wyss, 2004). This has also included restricting trans women from volunteering at rape crisis services, such as the well-documented case at Rape Relief in Vancouver, Canada (*Vancouver Rape Relief Society* v. *Nixon*, 2003). By refusing to acknowledge trans women as women, the issue was reframed as an attempt of a 'man' to penetrate a woman-only place, a common framing of the issue raised in debates about including trans people into the feminist movement:

> For supporters of Rape Relief, two things are at stake: preventing men from demanding access to women's organisations, and confirming women's rights to organise separately. Yet these related concerns are difficult to credit unless one reads trans women as men.
>
> (Elliot, 2012, p. 20)

Victims of naivety

In addition to framing trans women as 'men', this branch of radical feminism often positioned trans women as 'victims' of a patriarchal culture, naive to the societal pressures of femininity: 'On the other end are those who construe transsexuals as unwitting dupes of patriarchal norms or medical technologies and who believe that what they should be doing is transcending gender or transforming themselves' (Elliot, 2010, p. 24). Within this narrative, feminists were positioned as having a greater understanding of the issues, whereas trans women were just 'confused' or 'unaware' of their role as victim (e.g. Yudkin, 1978, pp. 100–101). Like psychology and psychiatry, feminism placed trans people in the position of the 'unknowing' and themselves in the position of 'expert', mimicking the dichotomy of medical expert and patient, which assumes incompetence on the part of the patient as a result of sanist oppression (Szasz, 2007). This victim discourse framed body-modification procedures as a cruel consequence of naive trans people living in a patriarchal society. Termed bodily 'mutilation' by the more polemical, the need for body modification was blamed on the profession of medicine capitalizing on the profit to be made by unsuspecting 'victims' (Greer, 2014; Jeffreys, 1994, 2000). As Raymond stated:

> What all of these events point to is the particularly instrumental role that medicine has played in the control of deviant or potentially deviant women. 'The Transsexual Empire' is ultimately a medical empire, based on a patriarchal medical model. This medical model has provided a 'sacred canopy' of legitimations for transsexual treatment and surgery. In the name of therapy, it has medicalized moral and social questions of sex-role oppression, thereby erasing their deepest meaning.
>
> (Raymond, 2006, p. 142)

Jeffreys (2014a) went further, stating that treatments in childhood amounted to 'eugenics', relating it to historic examples of forced sterilization. She stated that this analogy was made to highlight the harm of such treatments, but overlooked the harm that results from restricting young trans peoples' access to them as well as the alternatives offered, such as gender conversion therapy (see Chapters 3 and 5). In addition, she described treatments for trans and intersex children (which are within very different contexts regarding consensual bodily treatments); for example, she referred to 'sexual surgeries' in relation to transgender children (Jeffreys, 2012), but this is not an option or current practice (see Chapters 3 and 5).

The discourse constructs trans people as intellectually inferior for their lack of understanding of what is 'really' going on, and it fails to acknowledge the suicide rates and attempts when access to body-modification procedures is restricted, the difficulty in accessing such treatments, the distress from bodily incongruence, as well as the importance of self-determining gender (Butler and Williams, 2014). Thus, rather than victims of a cruel form of 'mutilation', body-modification procedures can be life saving. The discourse also centres on cisgender women, as some argued that the aim of such surgeries were 'male-mothered genetic engineering' to '"create" without women' (Daly, 1978) and to replace women (Raymond, 1979), thus making experiences of trans women centre on the lives of cisgender women.

Rape

Another contradiction within feminist thought regarding trans people is that they are simultaneously framed as naive victims, but also as violent perpetrators. Raymond's *The transsexual empire* (1979) 'demonized' trans people, causing much anger and offence, as well as promoting prejudice and discrimination (Stryker & Whittle, 2013). She argued that trans women were men, regardless of gender identity or bodily changes. Based on this assumption, she stated that transgender women 'raped' women through an invasion of women's spaces and commandeering the 'female form':

> Rape, of course, is a masculinist violation of bodily integrity. All transsexuals rape women's bodies by reducing the real female form to an artifact, appropriating this body for themselves . . . Because transsexuals have lost their physical 'members' does not mean that they have lost their ability to penetrate women – women's mind, women's space, women's sexuality. Transsexuals merely cut off the most obvious means of invading women so that they seem noninvasive. However, as Mary Daly has remarked, in the case of the transsexually constructed lesbian-feminists their whole presence becomes a 'member' invading women's presence and dividing us once more from each other.
>
> (Raymond, 2006, p. 134)

She goes on to state that this form of rape was based on deception rather than force. These polemical accusations promoted two of the most enduring and harmful narratives regarding trans people: that they were deceivers and sexual predators. These constructions have resulted in many issues for trans people, including exacerbating their exclusion from rape crisis centres, despite increasing evidence that trans people are particularly vulnerable to sexual assault (Gehring & Knudson, 2005; Grossman & D'Augelli, 2006; Wyss, 2004), and problems using public bathrooms which can result in violence and difficulty in participating in public life (Herman, 2013).

Raymond's (1979) theory had additional problems, such as her drawing on *Penthouse* as evidence for her 'rape' theory, neglecting to consider the unrepresentative and inaccurate portrayals the publication, which is designed to titillate, is likely to have. This is in addition to the long history of fetishizing and sexualizing cross-dressing and transgender people (see Chapter 3). Also, the theory mirrors the 'progress narrative' identified in the framing of cross-dressing as a means of accessing opportunities closed off to women (see Chapter 3), by framing the motivation of trans people to access women's spaces, but fails to consider the hostility, discrimination and exclusion that can occur when people are gender nonconforming or transgender (Grant et al., 2010; Jauk, 2013). Moreover, identifying sexual violence and the 'penetration' of women's spaces as the only motive for individuals to be transgender or to cross-dress ignores the possibility that there is value in being feminine, for its own sake. Thus, as identified by others in critiquing religious discourse from the Middle Ages (see Chapter 3), framing gender nonconformity for the purposes of sexual predation represents a profound devaluation of femininity.

Feminism or psychiatry?

Despite its critical stance on therapy, these radical perspectives parallel psychiatric and psychological perspectives that misgender trans people, in that they override trans individuals' ability to self-determine their body and gender identity, frame life-saving procedures as 'unnecessary', and aim to 'prevent' the existence of transsexuals. On the surface, they look like perfect allies. This is unsurprising, perhaps, due to the lack of engagement with critiques of the diagnosis. For example, in Jeffreys' (2014a) latest book, she declared a lack of critical literature on transgender issues and related diagnosis, despite there being an immense amount of criticism in this area that has accumulated over several decades (e.g. Ansara & Hegarty, 2012; Bryant, 2006; Burke, 1996; Hegarty, 2009; Isay, 1997; Lev, 2006; Winters, 2009). Therefore, there were feminist psychologists engaging with problematic psychiatric concepts uncritically for the purposes of gender equality, and radical feminists unaware of the wide range of clinical literature that promoted similar anti-trans arguments.

Another area of similarity between radical feminist and psychiatric perspectives on transgender people was the framing of gender nonconformity and transgender identities as being a result of sexual abuse (Jeffreys, 2000): 'Another cause lies in histories of sexual and physical abuse by men which make women want to exit the body they associate with victimhood, and gain safety by identifying with the abuser' (Jeffreys, 2005, p. 53). While Jeffreys (2005) stated that this was an 'under-recognised contributor' to transgender identities, there is a wealth of psychiatric literature that refutes her claim that it is 'under-recognised' (e.g. Beitchman et al., 1992, 1991; Roberts et al., 2012; Zucker & Kuksis, 1990). In fact, it is so regularly referred to in the literature, that there is little critical examination of the problems with the theory. For example, if sexual abuse was a causal factor in the development of trans identities, it fails to address the lifelong victimisation of trans people (see Tosh, 2013b for a review). Furthermore, it does not account for the fact that children often identify as trans prior to abuse (e.g. Zucker & Kuksis, 1990). Instead, it reflects a long-standing and problematic psychiatric narrative that frames gender non-conformists as sexual 'deviants' (see Chapter 3).

Another key area where radical feminism and psychiatry overlap is the framing of transgenderism as masochism (e.g. Jeffreys, 2005). This perspective argues that transgender people enjoy playing the subordinate role of women, and that the motivation for body-modification procedures is for the humiliation and degradation that presenting as a woman would offer: 'Femininity is sexually exciting to the men who seek it because it represents subordinate status and thus satisfies masochistic sexual interests' (Jeffreys, 2005, p. 46). Not only was this account of transvestism and transsexualism discounted by Hirschfield over a century ago (see Chapter 3), but the evidence that is drawn upon comes from pornography (Jeffreys, 2005). As feminism has a long history in challenging the inaccurate portrayals of women in porn, it is unclear why feminists would assume that its portrayal of any other group of people would be any more accurate. Moreover, it shows a lack of awareness of how psychiatry and psychology fetishize particular behaviours by framing them as sexualized and 'perverse'. Finally, it frames consensual BDSM and kink communities as pathological or 'deviant', also drawing on psychiatric discourse.

Conclusions

> Young women appear to be much more willing to listen to stories about transgender lives than previous generations were, and most are shocked by the anti-trans feminism they encounter.
>
> (Elliot, 2010, p. 26)

As stated at the beginning of this chapter, it is important not to essentialize feminism, or the different variations of feminism. Therefore, while there have been many problematic feminist perspectives, not all feminism is 'trans-exclusionary'. During the 1970s, Raymond (2006) noted how many feminists supported trans people, such as Elizabeth Rose who described her concern about feminists assuming the power of defining (and policing) who gets to use the term 'female'.

During the 1980s, feminists campaigned against the inclusion of gender identity disorder in the DSM and had a significant impact on the changes of the diagnosis (Bryant, 2006); in 2010, the Psychology of Women Section, the feminist section of the British Psychological Society, worked alongside gay, lesbian, trans and intersex individuals and groups to protest the Chair of the *DSM-5* Sexual and Gender Identity Disorders Work Group and the psychiatric treatment of transgender and gender-nonconforming children (Tosh, 2011). These are only a few examples of the many ways that feminists are working with and alongside transgender people, as well as the development of trans feminism (see Chapter 5). There have also been apologies and retractions by some feminists, acknowledging that their previous texts were harmful, or used terms and representations that were exclusionary and offensive to trans people. There is also the more trans-positive perspective that is associated with third-wave feminism (Davies, 2004; Stryker, 2007). However, there is less focus, at present, within third-wave texts and campaigns around diagnoses, depathologization and access to body-modification services. In that sense, third-wave texts do not construct a discourse around gender dysphoria.

In contrast, those who draw on psychiatric narratives and discourse (reframed as 'feminism') use the very source of harmful constructions that frame women as 'hysterical' and justified the use of electric shock treatments on homosexual individuals. It has in the past, and continues to, argue for unnecessary and non-consensual genital surgeries for women and intersex children (Ehrenreich & Barr, 2005; Tosh, 2013b; Tosh & Carson, in press). The uncritical use of psychiatric perspectives and discourses to argue *for* feminism and lesbianism is therefore paradoxical and absurd. Not only does it reject the increasingly well-documented discrimination, victimization and oppression of trans people (Bochenek & Brown, 2001; Grant et al., 2010; Jauk, 2013; Wyss, 2004), and the existence of cross-dressing, gender-nonconforming and trans people all over the world for millennia (see Chapter 3), but it also fails to consider the impact of sanism and how it has been used by some feminists to further their cause of silencing and discrediting trans people. Consequently, it adds to the criticisms of feminism that began in the 1970s, that many forms of feminism have disregarded other forms of oppression. In doing so, rather than offering a radical challenge to oppressive and sexist systems, they promoted conservative ideologies of gender (Willis, 1984).

Notes

1 I use the term 'essentialized' as described by Burr (2015) in her description of social constructionism as promoting 'anti-essentialism'. She states that 'Since the social world, including ourselves as people, is the product of social processes, it follows that there cannot be any given, determined nature to the world or people. There are no "essences" inside things or people that make them what they are' (p. 6).

2 For a discussion of feminist psychology, see Burman (1997), Clarke et al. (2005), Kitzinger (1990), Kitzinger & Perkins (1993), Ussher (1990) and Wilkinson (1997).

3 Money went further to state that child-adult sexual relations would 'not necessarily affect the child adversely' (Money, 1986b, p. 523) and spoke critically of the punishment of child molesters. Feminists, such as Bell (1993), have discussed at length the propensity for some who identified as 'sexually liberal' to overlook the abuse of power in relation to childhood sexual abuse.
4 An outdated and pathologizing term used by medical professionals to refer to intersex individuals, although some reclaimed the word within activist contexts (e.g. 'Hermaphrodites with Attitude').
5 Although, others acknowledge that the harms caused by previous texts, such as Steinem's framing of body-modification procedures as 'mutilation', had influence at a time when others, such as Janice Raymond were actively seeking to stop insurance coverage for such procedures. Therefore, some have called for more than apologies, but for action in addition to well-meaning words (Roberts, 2013).
6 Some psychologists used 'gender role' interchangeably with 'gender performance' (e.g. Cahill, 1983; Condry, 1984).
7 From www.dictionary.com (accessed 21 November 2015).
8 Hacking defines this as 'everything is socially constructed' (1999, p. 24).
9 Parker defines conservative relativists as not interested in 'the social implications of their arguments' and 'imagine that everything in the world and human nature can be made and remade at will' (1998, p. 2).

References

APA (American Psychiatric Association) (1980). *Diagnostic and statistical manual of mental disorders, third edition (DSM-III).* Washington, DC: Author.

APA (American Psychiatric Association) (1987). *Diagnostic and statistical manual of mental disorders, third edition revised.* Washington, DC: Author.

APA (American Psychiatric Association) (1994). *Diagnostic and statistical manual of mental disorders fourth edition (DSM-IV).* Washington, DC: Author.

APA (American Psychiatric Association) (2000). *Diagnostic and statistical manual of mental disorders, fourth edition text revision (DSM-IV-TR).* Washington, DC: Author.

Ansara, G., & Hegarty, P. (2012). Cisgenderism in psychology: Pathologising and misgendering children from 1999 to 2008. *Psychology & Sexuality, 3*(2), 137–60.

Barker, M. J., & Richards, C. (2015). Further genders. In C. Richards & M. J. Barker (Eds.), *The Palgrave handbook of the psychology of sexuality and gender* (pp. 166–82). Basingstoke: Palgrave Macmillan.

Beitchman, J. H., Zucker, K. J., Hood, J. E., da Costa, G. A., & Akman, D. (1991). A review of the short-term effects of child sexual abuse. *Child Abuse & Neglect, 15*(4), 537–56.

Beitchman, J. H., Zucker, K. J., Hood, J. E., da Costa, G. A., Akman, D., & Cassavia, E. (1992). A review of the long-term effects of child sexual abuse. *Child Abuse & Neglect, 16*(1), 101–18.

Bell, V. (1993). *Interrogating incest: Feminism, Foucault and the law.* London: Routledge.

Bem, S. (1981). Gender schema theory: A cognitive account of sex typing. *Psychological Review, 88*(4), 354–64.

Bem, S. (1986). Androgyny and gender schema theory: A conceptual and empirical integration. In T. Sondregger (Ed.), *Psychology and gender: Nebraska symposium on motivation, 1984* (pp. 179–226). Lincoln: University of Nebraska Press.

Bem, S. (1995). Dismantling gender polarization and compulsory heterosexuality: Should we turn the volume down or up? *Journal of Sex Research, 32*(4), 329–34.

Bem, S., & Lewis, S. (1975). Sex role adaptability: One consequence of psychological androgyny. *Journal of Personality and Social Psychology, 31*(4), 634–43.

Bevacqua, M. (2000). *Rape on the public agenda: Feminism and the politics of sexual assault.* Lillington, NC: Northeastern University Press.

Bevacqua, M. (2008). Reconsidering violence against women: Coalition politics in the antirape movement. In S. Gilmore & S. Evans (Eds.), *Feminist coalitions: Historical perspectives on second-wave feminism in the United States* (pp. 163–77). Champaign: University of Illinois Press.

Bochenek, M., & Brown, A. W. (2001). *Hatred in the hallways: Violence and discrimination against lesbian, gay, bisexual, and transgender students in U.S. schools.* New York: Human Rights Watch.

Bonilla-Silva, E. (2006). *Racism without racists: Color-blind racism and the persistence of racial inequality in the United States.* Oxford: Rowman & Littlefield Publishers.

Braidotti, R. (2003). Cyberfeminism with a difference. In M. Peters, M. Olssen, & C. Lankshear (Eds.), *Futures of critical theory: Dreams of difference* (pp. 239–60). Oxford: Rowman & Littlefield.

Brown, H. (1962). *Sex and the single girl.* New York: Geis.

Brown, L. (1989). New voices, new visions: Toward a lesbian/gay paradigm for psychology. *Psychology of Women Quarterly, 13*, 445–58.

Brownmiller, S. (1984). *Femininity.* New York: Simon and Schuster.

Bryant, K. (2006). Making gender identity disorder of childhood: Historical lessons for contemporary debates. *Sexuality Research & Social Policy, 3*(3), 23–39.

Burgess-Proctor, A. (2006). Intersections of race, class, gender, and crime future directions for feminist criminology. *Feminist Criminology, 1*(1), 27–47.

Burke, P. (1996). *Gender shock: Exploding the myths of male and female.* New York: Anchor Books/Doubleday.

Burman, E. (1997). *Deconstructing feminist psychology.* London: SAGE Publications.

Burr, V. (2015). *Social constructionism.* London: Routledge.

Butler, J. (1988). Performative acts and gender constitution: An essay in phenomenology and feminist theory. *Theatre Journal, 40*(4), 519–31.

Butler, J. (1990). *Gender trouble: Feminism and the subversion of gender.* New York: Routledge.

Butler, J. (2001). Doing justice to someone: Sex reassignment and allegories of transsexuality. *GLQ: A Journal of Lesbian and Gay Studies*, 7(4), 621–36.

Butler, J., & Williams, C. (2014). Gender performance: The TransAdvocate interviews Judith Butler: http://www.transadvocate.com/gender-performance-the-transadvocate-interviews-judith-butler_n_13652.htm (accessed 21 November 2015).

Cahill, S. E. (1983). Reexamining the acquisition of sex roles: A social interactionist approach. *Sex Roles, 9*(1), 1–15.

Campbell, K. (1973). The rhetoric of women's liberation: An oxymoron. *Quarterly Journal of Speech, 59*(1), 74–86.

Carrera, M. V., DePalma, R., & Lameiras, M. (2012). Sex/gender identity: Moving beyond fixed and 'natural' categories. *Sexualities, 15*(8), 995–1016.

Carr, L. G. (1997). *'Colorblind' racism.* London: SAGE Publications.

Clarke, V., Peel, E., Clarke, V., & Peel, E. (2005). LGBT psychology and feminist psychology: Bridging the divide. *Psychology of Women Section Review*, 7(2), 4–10.

Colapinto, J. (2000). *As nature made him: The boy who was raised as a girl.* New York: Harper Collins Publishers.

Condry, J. C. (1984). Gender identity and social competence. *Sex Roles*, *11*(5–6), 485–511.

Connell, N., & Wilson, C. (1974). *Rape: The first sourcebook for women*. New York: New American Library.

Conrad, P., & Angell, A. (2004). Homosexuality and remedicalization. *Society*, *41*(5), 32–9.

Cromby, J., & Nightingale, D. (1999). *Social constructionist psychology: A critical analysis*. Buckingham: Open University Press.

Daly, M. (1978). *Gyn/ecology: The metaethics of radical feminism*. Boston, MA: Beacon Press.

Davies, E. (2004). Finding ourselves: Postmodern identities and the transgender movement. In S. Gillis, G. Howie, & R. Munford (Eds.), *Third wave feminism: A critical exploration* (pp. 110–21). London: Palgrave Macmillan.

Dicker, R. C., & Piepmeier, A. (2003). *Catching a wave: Reclaiming feminism for the 21st century*. Lillington, NC: Northeastern University Press.

Dworkin, A. (2006). *Intercourse*. New York: Basic Books.

Ehrenreich, B., & Barr, M. (2005). Intersex surgery, female genital cutting, and the selective condemnation of 'cultural practices'. *Harvard Civil Rights-Civil Liberties Law Review*, *40*, 71–140.

Elliot, P. P. (2012). *Debates in transgender, queer, and feminist theory: Contested sites*. Farnham: Ashgate Publishing, Ltd.

Faludi, S. (2009). *Backlash: The undeclared war against American women*. New York: Crown/Archetype.

Fausto-Sterling, A. (2008). *Myths of gender: Biological theories about women and men*. New York: Basic Books.

Friedan, B. (2010 [1963]). *The feminine mystique*. New York: W. W. Norton & Company.

Friedman, J., & Valenti, J. (2008). *Yes means yes: Visions of female sexual power and a world without rape*. Berkeley, CA: Seal Press.

Gaard, G. (2011). Ecofeminism revisited: Rejecting essentialism and re-placing species in a material feminist environmentalism. *Feminist Formations*, *23*(2), 26–53.

Gallagher, C. (2003). Colour-blind privilege: The social and political functions of erasing the colour line in post race America. *Race, Gender & Class*, *10*(4), 22–37.

Garner, T. (2014). Chest surgeries of a different 'nature'. *Annual Review of Critical Psychology*, *11*, 337–56.

Gehring, D., & Knudson, G. (2005). Prevalence of childhood trauma in a clinical population of transsexual people. *International Journal of Transgenderism*, *8*(1), 23–30.

Gherovici, P. (2011). *Please select your gender: From the invention of hysteria to the democratizing of transgenderism*. London: Routledge.

Gilbert, L. A. (1981). Toward mental health: The benefits of psychological androgyny. *Professional Psychology*, *12*(1), 29–38.

Gottschalk, L. (2009). Transgendering women's space: A feminist analysis of perspectives from Australian women's services. *Women's Studies International Forum*, *32*(3), 167–78.

Grant, J., Mottet, L., Tanis, J., Herman, J., Harrison, J., & Keisling, M. (2010). *National transgender discrimination survey report on health and health care*. National Center for Transgender Equality; National Gay and Lesbian Task Force: http://www.thetaskforce.org/static_html/downloads/resources_and_tools/ntds_report_on_health.pdf (accessed 21 November 2015).

Green, R. (1979). 'Sissies' and 'tomboys'. *SIECUS Report*, 7(3), 1–15.

Greer, G. (2014). *The whole woman*. London: Random House.

Grossman, A., & D'Augelli, A. (2006). Transgender youth: Invisible and vulnerable. In *Current issues in lesbian, gay, bisexual, and transgender health* (pp. 111–28). Binghamton, NY: Harrington Park Press.

Hacking, I. (1999). *The social construction of what?* Boston, MA: Harvard University Press.
Hagger-Johnson, G. (2015). Quantitative methods. In C. Richards & M. J. Barker (Eds.), *The Palgrave handbook of the psychology of sexuality and gender* (pp. 333–52). Basingstoke: Palgrave Macmillan.
Haraway, D. (2002). A cyborg manifesto: Science, technology and socialist-feminism in the late twentieth century. In D. Bell & B. Kennedy (Eds.), *The cybercultures reader* (pp. 291–324). London: Routledge.
Harris, D. A. (1974). Androgyny: The sexist myth in disguise. *Women's Studies, 2*(2), 171.
Hegarty, P. (2009). Toward an LGBT-informed paradigm for children who break gender norms: Comment on Drummond et al. (2008) and Rieger et al. (2008). *Developmental Psychology, 45*(4), 895–900.
Herman, J. (2013). Gendered restrooms and minority stress: The public regulation of gender and its impact on transgender people's lives. *Journal of Public Management & Social Policy, 19*(1), 65–80.
Hoeflinger, E. (2008). Talking waves: Structures of feminist moments and the potential of a wave economy. *Thirdspace: A Journal of Feminist Theory & Culture, 8*(1): http://journals.sfu.ca/thirdspace/index.php/journal/article/view/hoeflinger (accessed 21 November 2015).
hooks, b. (1989). Feminism and black women's studies. *Sage: A Scholarly Journal on Black Women, 6*(1), 54–6.
Isay, R. (1997). Remove gender identity disorder from the DSM. *Psychiatric News, 32*(22), 9.
Jauk, D. (2013). Gender violence revisited: Lessons from violent victimization of transgender identified individuals. *Sexualities, 16*(7), 807–25.
Jeffreys, S. (1994). The queer disappearance of lesbians: Sexuality in the academy. *Women's Studies International Forum, 17*(5), 459–72.
Jeffreys, S. (2000). 'Body art' and social status: Cutting, tattooing and piercing from a feminist perspective. *Feminism & Psychology, 10*(4), 409–29.
Jeffreys, S. (2005). *Beauty and misogyny: Harmful cultural practices in the West*. London: Routledge.
Jeffreys, S. (2012). The transgendering of children: Gender eugenics. *Women's Studies International Forum, 35*(5), 384–93.
Jeffreys, S. (2014a). *Gender hurts: A feminist analysis of the politics of transgenderism*. London: Routledge.
Jeffreys, S. (2014b). The politics of the toilet: A feminist response to the campaign to 'degender' a women's space. *Women's Studies International Forum, 45*, 42–51.
Jervis, L. (2006). Goodbye to feminism's generational divide. In M. Berger (Ed.), *We don't need another wave: Dispatches from the next generation of feminists* (pp. 13–18). Emeryville, CA: Seal Press.
Kitzinger, C. (1990). Resisting the discipline. In E. Burman (Ed.), *Feminists and psychological practice.* (pp. 119–36). London: SAGE Publications.
Kitzinger, C., & Perkins, R. (1993). *Changing our minds: Lesbian feminism and psychology.* New York: New York University Press.
Kłonkowska, A. M. (2014). Dual-unity or dichotomy? Androgyny and social construction of gender bipartition. *Creativity Studies, 7*(2), 118–34.
LeFrançois, B. A., & Diamond, S. (2014). Queering the sociology of diagnosis: Children and the constituting of 'mentally ill' subjects. *Journal of Critical Anti-Oppressive Social Inquiry, 1*(1), 39–61.
Lev, A. I. (2006). Disordering gender identity: Gender identity disorder in the *DSM-IV-TR*. *Journal of Psychology & Human Sexuality, 17*(3–4), 35–69.

Lombardo, E., & Verloo, M. (2009). Contentious citizenship: Feminist debates and practices and European challenges. *Feminist Review, 92*(1), 108–28.

Marilley, S. M. (1996). *Woman suffrage and the origins of liberal feminism in the United States, 1820–1920*. Boston, MA: Harvard University Press.

Millett, K. (2000). *Sexual politics*. Champaign: University of Illinois Press.

Money, J. (1975). Ablatio penis: Normal male infant sex-reassigned as a girl. *Archives of Sexual Behavior, 4*(1), 65–71.

Money, J. (1985). Gender: History, theory and usage of the term in sexology and its relationship to nature/nurture. *Journal of Sex & Marital Therapy, 11*(2), 71–9.

Money, J. (1986a). *Lovemaps: Clinical concepts of sexual/erotic health and pathology, paraphilia, and gender transposition in childhood, adolescence and maturity*. New York: Irvington Publishers.

Money, J. (1986b). *Venuses penuses: Sexology, sexosophy and exigency theory*. New York: Prometheus Books.

Money, J. (1991). The development of sexuality and eroticism in human kind. In M. Haug, P. F. Brain, & C. Aron (Eds.), *Heterotypical behaviour in man and animals* (pp. 127–66). Padstow: Chapman and Hall.

Money, J., & Ehrhardt, A. (1972). *Man and woman, boy and girl: Differentiation and dimorphism of gender identity from conception to maturity*. Oxford: Johns Hopkins University Press.

Money, J., & Tucker, P. (1975). *Sexual signatures: On being a man or a woman*. Oxford: Little, Brown.

Money, J., Hampson, J., & Hampson, J. (1957). Imprinting and the establishment of gender role. *A.M.A. Archives of Neurology & Psychiatry, 77*(3), 333–6.

Nicki, A. (2006). Women's spaces are not trans spaces: Maintaining boundaries of respect. In K. Scott-Dixon (Ed.), *Trans/feminist voices speak out* (pp. 154–60). Toronto: Sumach.

Norden, B. (1990). Campaign against pornography. *Feminist Review, 35*, 1–8.

Parker, I. (1998). Realism, relativism and critique in psychology. In I. Parker (Ed.), *Social constructionism, discourse and realism*. (pp. 1–10). London: SAGE Publications.

Penley, C., Shimizu, C., Miller-Young, M., & Taormino, T. (2013). Introduction: The politics of pleasure. In T. Taormino, C. Penley, C. Shimizu, & M. Miller-Young (Eds.), *The feminist porn book: The politics of producing pleasure* (pp. 9–22). New York: Feminist Press.

Raymond, J. (1979). *The transsexual empire*. London: Women's Press.

Raymond, J. (2006). Sappho by surgery: The transsexually constructed lesbian-feminist. In S. Stryker & S. Whittle (Eds.), *The transgender studies reader* (pp. 131–43). London: Routledge.

Rekers, G. A. (1977). Atypical gender development and psychosocial adjustment. *Journal of Applied Behavior Analysis, 10*(3), 559–71.

Riddell, C. (2006). Divided sisterhood: A critical review of Janice Raymond's The Transsexual Empire. In S. Stryker & S. Whittle (Eds.), *The transgender studies reader* (pp. 144–58). New York: Routledge.

Roberts, A. L., Rosario, M., Corliss, H. L., Koenen, K. C., & Austin, S. B. (2012). Childhood gender nonconformity: A risk indicator for childhood abuse and posttraumatic stress in youth. *Pediatrics, 129*(3), 410–17.

Roberts, M. (2013). TransGriot: Gloria Steinem-Trans ally?: http://transgriot.blogspot.ca/2013/10/gloria-steinem-trans-ally.html (accessed 21 November 2015).

Rogers, L. J. (1983). Hormonal theories for sex differences – politics disguised as science: A reply to DeBold and Luria. *Sex Roles, 9*(11), 1109–13.

Salamon, G. (2008). Transfeminism and the future of gender. In J. Wallach Scott (Ed.), *Women's studies on the edge* (pp. 115–29). London: Duke University Press.

Sayers, J. (1982). *Biological politics: Feminist and anti-feminist perspectives*. London: Tavistock.

Serano, J. (2012). Reclaiming femininity. In A. Enke (Ed.), *Transfeminist perspectives: In and beyond transgender and gender studies*. (pp. 170–83). Philadelphia, PA: Temple University Press.

Shields, S. (1982). The variability hypothesis: The history of a biological model of sex differences in intelligence. *Signs*, 7(4), 769–97.

Showalter, E. (1987). *The female malady: Women, madness and English culture, 1830–1980*. London: Virago Press.

Smith, A. (2005). Native American feminism, sovereignty, and social change. *Feminist Studies*, *31*(1), 116–32.

Sorisio, C. (2003). A tale of two feminisms: Power and victimization in contemporary feminist debate. In L. Heywood & J. Drake (Eds.), *Third wave agenda: Being feminist, doing feminism* (pp. 134–49). Minneapolis: University of Minnesota Press.

Steinem, G. (2013). Op-ed: On working together over time: http://www.advocate.com/commentary/2013/10/02/op-ed-working-together-over-time (accessed 21 November 2015).

Stevens, P. E., & Hall, J. M. (1991). A critical historical analysis of the medical construction of lesbianism. *International Journal of Health Services*, *21*(2), 291–307.

Stimpson, C. R. (1974). The androgyne and the homosexual. *Women's Studies*, *2*(2), 237.

Stoller, R. J. (1974). *Sex and gender: The development of masculinity and femininity*. London: Karnac Books.

Stryker, S. (2007). Transgender feminism: Queering the woman question. In S. Gillis, G. Howie, & R. Munford (Eds.), *Third wave feminism: A critical exploration* (pp. 59–70). London: Palgrave Macmillan.

Stryker, S. (2013). Lesbian generations: Transsexual . . . lesbian . . . feminist. *Feminist Studies*, *39*(2), 375–83.

Stryker, S. & Whittle, S. (2013). *The transgender studies reader*. London: Routledge.

Sweeney, B. (2004). Trans-ending women's rights: The politics of trans-inclusion in the age of gender. *Women's Studies International Forum*, *27*(1), 75–88.

Szasz, T. (2007). *The medicalization of everyday life*. New York: Syracuse University Press.

Tosh, J. (2011). 'Zuck off!' A commentary on the protest against Ken Zucker and his 'treatment' of childhood gender identity disorder. *Psychology of Women Section Review*, *13*(1), 10–16.

Tosh, J. (2013a). 'Rape is . . . ': A feminist analysis of the production and transformation of rape discourses (Unpublished PhD thesis). Manchester Metropolitan University, Manchester, UK.

Tosh, J. (2013b). The (in)visibility of childhood sexual abuse: Psychiatric theorizing of transgenderism and intersexuality. *Intersectionalities: A Global Journal of Social Work Analysis, Research, Polity, and Practice*, *2*(1), 71–87.

Tosh, J., & Carson, K. (in press). The desire to be normal? A discursive and intersectional analysis of 'penetration disorder'. *Intersectionalities: A Global Journal of Social Work Analysis, Research, Polity, and Practice*.

Trebilcot, J. (1977). Two forms of androgynism. In M. Vetterling-Braggin, F. Ellison, & J. English (Eds.), *Feminism and philosophy* (pp. 70–78). Totowa, NJ: Rowman & Littlefield.

Ussher, J. (1990). Choosing psychology or not throwing the baby out with the bath water. In E. Burman (Ed.), *Feminists and psychological practice* (pp. 47–61). London: SAGE Publications.

Vint, S. (2007). The new backlash: Popular culture's 'marriage' with feminism, or love is all you need. *Journal of Popular Film and Television, 34*(4), 160–69.

Walker, R. (1992). How does a supermodel do feminism? An interview with Veronica Webb. In R. Walker (Ed.), *To be real: Telling the truth and changing the face of feminism* (pp. 209–18). New York: Anchor House.

Warren, M. (1982). Is androgyny the answer to sexual stereotyping? In M. Vetterling-Braggin (Ed.), *Femininity, masculinity, and androgyny.* (pp. 170–86). Totowa, NJ: Rowman & Littlefield.

Warren, M. (1985). *Gendercide: The implications of sex selection.* Totowa, NJ: Rowman & Littlefield.

Weisstein, N. (1971). Psychology constructs the female: or the fantasy life of the male psychologist (with some attention to the fantasies of his friends, the male biologist and the male anthropologist). *Journal of Social Education, 35,* 362–73.

Weisstein, N. (2003). Adventures of a women in science. In D. Freedman & O. Frey (Eds.), *Autobiographical writing across the disciplines: A reader.* (pp. 397–416). Durham, NC: Duke University Press.

White, M. S. (1979). Measuring androgyny in adulthood. *Psychology of Women Quarterly, 3*(3), 293–307.

Wiggins, J. S., & Holzmuller, A. (1981). Further evidence on androgyny and interpersonal flexibility. *Journal of Research in Personality, 15*(1), 67–80.

Wilkinson, S. (1997). Prioritizing the political: Feminist psychology. In T. Ibanez & L. Iniguez (Eds.), *Critical social psychology* (pp. 178–94). London: SAGE Publications.

Willis, E. (1984). Radical feminism and feminist radicalism. *Social Text, 9*, 91–118.

Winters, K. (2009). *Gender madness in American psychiatry: Essays from the struggle for dignity.* Dillon, CO: BookSurge Publishing.

Wyss, S. (2004). 'This was my hell': The violence experienced by gender non-conforming youth in US high schools. *International Journal of Qualitative Studies in Education, 17*(5), 709–730.

Yudkin, M. (1978). Transsexualism and women: A critical perspective. *Feminist Studies, 4*(3), 97–106.

Yuval-Davis, N. (1997). *Gender and nation.* London: SAGE Publications.

Zucker, K. J., & Kuksis, M. (1990). Gender dysphoria and sexual abuse: A case report. *Child Abuse & Neglect, 14*(2), 281–3.

Zuger, B. (1966). Effeminate behavior present in boys from early childhood. *The Journal of Pediatrics, 69*(6), 1098–107.

Chapter 5

Transgender constructions of psychiatry and feminism

In Chapters 2 and 3, I showed how psychiatry frames femininity and gender nonconformity as pathological in different ways. I also discussed how feminine transgender individuals are subjected to pathologization based on both their expression of femininity and for their transgender identities. In Chapter 4, I examined how feminism added to this hostile environment, by drawing on psychological discourse and supporting it through similar feminist theories of transsexualism. In this chapter, I begin to outline the diverse responses to psychiatry and feminism from transgender perspectives. By this, I mean perspectives that foreground transgender issues and voices, such as transgender and gender-nonconforming academics, activists and allies, rather than those who study transgender people. Again, this is not an ultimate definition of the term 'transgender perspectives', nor am I implying that all those discussed identify as transgender, simply that they foreground trans issues and form part of a counter-narrative to those described in Chapters 3 and 4. I first address responses to psychiatry and psychology, which includes a range of arguments including support for the diagnoses as enabling access to medical interventions (Lev, 2006; Winters, 2009), and calls for the depathologization of trans people (International Network for Trans Pathologization, n.d.). In describing transgender responses to feminism, there is a range of diverse viewpoints, from feminism as oppressive (Green, 2006) to trans activism being considered feminist 'at its core' (Serano, 2009a). I examine how these texts construct the disciplines and institutions that have had the authority in defining gender conformity and nonconformity for many decades. I analyse this reverse discourse, defined by Foucault (1979) as a discourse that is produced when a marginalized group begins 'to speak on its own behalf . . . often in the same vocabulary, using the same categories by which it was medically disqualified' (p. 101). This can also be thought of as a 'looping effect', where groups can be influenced by how they are constructed, but they can also influence those constructions: 'People classified in a certain way tend to conform to or grow into the ways they are described; but they also evolve in their own ways, so that the classifications and descriptions have to be constantly revised' (Hacking, 1995, p. 21). Therefore, I examine the push back against pathologizing and fetishizing narratives, where those who have been labelled by psychiatry and feminism interject new constructions (and reconstructions), and define themselves.

Transgender

> We are all familiar with the word 'transcendent' as in transcendental meditation or transcendent experience, but to use it as a noun rather than as an adjective is a little unusual. Actually, the word comes from the Latin *trans* – meaning over or across, and *scendere* – to climb. Thus a transcendent is a person who climbs over and goes beyond some sort of limitation or barrier.
>
> (Prince, 2006a [1978], p. 39)

Virginia Prince is acknowledged as introducing the term 'transgenderist' in her 1978 article 'The "transcendents" of "trans" people' (Ekins & King, 2006; Stryker, 2009). Prince's influential works occupy a contradictory space within trans history: some frame her as a pioneer of transgender activism and theory and 'rightfully remembered, commended and honored' (Stryker, 2006, p. xi), and as a 'catalyst' for change (MacKenzie, 1994, p. 159), but she was also criticized for her perspective on transsexual people, her lack of consideration of transgender men, as well as being described as homophobic and sexist (Bullough, 2008; Ekins & King, 2006; MacKenzie, 1994). While Prince challenged the pathologization of cross-dressing individuals (Bruce, 2005 [1967]),[1] and set up much-needed spaces of support for cross-dressing communities at a time when such spaces were not available (such as creating and distributing the magazine *Transvestia* at great personal risk when it was illegal to do so at the time), her writing on transsexual identities were deeply problematic, as she often argued against body-modification surgery, stereotyped transsexual people as sex workers (e.g. 'many of them were and remain prostitutes', Prince, 2006a [1978], p. 44), and positioned them (much like feminism) as 'naive' individuals who misunderstood their own gender and bodies.

Prince originally defined the term 'transgender' as 'people who have adopted the exterior manifestations of the opposite sex on a full-time basis but without surgical intervention. Thus they are what may rightly be termed "male women"' (Prince, 2006a [1978], p. 43). Transgenderists were differentiated from cross-dressing individuals through their living as another gender, and from transsexual individuals through their lack of surgical intervention. The term has since adopted numerous additional meanings beyond its original proposed by Prince, including as a term that exists outside of the gender binary, as well as to refer to a gender-nonconforming (or 'pan-gender') community brought together for the purposes of politics and social justice (Feinberg, 1992; Vartabedian, 2014). As a result, it is often referred to as an 'umbrella' term that is inclusive of many identities, communities and individuals (Hill, 2012), although Prince asserted that her term had been 'hi-jacked' (Ekins & King, 2006). Serano defined it as follows:

> While the word originally had a more narrow definition, since the 1990s it has been used primarily as an umbrella term to describe those who defy societal expectations and assumptions regarding femaleness and maleness;

> this includes people who are transsexual (those who live as members of the sex other than the one they were assigned at birth), intersex (those who are born with reproductive or sexual anatomy that does not fit the typical definitions of female or male), and genderqueer (those who [identify] outside of the male/female binary), as well as those whose gender expression differs from their anatomical or perceived sex (including cross-dressers, drag performers, masculine women, feminine men, and so on).
>
> (Serano, 2009a, p. 25)

However, it is also described as 'one of the most confusing and misunderstood words in the English language', that changes often within a context where words can quickly become outdated or offensive (Serano, 2009a, p. 25). Even this definition provided by Serano is problematic, as many intersex individuals do not identify as transgender and oppose the subsuming of intersex people into the transgender category (OII Australia, 2011), as do some transsexual people (Hill, 2012). Others consider the term temporary, reflecting only their transition from one gender to another:

> Transgendered or transsexual to me . . . it was a transition phase for me for being a male to a woman . . . I don't even equate myself as a transsexual. I mean I know I am, but . . . my primary definition of myself is a woman, to be honest with you. It's quite simple. I think transgendered or transsexual is exactly what it means: trans meaning 'in between' or moving between sexes. I've passed that now.
>
> (Hill, 2012, p. 33)

Serano (2009a) herself notes that use of the term potentially masks the intersections of multiple forms of oppression related to gender. Others have rejected the framing of trans people as 'transcendent', showing that for many the desire to live as another gender is not to challenge gender binaries or for social justice, but to participate in 'normal' life as a man or woman (Namaste, 2000). Therefore, while the term 'transgender' is frequently used and is a useful term in some contexts, it has a problematic beginning and continues to be contested when applied too broadly.

For some, the term has come to represent a particular kind of institutionalized label that refers specifically to a US context (Valentine, 2007; Vartabedian, 2014), or as one of Hill's (2012) interviewees (Suzy) described it, a 'big transgender fad': 'Suzy's take on this issue reflected the narratives from several other respondents. Her narrative was simply this: transgender was a US identity, coined by a US transgenderist (Ms. Prince); it potentially erased her distinct Canadian transsexual experience . . . .' (p. 34). There have also been problems when using it as an 'umbrella' term for those who do not identify with it, or know of it, due to alternative concepts and gender experiences in other cultures beyond North America. In other words, as gender identity intersects with other personal identities and social categories, such as race and class (Hill, 2012), it can be problematic to apply a predominantly US term to a range of cultures. For example, Vartabedian's (2014) work with *travestis* – a term commonly used in Brazil and Latin America to refer to a highly marginalized (and often stigmatized) group – highlights the nuanced differences between many different forms of gender nonconformity that can be lost in the use of 'transgender' as a universal category. Based on her interviews, Vartabedian defines *travestis* thus: 'They seek to be *like* women and *look like* women . . . However, they are aware that they will never be women and they do not intend to be' (Vartabedian, 2014, pp. 283–4). She also notes how they do not fit the definition of drag queens or cross-dressers, as they live as women and pursue body modifications. As one of her interviewees, Samanta, stated, 'I am not a woman . . . I like that men see me as a *travesti* in the body of a pretty woman' (p. 283).

Vartabedian (2014) noted a discomfort in applying the term 'transgender' to her interviewees, as often they had not heard of it, or did not feel that it applied to them. She also drew on Bento's argument that the use of other more institutionalized terms (such as the medical term of 'transsexual') 'cleans and disinfects a category from the street' (Bento, 2008, p. 12), and represents a kind of 'conceptual colonialism' where a term from one context is applied and 'imported' into another often without consideration of the differing cultures, lived realities and subjectivities of those involved (Vartabedian, 2014, p. 293); a criticism that is mirrored by those who identify as two-spirited in Aboriginal communities and the appropriation of the concept in non-Aboriginal queer spaces (Cameron, 2005).

Therefore, like feminism, there are tensions and contradictions within transgender perspectives, as well as those who continue to be marginalized even within the movement that claims to represent them. Not everyone identifies with 'transgender', with the terms used to describe personal identities spanning non-binary, genderqueer, gender creative, gender nonconforming, and more to refer to those who do not identify with the gender that was assigned (or incorrectly assumed) at birth. To address these contradictions, some call for solidarity while also celebrating diversity (Winters, 2009). I use the term 'transgender' to refer to those whose body does not align with their gender identity, or with societal expectations of gender. This definition does not, however, override or define individuals; it is simply my explanation for my use of the term in this book. Consequently, there will be those who fit this definition but who use different words to describe their own personal identity, in which case my definition is best only applied to this book. It is also important to note that I only use the term 'transsexual' in this chapter. This is because it is in the context of those who use the term to define themselves. Due to the pathologizing psychiatric label of 'transsexualism' (APA, 1980) that is the focus of analysis in other chapters, I only use the term when it will not be mistaken for, or add to, pathologization. Like Vartabedian (2014) argues, these terms can be understood as fluid and context dependent, with more value being given to self-identifications over universal definitions.

Psychology and psychiatry

The use of the word 'transgender' is often framed as a non-medical alternative to pathologizing diagnostic labels. However, its initial coinage was influenced and shaped by some of the problematic psychological concepts discussed in Chapter 3. Prince was highly influenced by the work of John Money, which was based on his attempts to change the gender of intersex children through surgical and psychological means (see Chapter 3). Though such work has since been highly criticized, its influence in feminism and queer studies continued. Prince's uptake of his work shows the extensive influence that psychological discourse had in defining gender, being absorbed into spaces often deemed critical. For example, Prince draws on Money's conceptualization of gender and sex as a combination of anatomy ('sex'), psychology ('gender identity') and environment ('gender role'). However, she replaced Money's concept of 'gender identity' with the psychoanalytic idea of 'sexual object choice',[2] and therefore reframed or reinterpreted Money's theory as a combination of anatomy, sexuality and gender role. She theorized these three dimensions as continuums with 'hermaphroditism',[3] bisexuality, and androgyny as the mid-points (Prince, 2006a [1978]). As a consequence, like feminism, she disregarded Money's work on the influence of biology on behaviour and the inflexibility of gender after a short period of 'malleability' in childhood.

When defining gender in 'The "transcendents" of "trans" people', Prince used the following statement, attributed to Money:

> A gender role is not established at birth but is built up through experiences encountered and transacted, through casual and unplanned learning and through explicit instruction and inclination . . . a gender role is established in much the same way as a native language.
>
> (Prince 2006a [1978], p. 40)

She then concluded, as many others did also, 'Sex you are born with and gender you acquire . . . ' (p. 40). However she extended Money's definition of gender beyond its original meaning. In the statement, Money refers to gender role, not gender identity – the latter being something that Money considered more difficult to change. She also repeated the influential hierarchy within psychiatry that there were 'true' or 'classic' transsexuals that needed surgery and the rest were not to be trusted in their motivations for body modifications. Consequently, she opposed terms such as Fisk's (1973) 'gender dysphoria' due to its inclusiveness and the resulting increase in availability of medical procedures (Prince, 2006b [1978]).

However, Money's influence went beyond the underlying definition of gender and sex that Prince promoted; she also mirrored his dedication to the creation of labels to define people based on a combination of Latin and Greek. While Money introduced many diagnostic labels regarding sexual 'pathology' (Money, 1986), including the word 'paraphilia' which means 'abnormal' ('para') 'love' ('philia'), Prince introduced 'femmiphilia' to refer to cross-dressing:

> But today the word transvestite is used indiscriminately so that all it says is that someone is crossdressing. In short it says what he DOES, not what he IS. So I have coined the word 'femmiphilia' for the *condition* and 'femmiphile' for the individual. It comes from the combination of the Latin femina for woman or feminine and Greek philia for love and it therefore means, 'lover of the feminine'.
>
> (Prince, 2006a [1978], pp. 42–3, my emphasis)

Prince's definition as combining 'love' ('philia') with women or femininity ('femina') seems remarkably similar to Blanchard's (1989) highly contested 'autogynephilia', meaning 'love of oneself as a woman' (see Chapter 3). Drawing on psychological discourse, and using similar methods to define (and categorize) had the potential to continue to pathologize gender nonconformists. It also had the potential to further fetishize cross-dressing through its similarity to the description and definitions of paraphilias, and thus to reinforce it as a 'perversion'. This is evident in the term's uptake within clinical literature that described 'the clinical syndromes of femmiphilic transvestism' as sexual 'disorders' in need of 'treatment' (e.g. Buhrich, 1978; Buhrich & McConaghy, 1977; Croughan et al., 1981; Epstein, 1993).

These problematic assumptions – that gender was 'acquired' and that there was only a small minority of 'true' transsexuals – stemmed from a pervasive influence from pathologizing discourse and the reinterpretation of it. By replacing gender identity with 'sexual object choice', Prince negated the aspect of Money's work that described a biologically influenced experience of gender that became permanent early in childhood. In excluding this piece of Money's theory, Prince framed gender much like many feminists did, as fluid and androgynous. As a result, she minimized and underestimated the embodied, subjective and materiality of gender identity and the potential for distress when it is incongruent with the physical body.

Beyond discourse: Embodied gender and distress

> . . . transsexuality is embodied, and any attempt to make sense of transition must give full weight to the issue.
>
> (Connell, 2012, p. 866)

In a move away from social-constructionist accounts of gender, other trans perspectives described the importance of acknowledging the pain and distress that was felt with gender dysphoria. While those less supportive of transsexual individuals dismissed this distress too easily, such as Prince's (2006b [1978]) questioning of disclosures of suicidal thoughts, and the DSM's minimizing of 'profound' (Serano, 2009a, p. 123) or 'debilitating distress' as 'discomfort' (Winters, 2009, p. 23), others highlighted that the focus of intervention and a diagnostic label should be distress, not gender nonconformity (Winters, 2006, 2009). Therefore, it was argued that gender-nonconforming or transgender identities should not be pathologized. This included a move away from constructions of gender nonconformity as a 'perversion' based on sexual pleasure to an emphasis on emotional pain as the reason for physical changes and for changing from a gender that had been assigned by others. As one of Veale, Clarke and Lomax's survey respondents stated when challenging the diagnosis of autogynephilia: 'Transitioning is a horribly painful thing. I've lost friends, good friends, family, have been thrown on the street by my family. Why would someone go through that for a sexual thrill?' (Veale, Clarke & Lomax, 2011, p. 6).

In addition to the distress experienced due to an internal incongruence between gender identity and physical bodies, others have highlighted how there is also distress as a result of living in a society that assumes there are only two genders (male/female, man/woman), and having to pretend you are a gender that you are not (Serano, 2009b). Some argued that due to the distress having a social cause, gender identity disorder did not qualify as a 'mental illness' (Bartlett, Vasey & Bukowski, 2000; Hegarty, 2009).[4] This socially induced distress was often attributed to psychological and psychiatric discourse, the promotion of a wide range of diagnostic labels that were applied to gender nonconformists, and therapies that aimed to 'prevent transsexualism' (see Chapter 3). As Winters (2009) stated, 'These labels reinforce social stigma of madness and perversion for all gender variant people' (p. 3). While this kind of distress included individual experiences of stigma and discrimination (Lev, 2006), it also involved sanism as a form of oppression that resulted from being labelled as 'mentally ill' (Birnbaum, 1960; Perlin, 1992). While trans perspectives often describe these consequences and are critical of the psy-professions, cross-over between accounts of cisgenderism and transphobia with those of sanism, mad studies, or psychiatric survivor movements are rare. This is a compelling potential collaboration for challenges to the pathologization of trans people as well as the harms enforced upon many under the name of 'therapy' (see Chapter 1).

Unfortunately, despite criticism, the revised *DSM-5* (APA, 2013) did not further emphasize distress. While the name 'gender dysphoria' means 'abnormal distress' related to gender, the criteria continued to pathologize gender nonconformity, particularly in behaviours expressed in childhood (Tosh, 2014; Winters, 2011). As Winters (2011) stated, 'The workgroup has not reflected these principles in the diagnostic criteria for Gender Dysphoria. They retain much of the flawed language from the *DSM-IV*' (para. 4). The criteria for 'gender dysphoria' in children still contained 'a strong preference for the toys, games, or activities stereotypically used or engaged in by the other gender', as well as 'a strong desire for the primary and/or secondary sex characteristics that match one's experienced gender' (APA, 2013, p. 452), and consequently continued to pathologize gender nonconformity based on stereotypical ideas of gender (Langer & Martin, 2004; Lev, 2006), a notable constant in psychological and psychiatric discourse (Ansara & Hegarty, 2012).

The distress criterion, which states that an individual is distressed by their behaviour or experiences significant social or occupational impairment, is required for all diagnoses as a result of the removal of homosexuality from the DSM in the 1970s (Drescher, 2009). However, psychiatrists have encouraged therapists to intervene even when trans children do not experience distress (Winters, 2009). One argument given for this is that the social exclusion that trans people can face is evidence of 'impairment', which then opens the door for psychiatric treatment, even if the individual is not distressed by their gender identity. As Winters (2009) explained, children can fit this description when their peers victimize them *and* when they do not. This is because positive relationships with peers of the same gender identity are disregarded by psychiatric perspectives that view them as friendships with those of the 'opposite sex'.

Therefore, while trans perspectives have campaigned to highlight the issue of gendered distress, psychology and psychiatry have minimized its role, focusing more often on the distress caused by social ostracism (Zucker, 1999), dismissing, then, the distress of 'constantly [pretending] to be a member of a gender with which they do not identify' (Serano, 2009b, p. 117). The diagnosis and psychiatric systems in place to support trans people (particularly children), then, are not adequately addressing the primary concern or issue: that of emotional distress that results from an incongruence between gender identity and physical body. What it does address, especially in relation to the childhood diagnosis, is the distress experienced by oppression, described as 'social ostracism' and 'bullying'. Rather than prevent or stop such victimization, conversion therapy aims to change the gender-nonconforming child, not the environment, culture, or the behaviour of those who victimize others. The reasoning for this, it is argued, is that the child 'causes' the social ostracism by their behaviour, and thus changing their behaviour stops the victimization. For example, Zucker (2006) argued that 'When children with GID are socially ostracized by their peers, *it is their overt behavior that elicits negative reactions*, not an abstract label' (p. 548, my emphasis), or, as Rekers (1977) stated, 'Although the peer group's intolerance and rejection is morally wrong, the most benevolent and direct strategy is to change the child's individual behaviour to alleviate his suffering' (p. 561). Both perspectives have been highly criticized (Burke, 1996; Hird, 2003; Langer & Martin, 2004; Lev, 2006; Pickstone-Taylor, 2003; Pyne, 2014; Spiegel, 2008; Tosh, 2011; Wren, 2002) and this is why challenging gender-reparative or conversion therapies for children have been a key site of trans activism (InYourFace, 1996; Tosh, in press).

The distress felt by trans people remains a key site for awareness and intervention, as support is greatly needed. This is again well documented in terms of high suicide risk, depression and anxiety (Clements-Nolle, Marx & Katz, 2006; Goldblum et al., 2012; Haas, Rodgers & Herman, 2014). Support for the emotional consequences of living in a cisgender society is also needed, in addition to medical services to address identity/body incongruence. Promoting these needs and experiences of distress, as well as the problems with current approaches within psychology and psychiatry, challenged those theories that posited that gender was fluid, easily changed and culturally constructed. The dominance of those models, however, within psychology, psychiatry, feminism and queer perspectives was a barrier to the acknowledgement of the distress trans people could experience, as well as minimizing or dismissing the need for potentially life-saving body-modification procedures (Grant et al., 2010, p. 10). Therefore, while there are many problems with the diagnoses of transsexualism (APA, 1980) and gender dysphoria (APA, 2013), not least that they pathologize a wide range of people far beyond those from transgender and gender nonconformity communities, they did create previously non-existent avenues for treatment (Lev, 2006).

Beyond discourse: Structural oppression

> For the portion of the trans community who is transsexual and painfully distressed by physical sex characteristics or birth-assigned gender role (a distress known as gender dysphoria), access to hormonal or surgical transition procedures is a matter of medical necessity.
>
> (Winters, 2009, p. 3)

As Winters (2009) highlighted, diagnoses regarding transgender and gender-nonconforming people have divided both those from within the trans community as well as professionals providing services. For instance, Prince (2006b [1978]) was outspoken on her views regarding body-modification procedures. She considered 90–95 per cent of transsexual people to be 'pseudotranssexuals', who should not be recommended for surgery or hormones (Prince, 2006b [1978], p. 35). She also minimized the need for such surgery, by suggesting that this majority 'could be just as happy and comfortable being transgenderists and saving a lot of money . . . ' (Prince, 2006a [1978], p. 45). Prince only considered 'inadequate' men who were considered sexually 'unsuccessful' with women and as 'compensating' by engaging in homosexual activities eligible for surgery, and argued that the very idea of surgery was contagious among transsexual people, framing it as a 'communicable disease' (Prince, 2006b [1978], p. 36). This problematic framing of body-modification procedures as unnecessary has been thoroughly challenged since (Burrill & Fredland, 2012; Cox, 2009; Shield, 2006; Stroumsa, 2014).

Trans individuals and allies have also challenged some of the myths and assumptions about such treatments. For example, in Caplan's (2011) article, 'Psychiatric diagnosis arbiters decide how boys vs. girls should act and feel', she takes a position that is common in feminist and antipsychiatry or critical psychology perspectives, that of questioning the authority and power of the medical and psychiatric industries. In doing so, she frames trans children as 'victims' of a gendered society, who are exploited by a capitalist-driven medical system. This is a common feminist reading of medical procedures related to gender, such as cosmetic surgeries for the 'perfect' genitalia or breast augmentation for gender-conforming women who aspire to an 'ideal' of a female body (whatever that may be) (Braun, 2005; Tiefer, 2008). It also mirrors Prince's writings that claim doctors are 'unable or unwilling' and therefore certify surgeries due to a perception that there is no alternative (2006a [1978], p. 45). The decision to view trans people as 'victims' of their surgery highlights several misconceptions, which Winters and others address (e.g. Garner, 2014; Lev, 2006). For example, rather than these procedures being 'forced' onto trans children (like those surgeries and treatments that are performed on intersex children without consent, see Alexander, 1997; Ehrenreich & Barr, 2005; Hupf Jr, 2014), in reality, trans individuals struggle to get the support and procedures they need. For example, Garner (2014) completed a comparative analysis of gender-conforming men and transsexual men who were seeking breast/'breast' reduction surgery. Garner (2014) noted that the assumption that some bodies are 'natural' and others are 'disordered' means that those who are viewed as 'normal' face fewer barriers to these surgical procedures than those who are labelled as 'mentally ill'. Therefore, rather than being compared to non-consensual surgery, such as the experiences of intersex individuals, or the desire for cosmetic surgery due to societal pressures on young women for the 'perfect' body, the case is more similar to restricted access to abortion services (Fegan & Rebouche, 2003; Jacobson & Royer, 2011; King & Husting, 2003; Smyth, 2002) and other forms of medical treatment that are sought after but denied due to structural forms of oppression within medical systems, that reflect underlying assumptions about normative gender.

As outlined in Chapter 3, there can be a wide range of criteria that transgender and gender-nonconforming people need to overcome if they are to be considered for surgery, which can include strict policies such as living for a year as another gender, as well as less formalized policies such as how 'passable' and 'attractive' they would be as a man or women based on the judgements made by medical professionals (Serano, 2009b). While a diagnosis of 'gender dysphoria' can act like an 'admission ticket' to services, it does not guarantee surgery or hormones; thus it can exclude those it is designed to support despite labelling many people beyond the trans and gender-nonconforming communities as 'mentally ill' (Lev, 2006). The many writings about the difficulties of accessing medical procedures well illustrates that these surgeries are highly unlikely to be an example of 'forced' medical treatment (Burrill & Fredland, 2012; Garner, 2014; Shield, 2006; Snelgrove et al., 2012; Sperber, Landers & Lawrence, 2005; Stroumsa, 2014).

Similarly, Winters explains that surgical interventions are not applied to transgender and gender-nonconforming children. For children, 'Transition means simply creating an environment where gender-variant or transcendent children may safely express their inner sense of gender identity without shame or fear' (Winters, 2009, p. 20). She goes on to state that hormonal interventions to delay puberty would be introduced later, in some cases, so as to prevent the emotional distress related to bodily changes that are incongruent with gender identity as well as to prevent additional surgeries that would be required to undo such changes. This description of interventions as preventing or ending emotional distress related to gender is in stark contrast to those who frame the medical intervention as oppressive and harmful, or those who dismiss or minimize the distress in general. It also shows a fundamental difference in conceptualizations of gender, as Winters draws on the concept of an 'inner' 'gender identity' rather than the social and cultural (external/public) gender role. Therefore, this moves away from those theories promoted by feminist and queer scholars, but instead focuses on the aspect most often neglected in those writings. It also moves away from Money's conceptualization, as Winters (2009) and others (e.g. Ehrensaft, 2012; Hill et al., 2010; Lev, 2013; Wren, 2002) do not frame the identity as malleable, nor do they view it appropriate or ethical to try to change it. Therefore, while the emphasis on distress challenged socially constructed notions of gender as fluid and changeable, perspectives that highlighted the need for surgery and the difficulty in accessing it, challenged the medical systems and structural oppression that trans people face.

'Pseudoscientific rubbish'

While some activists and theorists drew on psychology, others framed psychological and psychiatric theories of trans and gender-nonconforming people as unscientific and incorrect. This was in addition to academics who acknowledged the politics involved in the science of psychiatric classification (Moser, 2008). These trans perspectives undermined the positioning of the professions as 'science' and authoritative voices on the topic of transgender people, positioning them, not as scientists or therapists, but as 'gatekeepers' (Serano, 2009a). For example, in Veale, Clarke and Lomax's (2011) research that looked at transsexual responses to Blanchard's (1989) 'autogynephilia' concept, one respondent described the theory as 'pseudoscientific rubbish' (p. 5); a sentiment that has been repeated in numerous texts (Conway, 2003; Serano, 2010). Psychiatry and psychology have also been framed as out-dated and representing a particularly conservative viewpoint on gender, such as Winter's (2009) description of the gender identity disorder diagnostic criteria as 'archaic' (p. 23).

Much like feminists who challenged psychology for its poor representation of women, so too have trans individuals and allies examined and criticized the profession for failing to understand their experiences or represent them in a way that seems accurate or helpful. For example, psychology and psychiatry most often misgender individuals, describing them in academic texts by their assigned sex at birth rather than the gender they identify with (Ansara & Hegarty, 2012). The autogynephilia theory in particular has been framed as 'incorrect, offensive, and potentially politically damaging to a marginalized group' (Veale, Clarke & Lomax, 2011, p. 3). Many have stated that the claim that there is a sexual and erotic motivation for body modification surgery for 'most' transsexual people (e.g. Blanchard, 2005; Lawrence, 2004) does not reflect their experience. Most state that transition is related to their gender identity not their sexuality (Doorn, 1997; Veale et al., 2011; Wyndzen, 2003). Serano (2008) explained that many transgender and gender-nonconforming people reject the concept

> . . . because such theories naively conflate sexual orientation with gender expression, gender identity, and sex embodiment in a way that contradicts our personal life experiences and that is inconsistent with the vast diversity of trans women that exist. In fact, most trans critiques of autogynephilia center on the fact that this scientifically unsubstantiated theory forces all trans women into one of two rigid categories, nonconsensually defines us in ways that contradict our own personal sense of selves . . . .
>
> (Serano, 2008, p. 492)

Others rejected this pathologizing perspective, but preferred to acknowledge that for some individuals there may be a sexual component and that to disallow such narratives '[creates] a hierarchy between "real" and "false" desires for surgeries or body modification – the real desire constructed as coming from identity claims and the false desire coming from paraphilia' (Baril & Trevenen, 2014, p. 392). Consequently, trans academics, activists and allies navigate the difficult terrain of voicing a legitimate validation of sexuality and gender identity in body modification, while simultaneously trying to avoid the fetishizing and pathologizing discourse that has framed cross-dressing and transgender people as 'perverse' for well over a century. However, this remains an area with diverse perspectives within transgender communities, as some oppose the association of transgender identities or body modification with sexuality entirely.

Trans individuals and allies have criticized the eroticized concept that is promoted by psychiatry, arguing that it is sexist, cisgenderist and homophobic (Baril & Trevenen, 2014; Buckwalter, 2001; Conway, 2003; Serano, 2009a). They have also asserted that the division between transitions based on gender identity and those on sexuality potentially continues psychiatry's division between 'true' transsexuals and 'pseudotranssexuals', or 'primary' and 'secondary' transsexuals (Baril & Trevenen, 2014; Prince, 2006b [1978]; Serano, 2009a), as prior criteria for surgery has included rejecting those with a prior diagnosis of transvestism on the basis that it was a paraphilia and not an identity disorder (Lev, 2006). While Lawrence (2004) argues that body-modification procedures are appropriate for a diagnosis of autogynephilia, the historical constructions of gender nonconformity as perverse, the demonizing of paraphilias (Douard, 2007), and the already difficult barriers that people face to access services, makes those sceptical of psychiatry even less confident in the use of this concept. This has resulted in real concerns about further reducing access to medical support. As Baril and Trevenen stated, ' . . . we believe that they are still rooted in pathological conceptions of sexuality and that they simplify the complexities that Serano points to' (Baril & Trevenen, 2014, p. 401). Despite this wealth of criticism and concern, the concept of autogynephilia is included in the DSM (APA, 2000, 2013), and those that disagree with it have been labelled as 'liars' (see Chapter 3). Therefore, while trans perspectives position psychiatry as 'unscientific' and 'rubbish', psychiatry positions trans people as unknowing and untrustworthy (Serano, 2008).

Feminism

Feminist perspectives produced several problematic narratives regarding gender nonconformity and body modification. These included the theory that gender was fluid and changeable, based on an underlying definition borrowed from psychology. It also positioned transgender and transsexual women as 'men', and rejected the possibility that anyone other than those assigned female at birth could be women (see Chapter 4). While some feminist theorists took this negative stance much farther, such as to claim that transsexual body modification was a form of rape against non-transsexual women (Raymond, 1979), there were some parallels to both of these problematic claims within early transgender theory. For instance, Prince (2006b [1978]) referred to transsexual women as embracing 'pseudo-femaleness', much like radical feminist Daly (1990 [1978]), who was writing at the same time, used the term 'pseudofemale'. This stemmed from a fundamental belief that it was not possible to 'change sex', and that surgery could not address the lived experience of being a woman, an argument that featured both in feminist and early trans perspectives:

> Part of the so-called transsexual sees womanhood as a condition impossible to attain unless one has a vagina. Ergo, have the penis and testicles removed, an orifice constructed and PRESTO, one is now a 'woman'. Not so! Womanhood is a gender phenomenon not a sexual one and moreover *it must be learned by living* . . . The only possible route to such an attainment is personal experience and social acceptance and that is a long, hard trip.
>
> (Prince, 2006b [1978], p. 34, my emphasis)

Prince was influenced by both psychology and feminism (Ekins & King, 2006), so it is unsurprising, then, that we see traces of both in her writings. For instance, she also paralleled feminist writings on androgyny, by arguing that society's division based on gender meant that we were incomplete, being unable to express both masculinity and femininity: 'Thus to become one kind of person manifesting all the proper patterns, interests and activities, etc. we must give up, voluntarily or involuntarily, all opposite potentials. In effect we all become HALF HUMANS!' (Prince, 2006a [1978], p. 41).

Prince (2006b [1978]) preferred the term 'gynandry' to 'androgyny' so as to emphasize femininity; she defined it as someone who expressed all aspects of themselves, rather than being confined to a strict gender role. Therefore, like feminist theories of androgyny, Prince positioned a blending of masculinity and femininity as superior to gender identities that emphasized more of one than the other. She also denied the role of gender nonconformity or 'androgyny'[5] at different times in history, and like psychology, prioritized evolutionary discourse in the account of human development. In doing so, she valorized biological discourse at the expense of a wide range of cultures:

> I must also strongly assert that there was NEVER such a condition [of 'androgynous beings'] in the history of the human race. Anyone who has any understanding of evolution would easily see this. Unfortunately Singer is deeply involved in mythology and religions and probably believes in the Genesis concept of man's origins.
>
> (Prince, 2006a [1978], p. 45)

This mirrored some perspectives from within radical feminism, which also negated the existence of transsexualism prior to the 1950s and the development of body-modification procedures (Raymond, 1979). Therefore, at this time, feminism, psychology and early transgender writings positioned transsexual individuals as 'male' or 'female' based on their assigned sex at birth. This was due to a separation between 'sex' (considered biological and unchangeable) and 'gender' or 'gender role' that was framed as fluid, and as a consequence, minimized embodied gender identity, distress, and the need for some individuals to undergo surgical intervention.

Also writing at the same time, was Carol Riddell (2006 [1980]) who penned an insightful critique to Raymond's (1979) *The transsexual empire*, entitled *Divided sisterhood*. Riddell provided an alternative perspective from theories developing from within radical feminism and those offered by Prince, as she challenged myths regarding transsexual people and body-modification procedures. She criticized Raymond's work directly, but her analysis highlighted the problems of many other similar texts. For example, she described how those who framed gender identity clinics as coercing or exploiting trans people with an over-eagerness to complete surgical changes were highly inaccurate, supported not only in theory but also her own experience of the London Gender Identity Clinic. She argued that trying to confront the patriarchal medical establishment via gender identity clinics was 'like trying to excise a monster by focusing on his little toe' (Riddell, 2006 [1980], p. 157).

She also overturned the radical feminist positioning of transsexual people as a danger to women through a coercive penetration of women's spaces (Raymond, 1979), by instead positioning Raymond's *book* as dangerous:

> 'The Transsexual Empire' is a dangerous book. It is dangerous to transsexuals because it does not treat us as human beings at all, merely as the tools of a theory; because its arguments may make things more difficult for trans-sexual women and men as they strive to come out; and because it seeks to create hostility towards us among women who have no actual experience of trans-sexual people, find the subject disturbing, and want some simple, straight-forward answer that allays their unease.
>
> (Riddell, 2006 [1980], p. 155)

This was in addition to showing how the 'threat' of transsexual people had been greatly exaggerated, by drawing on statistical data to illustrate their small percentage of the population (Riddell, 2006 [1980]). Riddell also challenged Raymond's 'objective' scholarship, asserting that in failing to analyse her own emotions on the topic, Raymond masked the underlying fear and hatred that fuelled her work:

> It makes me feel that, in spite of Ms. Raymond's claims of sympathy to the 'existential plight' of trans-sexuals, and her use of the conventional model of formal scholarship, which enables her not to present her emotions clearly, she actually experiences hatred and fear when thinking about trans-sexuals.
>
> (Riddell, 2006 [1980], p. 149)

Following this, she highlighted how Raymond's method of analysis silenced criticisms by positioning transsexual people as 'deluded' and denying their existence as women. This meant that their viewpoints were easily dismissed. The use of sanist language, combined with cisgenderism, shows how multiple forms of oppression can silence marginalized groups and position particular kinds of knowledge as 'truth' (Foucault, 1979). However, Riddell also used sanist language to frame Raymond as 'deluded', calling her theory of a transsexual empire a 'paranoid fantasy' (2006 [1980], p. 151). She also overlooked the role of coercive and patriarchal medicine in the 'treatment' of intersex children when she dreamed of a future where transsexual surgeries could be conducted at birth: 'By then, I expect, wise women will be able to divine the energy patterns involved, and correct biology at birth, as can now be done with various hermaphroditic conditions. Who knows?' (p. 155); and thus illustrated the importance of considering multiple axes of oppression simultaneously.

Another influential response to Raymond's (1979) work was Sandy Stone's (1991) 'The "empire" strikes back: A posttranssexual manifesto'. Her role at Olivia Records (a women-only collective) was included in Raymond's controversial analysis that criticised Stone directly (Stryker & Whittle, 2006). Drawing on the work of Donna Haraway and Judith Butler, Stone's article introduced a transgender and feminist theory that embraced postmodernism, postfeminism and poststructuralism (Stryker & Whittle, 2006). Stone (1991) aimed to provide a new beginning for transsexual scholarship beyond what was already being produced from within feminism and medicine, a move toward 'posttranssexualism'. This concept was taken up by Halberstam as an examination of

> . . . the strangeness of all gendered bodies, not only the transsexualized ones and [a rewriting] of the cultural fiction that divides a sex from trans-sex, a gender from a transgender. All gender should be transgender, all desire is transgendered, movement is all.
>
> (Halberstam, 1999, p. 132)

In her article, Stone commented: 'I want to briefly consider four autobiographical accounts of male-to-female transsexuals, to see what we can learn about what they think they are doing' (1991, p. 12). However, this added to the long history of the study, interrogation and analysis of trans people's experiences and the questioning of the validity of such accounts, something Serano (2009a) considers a form of objectification that she called 'trans-interrogation' (p. 187). Stone analysed the experiences of these few cases, concluding that they had similar descriptions of a fetishized woman, of reinforcing a gender binary, and concealing identities that lie 'between' the boundaries:

> All these authors replicate the stereotypical male account of the constitution of woman: Dress, makeup, and delicate fainting at the sight of blood. Each of these adventurers passes directly from one pole of sexual experience to the other. If there is any intervening space in the continuum of sexuality, it is invisible.
>
> (Stone, 1991, p. 33)

She demonstrated how autobiographical accounts could be unhelpful in their reproduction of gendered discourses (Stryker & Whittle, 2006), concluding, 'No wonder feminist theorists have been suspicious. Hell, I'm suspicious' (Stone, 1991, p. 33). This is a difficult argument to make, however, to enable gender fluidity for those who identify as such, but also not to minimize or devalue the experiences of those who want to conform. As such, it is often the case that gender conformity is framed negatively, such as transsexual individuals being framed as 'part of the problem' for replicating gender stereotypes (Raymond, 1979). This often occurs without consideration of the value in gender-conforming femininity, as well as how often these criticisms can reflect the pressures made upon trans people to 'pass' either within medical systems (see Chapter 3), or in a society where hostility is directed towards those who do not conform (Tosh, 2014). Within feminist and queer perspectives, transgender and transsexual individuals can often be framed as useful or positive examples for analysis only when they conform to feminist and queer ideals of 'transcending' gender binaries (Rubin, 1998), or 'subverting' the gender binary (Serano, 2009a, p. 336). Trans people, then, can be placed in the impossible position of being expected to live up to psychology's gendered norms (i.e. conformity), or those promoted by feminism and queer perspectives (i.e. nonconformity) to be accepted.

Namaste (2000, 2011) criticized work that negated the lived realities of transsexual and transgender people by focusing on abstract discourse (Elliot, 2012). For example, Stone (1991) stated, 'I suggest constituting transsexuals not as a class or problematic "third gender", but rather as a genre – a set of embodied texts whose potential for productive disruption of structured sexualities and spectra of desire has yet to be explored' (1991, p. 45), which was seen as dehumanizing, much in the same way as current criticisms of the use of the term 'transgenderism' (GLAAD, n.d.). Therefore, the use of transgender people and their experiences to antagonize rigid gender binaries and hierarchies appropriated their existence for the purposes of advancing gender theory and the liberation of gender nonconformists, not transsexual people (Prosser, 2006). Consequently, it was argued that the concept of gender nonconformity was a threat to the gender binary, rather than gender-nonconforming or transgender people (Vartabedian, 2014, p. 289).

Stone also framed the different views of medicine, feminism and transsexual people as 'meeting on the battlefield of the transsexual body', and described the bodies of transsexual people as 'a tactile politics of reproduction constituted through textual violence' (1991, p. 43), but failed to discuss the actual violence enacted on transsexual and transgender people. This was a criticism that Namaste also levied at other similar theoretical perspectives, such as Butler's analysis of the transsexual character Venus Extravaganza in the film *Paris is Burning*. Namaste highlights how Butler dismisses Extravaganza's transsexual identity and her role as a sex worker despite them being key to the film's narrative regarding violence against trans sex workers:

> Butler argues that Extravaganza enacts an imaginary relation to the category 'woman' in order to escape the cruel realities of her class and ethnicity (Latina) in New York City . . . Since Butler has reduced Extravaganza's transsexuality to allegory, she cannot conceptualize the specificity of violence with which transsexuals, especially transsexual prostitutes, are faced. This, to my mind, is the most tragic misreading of all.
>
> (Namaste, 2000, p. 13)

In relation to Garber's analyses on the representation of cross-dressing, Namaste again points out how the lived realities of cross-dressing individuals is discarded in place of abstract theorizing:

> But what is missing from her research is a conceptualization of transvestite identity as a real, lived, viable experience. Naming the second edition of her book 'transvestite effects', Garber implies that the transvestite is an effect of performance and nothing else.
>
> (Namaste, 2000, p. 14)

Therefore, while social constructionist perspectives promoted a disembodied gender fluidity that was problematized within trans scholarship, it was also influential to some trans perspectives (e.g. Stone, 1991). As problems with the term 'transgender' have highlighted, the predominance of theories and perspectives regarding gender-blending nonconformity marginalized those who conformed to either femininity or masculinity and pursued body modifications, not to 'transcend' gender binary notions, but to live as men and women. Namaste (2005) framed this latter group as the less privileged within feminist, queer and transgender discourse, with their experiences misappropriated for the purposes of challenging the gender binary by other non-transsexual people (Elliot, 2012, p. 35).

Others highlighted how feminism had been a part of transgender oppression. For example, Green (2006) stated:

> Cisgendered women have the distinct privilege of being a part of a legitimate social class – woman. While the class of woman is certainly one of a patriarchally oppressed 'other,' the legitimacy of its right to exist is not routinely under attack.
>
> (Green, 2006, p. 243)

Serano (2009a) agreed, describing feminists' (and psychologists') tendency to claim responsibility for defining people's gender as 'cissexual gender entitlement' (Serano, 2009a, p. 166), and made a call to action, or inaction on the part of cisgender academics:

> Instead of exploiting our experiences to further their own careers, they should insist that universities make a point of hiring transsexual and intersex faculty, and that their publishers put out books by gender-variant writers. And they should finally acknowledge the fact that they have no legitimate claim to use transsexual and intersex identities, struggles, and histories for their own purposes . . . But until that time comes, non-intersex, cissexual artists and academics should put their pens down, open up their minds, and simply listen to what we have to say about our own lives.
>
> (Serano, 2009a, p. 212)

This demand is reflected in increasing interest in trans feminism, where gender-nonconforming, transgender, and transsexual individuals reclaim a movement that had excluded them, demonized them, ignored their oppression, and sometimes contributed to it.

Trans feminism

> ... we trans women must join allies of all genders and sexualities to forge a new type of feminism ....
>
> (Serano, 2009a, p. 17)

While feminism produced influential texts that were deemed hateful and fearful of trans people, there were also many transgender and transsexual individuals who embraced feminism and identified as feminists (Riddell, 2006 [1980]; Serano, 2009a; Stone, 1991). As a result, these academics and activists disrupted the predominant narratives produced by feminism and medicine by interjecting the voices of trans people and those who supported them (Enke, 2012). Their work represented a form of feminism that is increasingly referred to as trans feminism (or transfeminism) (Salamon, 2008; Scott-Dixon, 2006), defined by Koyama in her transfeminist manifesto as

> ... primarily a movement by and for trans women who view their liberation to be intrinsically linked to the liberation of all women and beyond. It is also open to other queers, intersex people, trans men, non-trans women, non-trans men and others who are sympathetic toward needs of trans women and consider their alliance with trans women to be essential for their own liberation.
>
> (Koyama, 2003, p. 245)

Koyama stated that 'there are as many ways of being a woman as there are women' (p. 246), and put forward several key principles that she considered to be central to the movement. These included a respect for people's own gender identities, as well as their right to make decisions about their bodies without being impeded by oppressive systems or to have such bodily autonomy taken away from them. However, Koyama (2003) also noted that her initial definition overemphasized trans women at the expense of other gender identities, and needed a greater consideration of intersecting inequalities.

While these key principles are general, it would be a mistake to view trans feminism as a coherent and uniform concept or movement; much like the diversity of perspectives in relation to the term 'transgender'. For example, some wanted to draw on feminist work to 'enrich' transgender theory (Stone, 1991), while others wanted to redefine it and reclaim it (Serano, 2009a). Trans feminists also represented a wide range of theoretical positions and approaches, analysing the intersections of sexuality, dis/ability, race and more (Almassi, 2010; Green, 2015; Grzinic & Stojnic, 2014). Rather than a focus on pathologization or abstract notions of gender for the purposes of cisgender theories, research has examined complex issues impacting on the lives of trans people, such as racism, homelessness, incarceration and sexual violence (Battle & Ashley, 2008; Edney, 2004; Lombardi et al., 2002; Mananzala & Spade, 2008; Mottet & Ohie, 2006; Peek, 2003). This is changing the conversation from studying trans people as an example of abnormality or a conceptual curiosity, to activist campaigns aimed at improving the circumstances of marginalized trans individuals who stand at the epicentre of numerous intersecting inequalities.

Transmisogyny

> These pseudofeminists consistently preach feminism with one hand while practicing traditional sexism with the other.
>
> (Serano, 2009a, p. 17)

In contrast to those who denied the gender identity of transsexual people as 'pseudofemale', Serano (2009a) denied the feminist identity of those who argued that the term 'woman' could only apply to those who had lived as women from birth (Raymond, 1979; Daly, 1978). She called them 'pseudofeminists' (p. 16) due to their definition of gender, which Serano considered to be sexist due to its reduction of all women 'down to [their] mere body parts', or expecting them 'to live up to certain societally dictated ideals regarding appearance' (Serano, 2009a, p. 11).

Serano went on to define several forms of sexism in her analysis of how discrimination and victimization of transsexual women differed from prior feminist theory that focused solely on cisgender experiences. She defined 'traditional sexism' as the positioning of maleness and masculinity as superior to femaleness and femininity, and reframed the gender binary as a form of 'oppositional sexism' that positioned masculinity and femininity, or men and women, in an oppositional dichotomy where if men are strong, then women must be weak and so on. In addition to these forms of sexism, Serano described her experiences of discrimination and hostility that not only targeted her gender nonconformity, but her expression of femininity. She described how she was ridiculed and dismissed more so for her femininity than for her gender nonconformity – that there was more hostility towards her for being a transsexual woman, than her previous experiences of cross-dressing or as a 'bigendered queer boy' (2009a, p. 2).

Serano described this combination of cisgenderism (or cissexism), transphobia, and sexism as transmisogny. She argued that by being seen to choose femininity and to live as a woman deeply challenged, not only the gender binary, but also sexist perspectives that framed femininity as 'less than' masculinity. She also drew attention to the role feminism had played in further positioning femininity as inferior (Serano, 2009a), due to arguments that addressed the restrictiveness of the feminine role in society as well as it being perceived as compulsory for women (Brownmiller, 2013; Friedan, 2010); a criticism that was also noted by third-wave feminists (Baumgardner & Richards, 2004). However, rather than reject the movement based on its negative framing of trans people and femininity, Serano continued to promote its value in challenging sexism and transmisogny, arguing that 'No form of gender equality can ever truly be achieved until we first work to empower femininity itself' (2009a, p. 6).

Conclusions

In addition, then, to psychology and psychiatry's pathologization of gender nonconformity and femininity that results in trans people being labelled as 'mentally ill', they too experience oppression living in a world that devalues both gender nonconformity and femininity – that of transmisogyny. As a result, challenging sexism by focusing solely on dismantling the gender binary, or campaigning for the rights of (cisgender) women, not only restricts the activist potential of such movements, but simultaneously further oppresses those who do not identify as cisgender or gender nonconforming.

By drawing on the work of psychologists, which sought to impose gender conformity and made its research conclusions based on controversial and abusive therapies and practices on intersex and gender-nonconforming children, psychology's authoritative discourse influenced – not only feminism – but also queer and early trans perspectives. As a consequence, not only did psychology and psychiatry promote the pathologization of trans people and conversion approaches, but also feminism refused to acknowledge trans people as women, and transgenderist perspectives sought to stop sex-reassignment surgery for the vast majority of transsexual people. Therefore, we can see how the problematic discourse of psychology and psychiatry penetrated critical activist spaces, tainted it with its version of gender and displaced the feminist focus on listening to the experiences of the oppressed (such as consciousness raising) and instead focused on authoritative discourses and applied them to others. It also shows how drawing on psychological discourse can pervert the course of anti-oppressive practice, and how making value judgements on the identities and bodies of others can result in the production of further norms and ideals – feminist, queer and trans 'norms' that further exclude already marginalized individuals (Serano, 2013). While feminism promoted an overly simplistic 'gender as constructed' argument that marginalized transsexual people who pursued body-modification procedures, an overemphasis on the fixed gender identity in response to coercive psychiatric treatments that aim to change someone's identity also has the potential to marginalize non-binary, androgynous and genderqueer individuals. It is essential, then, to avoid further oppressing marginalized groups and individuals; rather than embracing binaries of sex/gender, nature/nurture, anatomy/culture, masculine/feminine, androgyny/conformity, that we embrace complexity, intersectionality, plurality and contradiction.

Notes

1 Prince published this paper under the name Virginia Bruce.

2 That was (controversially) relied upon within psychoanalytic and behaviourist reparative therapies to argue that homosexuality was learned, and thus could be changed (Bieber, 1976;

Burch, 1993; Friedman, 1976), prior to its uptake in psychological studies on gender identity (Green, Newman & Stoller, 1972; Green, Stoller, & MacAndrew, 1966).

3 A previous medical term that was applied to intersex individuals.

4 Although this perspective also underestimated the role of an internal incongruence experienced by those who pursue body modification.

5 Although not described using these terms.

References

Alexander, T. (1997). The medical management of intersexed children: An analogue for childhood sexual abuse: http://www.isna.org/articles/analog (accessed 21 November 2015).

Almassi, B. (2010). Disability, functional diversity, and trans/feminism. *IJFAB: International Journal of Feminist Approaches to Bioethics, 3*(2), 126–49.

APA (American Psychiatric Association) (1980). *Diagnostic and statistical manual of mental disorders, third edition (DSM-III)*. Washington, DC: Author.

APA (American Psychiatric Association) (2000). *Diagnostic and statistical manual of mental disorders, fourth edition text revision (DSM-IV-TR)*. Washington, DC: Author.

APA (American Psychiatric Association) (2013). *Diagnostic and statistical manual of mental disorders fifth edition (DSM-5)*. Washington, DC: Author.

Ansara, G., & Hegarty, P. (2012). Cisgenderism in psychology: Pathologising and misgendering children from 1999 to 2008. *Psychology & Sexuality, 3*(2), 137–60.

Baril, A., & Trevenen, K. (2014). Exploring ableism and cisnormativity in the conceptualization of identity and sexuality 'disorders'. *Annual Review of Critical Psychology, 11*, 389–416.

Bartlett, N. H., Vasey, P. L., & Bukowski, W. M. (2000). Is gender identity disorder in children a mental disorder? *Sex Roles, 43*(11–12), 753–85.

Battle, J., & Ashley, C. (2008). Intersectionality, heteronormativity, and black lesbian, gay, bisexual, and transgender (LGBT) families. *Black Women, Gender & Families, 2*(1), 1–24.

Baumgardner, J., & Richards, A. (2004). Feminism and femininity: Or how we learned to stop worrying and love the thong. In A. Harris (Ed.), *All about the girl: Culture, power, and identity* (pp. 59–67). New York: Routledge.

Bento, B. (2008). *O que e transexualidade*. Sao Paulo: Editora Brasiliense.

Bieber, I. (1976). Psychodynamics and sexual object choice. I: A Reply to Dr. Richard C. Friedman's paper. *Contemporary Psychoanalysis, 12*(3), 366–9.

Birnbaum, M. (1960). The right to treatment. *American Bar Association Journal, 46*(5), 499–505.

Blanchard, R. (1989). The concept of autogynephilia and the typology of male gender dysphoria. *Journal of Nervous and Mental Disease, 177*(10), 616–23.

Blanchard, R. (2005). Early history of the concept of autogynephilia. *Archives of Sexual Behavior, 34*(4), 439–46.

Braun, V. (2005). In search of (better) sexual pleasure: Female genital 'cosmetic' surgery. *Sexualities, 8*(4), 407–24.

Brownmiller, S. (2013). *Femininity*. New York: Open Road Media.

Bruce, V. (2005 [1967]). The expression of femininity in the male. *International Journal of Transgenderism, 8*(4), 21–7.

Buckwalter, L. (2001). Autogynephilia: All dressed up and no one to be. *Transgender Tapestry, 1*(93), 22–3.

Buhrich, N. (1978). Motivation for cross-dressing in heterosexual transvestism. *Acta Psychiatrica Scandinavica, 57*(2), 145–52.

Buhrich, N., & McConaghy, N. (1977). The clinical syndromes of femmiphilic transvestism. *Archives of Sexual Behavior, 6*(5), 397–412.

Bullough, V. (2008). Virginia Prince (1913–). In V. Bullough (Ed.), *Before Stonewall: Activists for gay and lesbian rights in historical context* (pp. 372–5). London: Routledge.

Burch, B. (1993). Heterosexuality, bisexuality, and lesbianism: Rethinking psychoanalytic views of women's sexual object choice. *Psychoanalytic Review, 80*(1), 83–99.

Burke, P. (1996). *Gender shock: Exploding the myths of male and female*. New York: Anchor Books.

Burrill, N., & Fredland, V. (2012). Forgotten patient: A health provider's guide to providing comprehensive care for transgendered patients. *Indiana Health Law Review, 9*, 69.

Cameron, M. (2005). Two-spirited Aboriginal people: Continuing cultural appropriation by non-Aboriginal society. *Canadian Woman Studies, 24*, 123–7.

Caplan, P. (2011). Psychiatric diagnosis arbiters decide how boys vs. girls should act and feel: http://www.psychologytoday.com/blog/science-isnt-golden/201106/psychiatric-diagnosis-arbiters-decide-how-boys-vs-girls-should-act (accessed 21 November 2015).

Clements-Nolle, K., Marx, R., & Katz, M. (2006). Attempted suicide among transgender persons. *Journal of Homosexuality, 51*(3), 53–69.

Connell, R. (2012). Transsexual women and feminist thought: Toward new understanding and new politics. *Signs, 37*(4), 857–81.

Conway, L. (2003). An investigative report into the publication of J. Michael Bailey's book on transsexualism by the National Academies: http://ai.eecs.umich.edu/people/conway/TS/LynnsReviewOfBaileysBook2.html (accessed 21 November 2015).

Cox, T. (2009). Medically necessary treatments for transgender prisoners and the misguided law in Wisconsin. *Wisconsin Journal of Law, Gender & Society, 24*, 341.

Croughan, J. L., Saghir, M., Cohen, R., & Robins, E. (1981). A comparison of treated and untreated male cross-dressers. *Archives of Sexual Behavior, 10*(6), 515–28.

Daly, M. (1990 [1978]). *Gyn/ecology: The metaethics of radical feminism*. Boston, MA: Beacon Press.

Doorn, C. D. (1997). Towards a gender identity theory of transsexualism (Unpublished PhD thesis). Vrije Universiteit, Amsterdam, The Netherlands.

Douard, J. (2007). Loathing the sinner, medicalizing the sin: Why sexually violent predator statutes are unjust. *International Journal of Law and Psychiatry, 30*(1), 36–48.

Drescher, J. (2009). Queer diagnoses: Parallels and contrasts in the history of homosexuality, gender variance, and the diagnostic and statistical manual. *Archives of Sexual Behavior, 39*(2), 427–60.

Edney, R. (2004). To keep me safe from harm: Transgender prisoners and the experience of imprisonment. *Deakin Law Review, 9*, 327.

Ehrenreich, B., & Barr, M. (2005). Intersex surgery, female genital cutting, and the selective condemnation of 'cultural practices'. *Harvard Civil Rights-Civil Liberties Law Review, 40*, 71–140.

Ehrensaft, D. (2012). From gender identity disorder to gender identity creativity: True gender self child therapy. *Journal of Homosexuality, 59*(3), 337–56.

Ekins, R., & King, D. (2006). *Virginia Prince: Pioneer of transgendering*. Binghamton, NY: CRC Press.

Elliot, P. P. (2012). *Debates in transgender, queer, and feminist theory: Contested sites*. Farnham: Ashgate Publishing, Ltd.

Enke, A. (2012). *Transfeminist perspectives in and beyond transgender and gender studies*. Philadelphia, PA: Temple University Press.

Epstein, A. W. (1993). Notes on penetrative identification in femmiphilic transvestism. *American Journal of Psychoanalysis, 53*(4), 353–6.
Fegan, E. V., & Rebouche, R. (2003). Northern Ireland's abortion law: The morality of silence and the censure of agency. *Feminist Legal Studies, 11*(3), 221–54.
Feinberg, L. (1992). *Transgender liberation: A movement whose time has come.* New York: World View Forum.
Fisk, N. (1973). Gender dysphoria syndrome (the how, what, and why of a disease). In *Proceedings of the second interdisciplinary symposium on gender dysphoria syndrome.* (pp. 7–14). Palo Alto, CA: Stanford University Press.
Foucault, M. (1979). *The history of sexuality volume one: An introduction.* New York: Random House.
Friedan, B. (2010). *The feminine mystique.* New York: W. W. Norton & Company.
Friedman, R. C. (1976). Psychodynamics and sexual object choice. *Contemporary Psychoanalysis, 12*(1), 94–108.
Garner, T. (2014). Chest surgeries of a different 'nature'. *Annual Review of Critical Psychology, 11*, 337–356.
GLAAD. (n.d.). GLAAD media reference guide – Transgender issues [Text]: http://www.glaad.org/reference/transgender (accessed 21 November 2015).
Goldblum, P., Testa, R. J., Pflum, S., Hendricks, M. L., Bradford, J., & Bongar, B. (2012). The relationship between gender-based victimization and suicide attempts in transgender people. *Professional Psychology: Research and Practice, 43*(5), 468–75.
Grant, J., Mottet, L., Tanis, J., Herman, J., Harrison, J., & Keisling, M. (2010). *National transgender discrimination survey report on health and health care.* National Center for Transgender Equality; National Gay and Lesbian Task Force: http://www.thetaskforce.org/static_html/downloads/resources_and_tools/ntds_report_on_health.pdf (accessed 21 November 2015).
Green, E. (2006). Debating trans inclusion in the feminist movement: A trans-positive analysis. *Journal of Lesbian Studies, 10*, 231–48.
Green, K. (2015). The essential I/Eye in we: A black transfeminist approach to ethnographic film. *Black Camera, 6*(2), 187–200.
Green, R., Newman, L., & Stoller, R. (1972). Treatment of boyhood 'transsexualism': An interim report of four years' experience. *Archives of General Psychiatry, 26*(3), 213–17.
Green, Stoller, R., & MacAndrew, C. (1966). Sex assignment and reassignment: Physicians' attitudes in the management of hermaphroditic children. *American Journal of Diseases of Children, 111*(5), 524–8.
Grzinic, M., & Stojnic, A. (2014). From feminism to transfeminism: From sexually queer to politically queer. In K. Kosmala (Ed.), *Sexing the border: Gender, art and new media in central and eastern Europe* (pp. 231–52). Newcastle upon Tyne: Cambridge Scholars Publishing.
Haas, A., Rodgers, P., & Herman, J. (2014). *Suicide attempts among transgender and gender non-conforming adults: Findings of the National Transgender Discrimination Survey.* New York: American Foundation for Suicide Prevention.
Hacking, I. (1995). The looping effect of human kinds. In D. Sperber, D. Premack, & A. Premack (Eds), *Causal cognition: A multidisciplinary debate* (pp. 351–83). Oxford: Oxford University Press.
Halberstam, J. (1999). F2M: The making of female masculinity. In J. Price & M. Shildrick (Eds), *Feminist theory and the body: A reader* (pp. 125–33). New York: Routledge.
Hegarty, P. (2009). Toward an LGBT-informed paradigm for children who break gender norms: Comment on Drummond et al. (2008) and Rieger et al. (2008). *Developmental Psychology, 45*(4), 895–900.

Hill, D. B. (2012). *Trans Toronto: An oral history*. New York: William Rodney Press.

Hill, D. B., Menvielle, E., Sica, K. M., & Johnson, A. (2010). An affirmative intervention for families with gender variant children: Parental ratings of child mental health and gender. *Journal of Sex & Marital Therapy*, *36*(1), 6–23.

Hird, M. J. (2003). A typical gender identity conference? Some disturbing reports from the therapeutic front lines. *Feminism & Psychology*, *13*(2), 181–99.

Hupf Jr, R. (2014). Allyship to the intersex community on nonconsensual genital 'normalizing' surgery: http://works.bepress.com/robert_hupf/1 (accessed 21 November 2015).

International Network for Trans Pathologization. (n.d.). Manifesto: http://www.stp2012.info/old/en/manifesto (accessed 21 November 2015).

InYourFace. (1996). NGLTF issues historic statement: Calls for gender disorder reform: http://www.gendertalk.com/articles/archive/ngltf1.htm (accessed 21 November 2015).

Jacobson, M., & Royer, H. (2011). Aftershocks: The impact of clinic violence on abortion services. *American Economic Journal: Applied Economics*, *3*(1), 189–223.

King, L., & Husting, G. (2003). Anti-abortion activism in the U.S. and France: Comparing opportunity environments of rescue tactics. *Mobilization: An International Quarterly*, *8*(3), 297–312.

Koyama, E. (2003). The transfeminist manifesto. In R. Dicker & A. Piepmeier (Eds), *Catching a wave: Reclaiming feminism for the 21st century* (pp. 244–62). York: Northeastern University Press.

Langer, S. J., & Martin, J. I. (2004). How dresses can make you mentally ill: Examining gender identity disorder in children. *Child and Adolescent Social Work Journal*, *21*(1), 5–23.

Lawrence, A. (2004). Autogynephilia: A paraphilic model of gender identity disorder. In U. Leli & J. Drescher (Eds), *Transgender subjectivities: A clinician's guide*. (pp. 69–87). Binghamton, NY: Haworth Medical Press.

Lev, A. I. (2006). Disordering gender identity: Gender identity disorder in the *DSM-IV-TR*. *Journal of Psychology & Human Sexuality*, *17*(3–4), 35–69.

Lev, A. I. (2013). *Transgender emergence: Therapeutic guidelines for working with gender-variant people and their families*. London: Routledge.

Lombardi, E., Wilchins, R., Priesing, D., & Malouf, D. (2002). Gender violence: Transgender experiences with violence and discrimination. *Journal of Homosexuality*, *42*(1), 89–101.

MacKenzie, G. O. (1994). *Transgender nation*. Bowling Green: Bowling Green State University Popular Press.

Mananzala, R., & Spade, D. (2008). The nonprofit industrial complex and trans resistance. *Sexuality Research & Social Policy*, *5*(1), 53–71.

Money, J. (1986). *Lovemaps: Clinical concepts of sexual/erotic health and pathology, paraphilia, and gender transposition of childhood, adolescence, and maturity*. New York: Ardent Media.

Moser, C. (2008). A different perspective. *Archives of Sexual Behavior*, *37*(3), 472–5.

Mottet, L., & Ohie, J. (2006). Transitioning our shelters: Making homeless shelters safe for transgender people. *Journal of Poverty*, *10*(2), 77–101.

Namaste, V. (2000). *Invisible lives: The erasure of transsexual and transgendered People*. Chicago, IL: University of Chicago Press.

Namaste, V. (2011). *Sex change, social change: Reflections on identity, institutions, and imperialism*. Toronto: Canadian Scholars' Press.

OII Australia. (2011). 'ISGD' and the appropriation of intersex: https://oii.org.au/13651/isgd-and-the-appropriation-of-intersex/ (accessed 21 November 2015).

Peek, C. (2003). Breaking out of the prison hierarchy: Transgender prisoners, rape, and the eighth amendment. *Santa Clara Law Review*, *44*, 1211.

Perlin, M. L. (1992). On sanism. *SMU Law Review, 46*, 373.
Pickstone-Taylor, S. (2003). Children with gender nonconformity. *Journal of the American Academy of Child and Adolescent Psychiatry, 41*, 1010–13.
Prince, V. (2006a [1978]). The 'transcendents' of 'trans' people. In R. Ekins & D. King (Eds), *Virginia Prince: Pioneer of transgendering* (pp. 39–46). Binghamton, NY: Haworth Medical Press.
Prince, V. (2006b [1978]). Transsexuals and pseudotranssexuals. In R. Ekins & D. King (Eds), *Virginia Prince: Pioneer of transgendering* (pp. 33–8). Binghamton, NY: Haworth Medical Press.
Prosser, J. (2006). Judith Butler: Queer feminism, transgender, and the transubstantiation of sex. In S. Stryker & S. Whittle (Eds), *The transgender studies reader* (pp. 257–80). New York: Routledge.
Pyne, J. (2014). The governance of gender non-conforming children: A dangerous enclosure. *Annual Review of Critical Psychology, 11*, 79–96.
Raymond, J. (1979). *The transsexual empire*. London: Women's Press.
Rekers, G. A. (1977). Atypical gender development and psychosocial adjustment. *Journal of Applied Behavior Analysis, 10*(3), 559–71.
Riddell, C. (2006 [1980]). Divided sisterhood: A critical review of Janice Raymond's *The transsexual empire*. In S. Stryker & S. Whittle (Eds), *The transgender studies reader* (pp. 144–58). New York: Routledge.
Rubin, 1998. (1998). Phenomenology as method in trans studies. *GLQ: A Journal of Lesbian and Gay Studies, 4*(2), 263–81.
Salamon, G. (2008). Transfeminism and the future of gender. In J. Wallach Scott (Ed.), *Women's studies on the edge* (pp. 115–29). London: Duke University Press.
Scott-Dixon, K. (2006). *Trans/forming feminisms: Trans/feminist voices speak out*. Toronto: Canadian Scholars' Press.
Serano, J. (2008). A matter of perspective: A transsexual woman-centric critique of Dreger's 'scholarly history' of the Bailey controversy. *Archives of Sexual Behavior, 37*(3), 491–4.
Serano, J. (2009a). *Whipping girl: A transsexual woman on sexism and the scapegoating of femininity*. Emeryville, CA: Seal Press.
Serano, J. (2009b). Psychology, sexualization and trans-invalidations. Presented at the 8th Annual Philadelphia Trans-Health Conference.
Serano, J. (2010). The case against autogynephilia. *International Journal of Transgenderism, 12*(3), 176–87.
Shield, S. (2006). The doctor won't see you now: Rights of transgender adolescents to sex reassignment treatment. *New York University Review of Law & Social Change, 31*, 361.
Smyth, L. (2002). Feminism and abortion politics: Choice, rights, and reproductive freedom. *Women's Studies International Forum, 25*(3), 335–45.
Snelgrove, J. W., Jasudavisius, A. M., Rowe, B. W., Head, E. M., & Bauer, G. R. (2012). 'Completely out-at-sea' with 'two-gender medicine': A qualitative analysis of physician-side barriers to providing healthcare for transgender patients. *BMC Health Services Research, 12*(1), 110.
Sperber, J., Landers, S., & Lawrence, S. (2005). Access to health care for transgendered persons: Results of a needs assessment in Boston. *International Journal of Transgenderism, 8*(2–3), 75–91.
Spiegel, A. (2008). Two families grapple with sons' gender preferences: www.npr.org/2008/ . . . /two-families-grapple-with-sons-gender-preference (accessed 7 December 2015).
Stone, S. (1991). The "empire" strikes back: A posttranssexual manifesto. In J. Epstein & K. Straub (Eds.) *Body guards: The cultural politics of gender ambiguity* (pp. 280–304). New York: Routledge.

Stroumsa, D. (2014). The state of transgender health care: Policy, law, and medical frameworks. *American Journal of Public Health, 104*(3), e31–e38.

Stryker, S. (2006). Foreword. In R. Ekins & D. King (Eds), *Virginia Prince: Pioneer of transgendering* (pp. xi–xii). Binghamton, NY: Haworth Medical Press.

Stryker, S. (2009). *Transgender history*. Berkeley, CA: Seal Press.

Stryker, S., & Whittle, S. (2006). *The transgender studies reader*. London: Taylor & Francis.

Tiefer, L. (2008). Female genital cosmetic surgery: Freakish or inevitable? Analysis from Medical Marketing, Bioethics, and Feminist Theory. *Feminism & Psychology, 18*(4), 466–79.

Tosh, J. (in press). Gender nonconformity or psychiatric noncompliance? How organised noncompliance can offer a future without psychiatry. In M. Morrow & L. Halinka Malcoe (Eds), *Critical inquiries: Theories and methodologies for social justice in mental health*. Toronto: University of Toronto Press.

Tosh, J. (2011). 'Zuck off!' A commentary on the protest against Ken Zucker and his 'treatment' of childhood gender identity disorder. *Psychology of Women Section Review, 13*(1), 10–16.

Tosh, J. (2014). Working together for an inclusive and gender creative future: A critical lens on 'gender dysphoria'. In E. Meyer & A. Pullen Sansfacon (Eds), *Supporting transgender and gender creative youth: Schools, families, and communities in action* (pp. 41–53). New York: Peter Lang.

Valentine, D. (2007). *Imagining transgender: An ethnography of a category*. Durham, NC: Duke University Press.

Vartabedian, J. (2014). The political scope of travestilities: On the transgressive potential of travestis. *Annual Review of Critical Psychology, 11*, 279–97.

Veale, J., Clarke, D., & Lomax, T. (2011). Male to female transsexuals' impressions of Blanchard's autogynephilia theory. *International Journal of Transgenderism, 13*(3), 131–9.

Winters, K. (2006). Gender dissonance. *Journal of Psychology & Human Sexuality, 17*(3–4), 71–89.

Winters, K. (2009). *Gender madness in American psychiatry: Essays from the struggle for dignity*. Dillon, CO: BookSurge Publishing.

Winters, K. (2011). The proposed gender dysphoria diagnosis in the *DSM-5*: http://gidreform.wordpress.com/2011/06/07/the-proposed-gender-dysphoria-diagnosis-in-the-dsm-5/ (accessed 7 December 2015).

Wren, B. (2002). 'I can accept my child is transsexual but if I ever see him in a dress I'll hit him': Dilemmas in parenting a transgendered adolescent. *Clinical Child Psychology and Psychiatry*, 7(3), 377–97.

Wyndzen, M. (2003). Autogynephilia and Ray Blanchard's mis-directed sex-drive model of transsexuality: http://www.genderpsychology.org/autogynephilia/ray_blanchard/ (accessed 21 November 2015).

Zucker, K. J. (1999). Commentary on Richardson's (1996) 'setting limits on gender health'. *Harvard Review of Psychiatry*, 7(1), 37–42.

Zucker, K. J. (2006). Commentary on Langer and Martin's (2004) 'How dresses can make you mentally ill: Examining gender identity disorder in children.' *Child and Adolescent Social Work Journal, 23*(5–6), 533–55.

Chapter 6

Conclusions

A trans feminist antipsychology

Feminism has a long history of replicating oppressive hierarchies. While some radical feminist texts have been criticized for their representation of trans individuals, they have also been highlighted for their failure to consider issues regarding race and racism. In Audre Lorde's (2012 [1979]) open letter to Mary Daly, she described how *Gyn/Ecology* (Daly, 1978) distorted the history and images of her foremothers, with only examples given when it supported the overall theory or perspective of white women:

> Have you read my work, and the work of other Black women, for what it could give you? Or did you hunt through only to find words that would legitimize your chapter on African genital mutilation in the eyes of other Black women? And if so, then why not use our words to legitimize or illustrate the other places where we connect in our being and becoming? If, on the other hand, it was not Black women you were attempting to reach, in what way did our words illustrate your point for white women?
>
> (Lorde, 2012 [1979], p. 69)

She concluded that neglecting the history and experiences of black women from feminist theorizing, 'serves the destructive forces of racism and separation between women' (p. 69).[1] This is an ongoing criticism within the feminist movement (Daniels, 2015; Ortega, 2006; Thomlinson, 2012), in addition to those voicing concerns for not considering issues related to class (Bettie, 2014; Mink, 1998) and dis/ability (May & Ferri, 2005; Schriempf, 2001). The production of texts related to transgender and gender-nonconforming people can be added to this list of areas where feminism has too often neglected their experiences, selected examples for theories about cisgender women, or furthered their oppression. These criticisms are not separate either, as there can also be a failure to consider how these multiple areas intersect, such as the issues of poverty, homelessness, racism and violence that can impact on the lives of trans people.

This perpetuation of oppression has gone beyond abstract theorizing, and has wide-ranging and material consequences. In a context where hostility and violence towards trans individuals is widespread, particularly the victimization of black trans women (Black Girl Dangerous, 2014; O'Hara, 2014; Starr, 2015; Vries, 2015), the perpetuation of negative discourses of this community enables persecution to continue. There are also numerous examples of how some feminist definitions of gender and 'woman' have resulted in harm and exclusion for trans people, such as the well-documented case of a transsexual woman, Kimberly Nixon, being prevented from volunteering for a Rape Relief centre in Vancouver, Canada (Elliot, 2012). Preventing access to services, whether for victims of violence or for medical support, are some of the serious consequences of feminist work that focused on only one form of oppression. Consequently, anti-oppressive approaches cannot focus on single issues or look at only one form of discrimination (Spade, 2015).

While many approaches to feminism were criticized for this neglect, factions of radical feminism explicitly positioned other forms of oppression as less significant, creating a kind of hierarchy of oppression with sexism at the top: 'Very early in the game radical feminists tried to make an end run around this problem by advancing the thesis that women's oppression was not only the oldest and most universal form of domination but the primary form' (Willis, 1984, p. 96).

As a consequence, not only did the movement marginalize class oppression and racism, it did not consider the possibility that trans people could experience oppression. This was based on several fundamental assumptions from within this form of radical feminism. These included that, as women were victims of the 'universal' and 'primary' form of oppression (i.e. male supremacy), for those who were thought to have lived a part of their life as another gender meant that they were not a victim of sexism, and therefore were privileged. As others have stated, this failed to consider the complexity of oppression and privilege, such as the wealthy white women who accused black men of rape during and after slavery (Hodes, 1997), which illustrates how intersecting inequalities challenges this assumption about power, racism and sexism (Davis, 1983). By employing a binary of privileged/oppressed, trans people were excluded from any claim to oppression. This highlights the crucial role of analysing multiple intersecting oppressions simultaneously for anti-oppressive practice and theory.

In her analysis of violence against black women, Crenshaw (1991) introduced the term intersectionality, highlighting that intersections of multiple forms of oppression (such as sexism and racism) cannot be analysed, challenged, or understood as separate or disconnected experiences. The concept has been taken up within many sections of feminism, with others additionally proposing the concept of kyriarchy in an attempt to move away from a sole focus on patriarchy. Kyriarchy is a 'theory of power that describes the power structures intersectionality produces' (Osborne, 2015, p. 130). Fiorenza (2013) coined the term, based on a combination of the Greek *kyrios* (i.e. lord, master) and *archein* (i.e. to dominate). She defined the concept as

> . . . a complex pyramidal system of interlocking multiplicative social and religious structures of superordination and subordination, of ruling and oppression. Kyriarchal relations of domination are built on elite male property rights as well as on the exploitation, dependency, inferiority, and obedience of wo/men who signify all those subordinated. Such kyriarchal relations are still today at work in the multiplicative intersectionality of class, race, gender, ethnicity, empire, and other structures of discrimination.
>
> (Fiorenza, 2013, p. 7)

However, the ongoing perpetuation of transphobia, racism, classism and ableism within feminism shows that there are some factions within this diverse movement that continue to position sexism as the 'primary' form of oppression. With that in mind, I consider the consequences of how some feminist, queer and transgender perspectives can overlook and perpetuate sanism.

Sanism, sexism and cisgenderism

> A fourth rationale for the treatment of cross-gender identification in children is the prevention of transsexualism in adulthood. There is little controversy in this rationale.
>
> (Zucker, 1990, p. 30)

Zucker's proclamation that preventing transsexualism is uncontroversial not only assumes that transsexual identities are something that can be prevented, but that they should be prevented. It also denies and ignores the extensive criticisms and protests addressing the diagnosis and this very rationale for treatment. As the previous chapters of this book have shown, the diagnosis and preventative treatment approaches regarding transsexualism (and its subsequent terms and conceptualizations) are *highly* controversial within psychology and psychiatry.

In addition to viewing transsexual, transgender and gender-nonconforming people as fundamentally 'abnormal', and underestimating and dismissing criticisms from a wide range of professionals and activists, statements like this show how the label of 'mental illness' is used to ignore or deny the voices of those who are labelled. The 'prevention of transsexualism' as a therapeutic aim has resulted in an immense amount of criticism both inside and outside of the academy; therefore, to state that it is not a controversial aim of therapy is to ignore the perspectives of those who are transgender and gender-nonconforming people, or those who support them. This is one way that sanism impacts on the lives of those labelled as 'mentally ill', where their perspective and experience is constantly questioned, disbelieved, interpreted, discredited and silenced.

However, the failure of feminist, queer, and trans perspectives to fully interrogate sanism as part of their intersectional analysis of sexism, heterosexism and cisgenderism has resulted in the production of harmful theories and perspectives due to analyses that view trans people through the lens of abnormality. In doing so, the collusion with pathologizing discourse promoted division, hierarchies and hate within movements that have a mutual interest in challenging psychology and psychiatry – due to their abuse and pathologization of women,[2] as well as queer and trans people. Squire described 'feminist antipsychology' as 'an approach which grants all psychological data and theories a severely limited validity, or even rejects them completely', which she argued was developed, 'through a discovery of how other social differences, like those of class, sexuality and "race", affect psychology' (1990, p. 80). Therefore, perhaps it is time for a renewed trans feminist antipsychology, where sanism is included in intersectional analyses, where psychological and psychiatric approaches promoted by cisgender men are approached with scepticism, and with good reason. Psychology and psychiatry have abused women and gender nonconformists for well over a century. They are unlikely to provide solutions, because they are part of the problem.

Drawing on discourses that pathologize, and the profession that harms, only causes further harm to those movements and pits communities against each other. It penetrates and perverts. Psychology is the deceiver who seeks access to women's/trans/queer spaces under the guise of 'science', 'knowledge' and 'help'. It is imperative that critical perspectives remain critical of not only the professions and the harmful treatments they can promote, but also of their concepts, theories, explanatory models and labels. What may appear neutral, or useful, masks the power in the disciplines' ability to define, which is a power to include, exclude, normalize, or pathologize. We cannot challenge or bring an end to gender 'norms' without first dismantling the profession that produced, promoted and authenticated them – as well as the social conditions that make their existence and influence possible. Psychiatric theories that have been developed from the abuse of intersex and trans children should not be decontextualized within feminist or queer spaces to challenge the oppression of gender-conforming and cisgender people. Knowledge that is gained or developed through such abuse is tainted with that abuse, it cannot be used uncritically for anti-oppressive practice or social justice.[3] Drawing on sanist and sexist theories will not provide a future free from either.

Notes

1 This is in addition to Daly's (1978) comparison of trans people to 'black face' and Raymond's (1979) argument that transsexual surgery should not be accepted, drawing on the hypothetical example of individuals wanting to change their skin to become 'black' – an argument that Zucker (2006) also draws on in his discussion of 'ethnic identity disorder'.

2 This includes gender-conforming/cisgender, gender-nonconforming and trans women.

3 It is important to note, however, that knowledge from abuse can be used for anti-oppressive practice in some circumstances. For example, when it derives from the experiences of victims and survivors to challenge abusive and violent structures and modes of practice.

References

Bettie, J. (2014). *Women without class: Girls, race, and identity*. Oakland: University of California Press.

Black Girl Dangerous. (2014). Whose lives matter? Trans women of color and police violence: http://www.blackgirldangerous.org/2014/12/whose-lives-matter-trans-women-color-police-violence/ (accessed 24 November 2015).

Crenshaw, K. (1991). Mapping the margins: Intersectionality, identity politics, and violence against women of color. *Stanford Law Review*, *43*(6), 1241–99.

Daly, M. (1978). *Gyn/ecology: The metaethics of radical feminism*. Boston, MA: Beacon Press.

Daniels, J. (2015). *The trouble with white feminism: Whiteness, digital feminism and the intersectional Internet* (SSRN Scholarly Paper No. ID 2569369). Rochester, NY: Social Science Research Network: http://papers.ssrn.com/abstract=2569369 (accessed 25 November 2015).

Davis, A. (1983). Rape, racism and the myth of the black rapist. In A. Davis (Ed.), *Women, race, and class* (pp. 172–201). New York: Vintage Books.

Elliot, P. P. (2012). *Debates in transgender, queer, and feminist theory: Contested sites*. Farnham: Ashgate Publishing, Ltd.

Fiorenza, E. S. (2013). *Changing horizons: Explorations in feminist interpretation*. Minneapolis, MN: Fortress Press.

Hodes, M. (1997). *White women black men: Illicit sex in the nineteenth century south*. New York: Yale University Press.

Lorde, A. (2012). *Sister outsider: Essays and speeches*. New York: Crown Publishing Group.

May, V. M., & Ferri, B. A. (2005). Fixated on ability: Questioning ableist metaphors in feminist theories of resistance. *Prose Studies*, *27*(1–2), 120–40.

Mink, G. (1998). The lady and the tramp (II): Feminist welfare politics, poor single mothers, and the challenge of welfare justice. *Feminist Studies*, *24*(1), 55–64.

O'Hara, M. (2014). Trans women of color face an epidemic of violence and murder. *VICE Canada*: http://www.vice.com/en_ca/read/trans-women-of-color-face-an-epidemic-of-violence-and-murder-673 (accessed 25 November 2015).

Ortega, M. (2006). Being lovingly, knowingly ignorant: White feminism and women of color. *Hypatia*, *21*(3), 56–74.

Osborne, N. (2015). Intersectionality and kyriarchy: A framework for approaching power and social justice in planning and climate change adaptation. *Planning Theory*, *14*(2), 130–151.

Raymond, J. (1979). *The transsexual empire*. London: Women's Press.

Schriempf, A. (2001). (Re)fusing the amputated body: An interactionist bridge for feminism and disability. *Hypatia*, *16*(4), 53–79.

Spade, D. (2015). *Normal life: Administrative violence, critical trans politics, and the limits of law*. Durham, NC: Duke University Press.

Squire, C. (1990). Feminism as antipsychology: Learning and teaching in feminist psychology. In E. Burman (Ed.), *Feminists and psychological practice*. (pp. 76–88). London: SAGE Publications.

Starr, T. J. (2015, January 23). Violence against black transgender women goes largely ignored: http://www.theroot.com/articles/culture/2015/01/violence_against_black_transgender_women_goes_largely_ignored.html (accessed 25 November 2015).

Thomlinson, N. (2012). The colour of feminism: White feminists and race in the women's liberation movement. *History*, *97*(327), 453–75.

Vries, K. M. de. (2015). Transgender people of color at the center: Conceptualizing a new intersectional model. *Ethnicities, 15*(1), 3–27.

Willis, E. (1984). Radical feminism and feminist radicalism. *Social Text, 9*, 91–118.

Zucker, K. (1990). Treatment of gender identity disorders in children. In R. Blanchard & B. W. Steiner (Eds), *Clinical management of gender identity disorders in children and adults.* (pp. 25–46). Washington, DC: American Psychiatric Press, Inc.

Zucker, K. J. (2006). Commentary on Langer and Martin's (2004) "How Dresses Can Make You Mentally Ill: Examining Gender Identity Disorder in Children." *Child and Adolescent Social Work Journal, 23*(5–6), 533–55.

Index

For Product Safety Concerns and Information please contact our EU
representative GPSR@taylorandfrancis.com
Taylor & Francis Verlag GmbH, Kaufingerstraße 24, 80331 München, Germany

www.ingramcontent.com/pod-product-compliance
Ingram Content Group UK Ltd.
Pitfield, Milton Keynes, MK11 3LW, UK
UKHW022122190926
475702UK00013B/1600

* 9 7 8 0 8 1 5 3 5 9 9 6 8 *

ROUTLEDGE LIBRARY EDITIONS:
DEVELOPMENT

SOCIAL POLICY IN DEVELOPING COUNTRIES